THE WRONG WAR

The Wrong War

WHY WE LOST

IN VIETNAM

Jeffrey Record

Naval Institute Press • Annapolis, Maryland

Library of Congress Cataloging-in-Publication Data

Record, Jeffrey.

    The wrong war : why we lost in Vietnam / Jeffrey Record.

      p.   cm.

    Includes bibliographical references (p.   ) and index.

    ISBN 1-55750-699-X (alk. paper)

    1. Vietnamese Conflict, 1961–1975—United States. 2. United States—History—1945–   I. Title.

    DS558.R43   1998

    959.704'3—dc21   97-47706

Printed in the United States of America on acid-free paper ∞

05 04 03 02 01 00 99 98   9 8 7 6 5 4 3 2

Contents

Introduction

THE VIETNAM WAR has divided Americans as has no other foreign conflict since the War of 1812. It continues to be fought in the United States, even though a quarter of a century has elapsed since the last American combat troops were withdrawn from that unfortunate country. Witness the bitter controversies provoked by the POW-MIA issue; the design of the Vietnam War Memorial; the appearance of such movies as *Apocalypse Now, Coming Home, Platoon,* and *Full Metal Jacket;* Vice President Dan Quayle's wartime service in the Indiana National Guard; President Bill Clinton's lack of military service; publication of Robert S. McNamara's belated confession, *In Retrospect: The Tragedy and Lessons of Vietnam;* and subsequent U.S. normalization of diplomatic relations with Vietnam. George McGovern, politically both product and victim of the war, has rightly declared Vietnam to be "our second civil war. We are going to be fighting [it] for the rest of our lives."[1]

The war remains an open wound in the United States, in part because for Americans it was an exceptional twentieth-century historical and psychological experience: a lost war. The immediate American purpose in Indochina—the preservation of a noncommunist South Vietnam—was defeated, notwithstanding a twenty-year investment of billions of dollars and millions of troops.[2]

Wars are unpleasant to wage, and even more unpleasant to lose, especially for a country which entered the Vietnam War convinced of the justness of its cause and the invincibility of its military power. To be defeated by what was regarded at the time as (in Lyndon B. Johnson's words) "a piddling piss-ant little country"[3] simply intensified the rancor with which postwar fingers of blame were pointed. Most of the blame was directed, and continues to be directed, at civilian policymakers, the so-called "best and the brightest," who made the key decisions that propelled the United States into Vietnam and set the parameters of U.S. military power's application. The military, in contrast, has more often than not been portrayed as an innocent victim of not only misguided, even malevolent, White House and Defense Department civilians, but also a hostile media and perfidious antiwar movement. In his presidential nomination acceptance speech at the 1996 Republican Party convention, Robert Dole declared that "in Vietnam the long gray line did not fail us, we failed it. The American soldier was not made for the casual and arrogant treatment he suffered there, where he was committed without clear purpose or resolve, bound by rules that prevented victory, and kept waiting in the valley of the shadow of death for ten years while the nation debated the undebatable question of his honor."[4]

If Vietnam was a lost war, it was no less a war of serious and enduring negative legacies for the United States. Abroad, the war caused— or encouraged—decreased economic competitiveness, strategic exhaustion, relative military decline, and perceptions of American timidity, even paralysis. At home, the war crippled the Democratic Party, destroyed much of what remained of the post-World War II tradition of bipartisanship in foreign policy, exacerbated domestic political divisions already inflamed by the civil rights movement, and laid the groundwork for the gold crisis and disastrous inflation of the 1970s. Worse still, it contributed (along with Watergate) to a sharp erosion of public trust in the competence and integrity of governmental institutions and seriously damaged Americans' psychological self-confidence and sense of uniqueness. Before the war, the vast majority of Americans believed what their government told them, especially about overseas events. They also believed that their government, by virtue of its possession of "superior" information, was in a position to make the best judgments on what to do or not to do in situations involving war and peace. Americans entered the war further convinced that they occupied a special and virtuous place in human affairs, and that they could prevail over any challenge via a combination of technological and organizational know-how, "can do" spirit, and the inherent attractiveness of the American model for others to follow. For many Americans, these convictions died in the rice paddies and mountainous jungles of Indochina.

Americans have yet to come to terms with the war precisely because they cannot agree on what happened to the United States in Vietnam and why. Presidential assassinations and plane crashes prompt painstaking official examinations, but there has been no such inquiry into the cause of America's failure in Vietnam. Was the war a noble cause, a crime, or simply a monumental strategic mistake? Did 58,000 Americans die in vain? What was the cause and nature of the conflict, and did the United States correctly understand both? Was U.S. intervention—and subsequent Americanization of the war—justified? What were the causes of U.S. defeat, and who and what are to blame? Was, in fact, the United States defeated? To what extent can accountability for whatever happened to the United States be accurately assigned?

In 1982, the neoconservative Norman Podhoretz published a controversial book entitled *Why We Were in Vietnam*. In it he concluded that the United States was doomed in Vietnam: "The only way the United States could have avoided defeat in Vietnam was by staying out of the war altogether."[5] But he also argued that America's motive—to save South Vietnam from communism—was noble. Intervention was, he concluded, "an act of imprudent idealism whose moral soundness has been . . . overwhelmingly vindicated by the hideous consequences [for South Vietnam] of our defeat."[6] Unfortunately, nobility of purpose does not redeem an otherwise disastrous enterprise. (Nor does nobility of effort redeem an unjust cause.) On the contrary, in international politics, strong convictions of moral superiority can obscure imperative considerations of feasibility; the right thing may simply not be attainable. Vietnam, like the Charge of the Light Brigade at Balaclava and like Custer's last stand at the Little Big Horn, was the product of bad decisions by well-intentioned though arrogant—and ignorant—individuals. Was it better to have intervened and lost than not to have intervened at all? Did the hideous consequences for South Vietnam of a communist victory surpass those for the United States of an agonizing defeat in that country?

Declared reasons for intervention, however noble or nonsensical, are a matter of record. The government may have repeatedly lied to the public (and to itself) about the war's origins, nature, and progress, but it was very clear (if not always convincing) about what it believed were the stakes in Vietnam. The United States was in Vietnam to contain communism's spread, curb Chinese expansionism, stop other Asian "dominoes" from falling, demonstrate resolve, underline the integrity of U.S. commitments everywhere, and meet the tactical challenge posed by indirect aggression in the form of communist-sponsored "wars of national liberation." Equally indisputable was the significance, especially for the Kennedy and Johnson administrations, of domestic political imperatives in steering the United States into Vietnam. Fear of appearing "soft on communism" became a phobia within the Democratic Party in the wake of Mao Tse-tung's victory in China and McCarthyism's subsequent assault on the very loyalty of prominent Americans and gifted civil servants, many of them Truman administration decision makers. Johnson believed that no Democratic president could abandon Vietnam and expect to remain in office. After he left the White House he told Doris Kearns: "I knew that if we let Communist aggression succeed in taking over South Vietnam, there would follow in this country . . . a mean and destructive debate . . . that would shatter my Presidency. . . . I knew that Harry Truman and Dean Acheson had lost their effectiveness the day that the Communists took over China."[7]

The United States also believed it could win. Most enterprises are undertaken in the expectation that they will produce enough of desired results to justify the resources invested. In the case of Vietnam, many policymakers understood that intervention would be a long and difficult affair. But from the end of the French-Indochina War onward, both civilians and military men were confident that the combination of American arms and nation-building efforts in South Vietnam eventually would prevail. Surely, a country that had defeated Germany and

Japan, and that had subsequently transformed both into prosperous democracies, could do the same in a little piece of Southeast Asia. In 1966, an ebullient Vice President Hubert Humphrey declared, "We ought to be excited about this challenge [in Vietnam] because here's where we can put to work some of the ideas about . . . nation-building, of new concepts of education, development of local government, the improvement of health standards of people and really the achievement and fulfillment of full social justice."[8]

In contrast to the relative consensus on the reasons why the United States entered Vietnam, great disagreement surrounds the issue of why it was beaten there. The literature on the subject is voluminous, albeit all too often anecdotal, emotional, argumentative, and ill-informed. Some, like Podhoretz, argue that defeat was inevitable, given such things as the nature of the war, the disparity of interests and will between the two sides, the limited utility of U.S. military power in Indochina's operational setting, and the inability of America's client in Saigon to compete politically with Hanoi. Others, like McNamara, who claims that he now sees "Vietnam far more clearly than I did in the 1960s," contend that we simply didn't know what we were doing in Vietnam, that "in our judgment and capabilities . . . we were wrong, terribly wrong."[9]

Considerably more numerous are those who remain convinced that the war was winnable, but that victory was self-denied by civilian mistakes, inadequate military performance, or both. Within this group fall those who contend that the war was winnable, even easily so, but for the fact that the armed forces were stabbed in the back by a timorous and meddlesome White House and Office of Secretary of Defense (McNamara and his "whiz kids"). The influential *New York Times* military correspondent, Hanson Baldwin, gave pungent expression to this view shortly after the war ended: "The blame for this war rests, *not* upon the men in uniform, but upon the civilian policy makers in Washington and those who evolved and developed the policies of gradualism, flexible response, off-again-on-again bombing, negotiated victory, and, ultimately, one-arm-behind-the-back restraint, and scuttle-and-run."[10] Gen. William C. Westmoreland himself has argued that "it was a mistake to permit appointive civilian officials lacking in military experience and knowledge of military thinking and oblivious to the lessons of communist diplomatic machinations to wield undue influence in the decision-making process. Overall control of the military is one thing; shackling professional military men with restrictions in professional matters imposed by civilians who lack military understanding is another."[11]

Still others, including the late Richard Nixon, believe that the United States was in fact not beaten in Vietnam, that, on the contrary, by January 1973 (when the Paris peace accords were signed), "We had won the war in Vietnam. We had attained the one political goal for which we had fought the war. The South Vietnamese would have the right to determine their own political future," and would have been able to do so but for "a spasm of congressional irresponsibility" that deprived South Vietnam of further U.S. military and economic assistance.[12]

I reject this judgment. As the title of this book implies, I believe the U.S. cause in Vietnam was beaten—and beaten before 1973. Regardless of who is to blame, the fact remains that the United States failed to avert a communist takeover of Vietnam, and that it suffered defeat's attendant humiliation, loss of prestige, and domestic recrimination. The real questions are why the United States lost in Vietnam, who was responsible, and whether defeat was avoidable.

To be sure, the U.S. military in Vietnam was not defeated in the narrow, conventional military sense of being destroyed or driven from the field. No white flag was raised. The People's Army of Vietnam (PAVN) and National Liberation Front (NLF) did not succeed in directly evicting U.S. forces from South Vietnam, nor did they ever inflict upon them a set-piece battlefield defeat approaching the magnitude of the Viet Minh defeat of the French at Dien Bien Phu in 1954. On the contrary, on almost every occasion where communist forces elected to expose themselves en masse to American firepower (for example, Khe Sanh, the Tet Offensive of 1968, and the so-called "Easter Offensive" of 1972) they were repulsed with severe losses. Westmoreland has proudly noted that fully two years separated the departure of the last U.S. combat troops from Indochina in 1973 and the fall of South Vietnam in 1975.[13]

But if U.S. forces were not defeated, neither did they inflict a strategically decisive defeat on the communist side. Years of bombing North Vietnam and "attriting" communist forces in South Vietnam neither broke Hanoi's will nor decisively crippled its capacity to fight—

notwithstanding the confidence of both the Joint Chiefs of Staff (JCS) and the U.S. Military Assistance Command, Vietnam (MACV) in Saigon that the combination of bombing and attrition would produce a military victory sufficient to preserve a noncommunist South Vietnam. In the end it was America's will, not North Vietnam's, that faltered, and it faltered because Hanoi recognized, if Washington did not, that a condition of enduring military stalemate, given American impatience and North Vietnam's far greater stake in the war, would ultimately produce an American withdrawal from the fight.

The absence of an outright U.S. military defeat was, in short, simply not sufficient to guarantee political success. Nothing testifies better to the defeat of the American cause in Vietnam than the appearance since 1975 of Saigon as Ho Chi Minh City on maps of Southeast Asia.

Nixon, hardly a disinterested retrospective observer of events in Indochina during his presidency, is disingenuous in ascribing a U.S. victory by 1973 to the combination of a military stalemate, a peace agreement that preserved (at least temporarily) Saigon's Thieu regime in power, and a White house pledge to employ U.S. air power on behalf of South Vietnam in response to any major communist violations of the agreement. By 1973, President Nixon was in no position to make such a pledge absent congressional consent. More important, the Paris accords remained silent on the very issue that had elicited U.S. intervention in the first place: the aggressive North Vietnamese military presence in the South. The agreement mandated the departure of remaining U.S. forces from Vietnam, but not that of the estimated 145,000–160,000 readily and massively reinforcible PAVN regulars encamped in the Central Highlands,[14] to whose tender mercies the Thieu regime was effectively abandoned. The U.S. Army out of South Vietnam, but the PAVN left in South Vietnam: this was a win? Former NLF Minister of Justice Truong Nhu Tang has observed of Hanoi's accession to the Paris accords that "the Politburo's two primary objectives had already been satisfied: first, a complete American withdrawal . . . . second, the permanent emplacement of the North Vietnamese army [inside South Vietnam]. In our view, these two objectives, by themselves, assured the eventual destruction of the Saigon regime."[15] His assessment is shared by former South Vietnamese military Chief of Staff

Cao Van Vien: "The Paris Agreement was served on South Vietnam like a death warrant. The downhill course was set. Small wonder that the enemy claimed it was his victory; he had indeed won the first round. With U.S. forces completely gone, the enemy set about making preparations for the final push. His hands were now completely free; no more U.S. air strikes, not even the remote chance of token retaliation."[16]

It is understandable that the Nixon White House signed an agreement that left the PAVN in South Vietnam; no piece of paper could accomplish what the force of U.S. arms had failed to achieve for eight years. But in so doing, Nixon and Henry Kissinger, as savvy and cynical a pair of practitioners of realpolitik as have ever conducted U.S. foreign policy, surely recognized (Thieu certainly did) that the Paris agreement, like the Geneva Accords of 1954, constituted little more than a short military recess in a struggle that Hanoi would certainly resume sooner or later. The agreement left North Vietnam's political will and military capacity intact, and neither Nixon nor Kissinger should have been under any illusions about either. As Kissinger later remarked about the U.S. decision to intervene in Vietnam, "If America had searched the world over, it could not have found a more intractable adversary."[17]

And surely, both men must have anticipated the probability of congressional attempts to cripple any proposed U.S. reentry into what by 1973 had become the most divisive and unpopular war in living memory. By the time of the Paris accords it was hardly a secret that public opinion on the war had soured, and that Congress, reflecting that opinion, was becoming increasing hostile to any further U.S. participation—direct or indirect—in the war. Even Nixon concedes that "Congress was in part the prisoner of events. The leaders of the United States in the early and mid-1960s . . . misled the public by insisting we were winning the war and thereby prepared the war for defeatism . . . later on. The American people could not be expected to continue indefinitely to support a war in which they were told victory was around the corner, but which required greater and greater effort without any obvious signs of improvement."[18]

The communists may not have won the war in 1973, but they certainly did two years later, and they did so because they correctly gauged, as did Congress, the paralytic depth of U.S. public aversion to jumping back into the war. All of this points to the conclusion that the Paris agreement may have been intended by the Nixon White House as simply a face-saving device to provide a "decent interval" (Kissinger's choice of words at various academic symposia on the war in 1967 and 1968)[19] between the departure of the MACV and the arrival of the PAVN. Westmoreland has declared that the "so-called Paris Peace Agreement . . . had practically little if any chance of success."[20] The late Dean Rusk went even further: the accords "were in effect a surrender. Any agreement that left North Vietnamese troops in South Vietnam meant the eventual takeover of South Vietnam."[21]

In this book I seek to identify and examine the main causes of U.S. defeat in Vietnam, and then to render an informed judgment on: (1) how responsibility for that defeat may reasonably be apportioned between the civilian and military decision-making establishments, and (2) whether defeat was avoidable via a different U.S. war policy. I do not believe that the Vietnam War's outcome was predetermined by forces over which parties to the war had no control. I believe that the outcome of any war is largely the product of unfolding and interlocking actions and responses made by both sides: the communist side won the war in Vietnam as much as the United States lost it. Though I focus, as does the vast bulk of the literature on the Vietnam War, on the behavior of the American side, I reject the notion implicit in that focus that the war was America's to win or lose. The war may indeed have been winnable; it was certainly within U.S. capacity to destroy the state of North Vietnam and most of its people. The real issue is whether it was winnable at an acceptable moral, material, and strategic cost.

With respect to the issue of why the United States lost, I contend that the main causes of America's defeat were:

- Misinterpretation of both the significance and nature of the struggle in Vietnam. American policymakers in the 1950s and 1960s accorded events in Indochina far greater political and strategic significance than they warranted, and in so doing set the stage not only for intervention but also for a prolongation of that intervention that ultimately produced strategic exhaustion and loss of essential public support.

Obviously, a decision early on, say, following Ngo Dinh Diem's over-throw in late 1963, to cut U.S. losses in Vietnam (as did the Truman administration in China in 1947–48) would have spared the United States great agony. Policymakers were also wont, especially in the critical years leading up to the Tet Offensive, to read the war as a simple case of international aggression conducted by a communist enemy who by definition could not capture or speak for the legitimate national aspirations of the Vietnamese people. Such an interpretation ignored the powerful social and political foundations of the war in Vietnam and encouraged an emphasis on military solutions.

- Underestimation of the enemy's tenacity and fighting power. Policymakers never fully grasped the fact that whereas for the United States the conflict in Vietnam was a war fought with limited means for limited ends, for the communists it was a total war in which the main issue at stake was nothing less than the survival of the Vietnamese revolution. American officials were repeatedly astounded by the communist capacity to accept and replace staggering losses, notwithstanding a history of fanatical Vietnamese resistance to foreign domination stretching back for almost two millennia. And though some of the same American officials respected the demonstrated generalship and fighting prowess of the communist military, they more often than not approached the war confident that no amount of either could ultimately withstand the sheer weight of American firepower.

- Overestimation of U.S. political stamina and military effectiveness. Failing to recognize the strategic implications of the great disparity of stakes in the Vietnam War between the United States and the Vietnamese communists, key American decision makers concluded early on that the United States could awe the enemy into submission or, failing that, grind him down in a war of attrition. As a military strategy, attrition was certainly in keeping with America's mastery of industrial warfare and had paid off twice in Europe and once in Korea. Attrition, however, presupposed both a capacity to inflict irreplaceable losses on the enemy and a degree of political patience at home capable of surviving years of apparent military stalemate and constant official dissembling on the war. Both assumptions proved false. Nor did the U.S. military leadership properly appreciate the inherently limited effectiveness—and in some respects, counter-productiveness—of U.S.-style conventional warfare in the Vietnamese operational and political setting.

- Absence of a politically competitive South Vietnam. The Republic of Vietnam was an artificial creation that, notwithstanding massive infusions of American assistance and advice, never succeeded in acquiring a degree of legitimacy sufficient to stimulate the kind of sacrifices on the part of its citizenry that might have ensured its survival. Indeed, its utter and obvious dependence on the United States for its very existence, coupled with a highly destructive and culturally offensive American military presence, undermined all attempts to confer legitimacy upon the regime. Only a continuing and substantial post-1973 U.S. military presence could have preserved a noncommunist political order in the South.

To be sure, these judgments have been made before. But they bear reexamination as a prelude to addressing the most contentious of all the causes cited for U.S. defeat in Vietnam: a war policy crippled by civilian intrusion upon professional military prerogatives. Is it possible that the Vietnam War simply may not have been America's to win, given the tremendous and enduring disparity in political skill and fighting power separating the Vietnamese parties to the conflict? Would White House accession to all the military's desiderata regarding the war's conduct have made a decisive difference in its outcome?

I should note in passing that I do not regard the U.S. media and domestic antiwar movement as significant causes of America's defeat in Vietnam, though both remain prime targets of recrimination among those who believe that victory in Vietnam was stolen from the American military. Condemnation of the media is a dog that won't hunt. To be sure, the media's professional performance in covering the war left much to be desired. The fact remains, however, that until the Tet Offensive, which prompted a dramatic lowering of U.S. war aims (from seeking a military victory to searching for an "honorable" way out of Vietnam), both print and broadcast media editorials by and large supported the war, in many cases buying the official and congenitally optimistic line on the war's course. Moreover, the early skepticism of such bright and ambitious young journalists as Neil Sheehan, Peter Arnette, and David Halberstam over official prognoses of the war's progress was justified. That skepticism was fueled by the yawning gap between, on the one hand, what they saw in the field with their own eyes—and were told by such U.S. Army advisors as the legendary John Paul Vann—and, on the other, the perceptions to which they were treated back in Saigon by such career optimists as Ambassador Fritz Nolting and Westmoreland's predecessor, Paul Harkins (who, among other things, called the South Vietnamese Army's calamitous performance in the January 1973 Battle of Ap Bac a victory). The press was rightly suspicious of an official reporting system whose integrity was constantly threatened by a near manic preoccupation with quantification and with pleasing superiors.

As for the organized antiwar movement, which is not to be confused with the broader and far more influential phenomenon of antiwar sentiment, there is still no persuasive evidence that it had a significant impact on the formulation and implementation of U.S. war policy. On the contrary, to the extent that the antiwar movement became a vehicle for the emerging counterculture of the 1960s, it probably turned off many more Americans than it turned on. Most Americans, including the tens of millions who gave Richard Nixon his landslide 1972 victory over George McGovern and the ascendant antiwar wing of the Democratic Party, simply did not wish to be associated with unwashed hippies, and certainly not with political radicals shrieking condemnation of American society and mores. Michael Mandlebaum is certainly correct in his observation that although "the war became unpopular, the antiwar movement was always *more* unpopular."[22] The most effective antiwar initiatives came not in the form of street demonstrations, but rather in post–Johnson administration congressional amendments that progressively limited White House freedom of military action in Indochina.

On the matter of apportioning responsibility for defeat, I contend that, whereas the primary responsibility for the U.S. share of the war's outcome clearly rests with civilian decision-making authorities—which were, after all, Constitutionally and politically responsible— the military's accountability was significant and cannot and should not be overlooked. No debacle as monumental as America's in Vietnam can be ascribed solely to the White House and Office of the Secretary of Defense, and the interests of neither history nor the future formulation and implementation of foreign policy are promoted by a portrayal of the military as innocent and hapless victims of civilian perfidy. The Joint Chiefs of Staff, Pacific Command, and MACV were not well-served by their civilian superiors, but neither did they serve their country well.

I believe that, whatever the case to be made that the military was stabbed in the back by an arrogant and intrusive White House and OSD, a hostile press, and a subversive antiwar movement, the military nonetheless spent much of its time in Vietnam shooting itself—and the American cause in Vietnam—in the foot. The U.S. armed forces contributed to their own defeat in Vietnam by fighting the war they wanted to fight rather than the one at hand. Vietnam was hardly the first or the last time a great power came to grief militarily at the hands of a lesser foe.

To be sure, civilian authority was in charge and made the crucial decisions that thrust the United States into Vietnam and imposed the limits with which U.S. military power would be applied in Indochina. Yet U.S. military leadership not only warmly supported the Johnson administration's decision to enter the very kind of open-ended land war on the Asian mainland whose avoidance had been a traditional—and strategically wise—staple of American military planning. It also submitted, without effective protest, to civilian-imposed restrictions on military operations that it regarded as crippling to reasonable prospects for a decisive resolution of the conflict in Vietnam. Rather than confront the White House and OSD and place their careers on the line, key military leaders chose to go along with civilian decisions they regarded as ruinous to chances for victory and entailing an unnecessary expenditure of American lives.

Stab-in-the-back proponents argue that a politically unconstrained U.S. military effort would have prevailed in Vietnam. Civilian intrusion upon the conduct of military operations was indeed extensive and in some cases nonsensical. Civilian authority pursued a policy of graduated response that conveyed to the enemy a lack of resolve and permitted him to adapt and perfect his responses to slowly escalating U.S. military pressure. The Johnson White House and McNamara OSD, in their relationship with the JCS, exhibited a combination of arrogance and contempt that compromised the war's prosecution and poisoned civil-military relations. And in his refusal to mobilize both the reserves and public opinion early on in the war, Lyndon Johnson laid the foundation for popular disenchantment with the war that ultimately compelled a unilateral withdrawal of U.S. military forces from Vietnam. But none of this proves that the military could have won the war on its own—even assuming one could reach a consensus on a definition of victory.

Whatever the deficiencies in the performance of civilian authority— and they were many and serious— the fact remains that the military's performance left much to be desired even within the political limits imposed on the use of force within Indochina, which were much more stringent in North Vietnam, Laos, and Cambodia than they were in South Vietnam itself, where the MACV had a more or less free hand.

Thoughtful military professionals and other informed observers during the war and since have criticized various features of the U.S. military's performance, responsibility for none of which can be laid at the doorsteps of Lyndon Johnson, Robert McNamara, Peter Arnette, or Jane Fonda. Among them: an ill-conceived attrition strategy, an excessive use of firepower, an essentially superfluous bombing campaign, fractured command authority, self-defeating personnel rotation policies, and low combat-to-support-ratios. The military certainly shared with civilian authority that combination of unwarranted self-confidence in America's ability to prevail in Indochina and abominable ignorance of Vietnamese history and culture that so ill served the United States in Vietnam. It also shared with the civilians a capacity to avoid coming to grips with unpleasant truths. Colin Powell recounts that, "Our senior officers knew the war was going badly. Yet they bowed to group think pressure and kept up pretenses, the phony measure of body counts, the comforting illusion of secure hamlets, the inflated progress reports. As a corporate entity, the military failed to talk straight to its political superiors or to itself."[23]

The sources of America's defeat in Vietnam and of institutional responsibility for that defeat have been the subject of much discussion during the past quarter century. I recognize that I am taking a new crack at some old issues. But I believe that the passage of time has afforded a capacity for more informed and comprehensive judgment. Much more is now known about the consequences of decisions made than was known at the time they were made. Long-silent key policy-makers, including McNamara and the late Dean Rusk, have recently provided their unique perspectives on the war, and there have been important recent additions to the war's burgeoning literature on the issues of civil-military relations, domestic antiwar protest, the role of the press in shaping public attitudes towards the war, and North Vietnam's military calculations and strategy. Distance, together with the Cold War's demise, offers opportunities to develop new political perspectives on the war, perspectives less contaminated by blind passion and by the once unquestioned verities of what in hindsight seems a strategically hysterical anticommunism. Additionally, over three decades of substantial post–Vietnam War military reform and reorganization, highlighted by the masterful performance of the U.S. armed forces during the Persian Gulf crisis of 1990–91, offer fresh military perspectives on the Vietnam War.

My examination of the Vietnam War has driven me to an unusual conclusion: namely, that the ongoing debate over whether a U.S. victory was self-denied because of a flawed war policy may be irrelevant because a decisive U.S. military victory in Vietnam was probably unattainable except via measures—an invasion of North Vietnam or an unrestricted air attack on its population—that were never seriously considered by either civilian or military authorities. In other words, in terms of operational latitude, U.S. military authorities asked for too *little* rather than too much from their civilian superiors.

On a personal note, I should declare that my views on the Vietnam War are shaped in part by Vietnam-related personal experiences. I wrote my College Honors thesis in 1965 on the French-Indochina War. In 1967 I entered the State Department's Vietnam Training Program, and shortly after the beginning of the Tet Offensive in January 1968, began serving in Vietnam under the auspices of the Office of Civil Operations for Revolutionary Development Support (CORDS), an historically unique, integrated civilian-military advisory effort that conducted pacification programs in the so-called "other war." I served in the lower Mekong Delta as psychological operations advisor, initially as deputy assistant province advisor in Ba Xuyen Province and later as assistant province advisor in Bac Lieu Province. In these positions I worked closely with the Chieu Hoi (Open Arms) program, which sought, with considerable success in the Mekong Delta, to induce enemy soldiers and cadre to defect to the South Vietnamese government. I returned from Vietnam in August 1969 to the Johns Hopkins School of Advanced International Studies, where I wrote my Ph.D. dissertation, *The Viet Cong: Shadow and Substance,* a socioeconomic profile of Viet Cong defectors in Bac Lieu. Since then I have taught courses on the Vietnam War at the Georgia Institute of Technology's Sam Nunn School of International Affairs, Georgia State University, North Georgia College, and the U.S. Air Force's Air War College.

Throughout the Vietnam War I remained skeptical of both the wisdom of U.S. intervention and the prospects for its success. I observed at first hand not only the endemic corruption and incompetence of the South Vietnamese military and governmental institutions (the two were more often than not synonymous) at the regional, provincial, and district levels, but also the politically self-defeating consequences of an excessive U.S. and South Vietnamese reliance on firepower in the countryside. I also witnessed some of the first signs of the deterioration in the morale and discipline of U.S. forces that subsequently brought the U.S. Army in Vietnam to a state of near disintegration by the early 1970s.

I returned home convinced that the United States had to terminate its military intervention in Vietnam, and that an independent, noncommunist South Vietnam had no chance of survival in the long run unless it was transformed into a permanent and costly military ward of the United States.

The pages that follow are divided into seven chapters. Chapter 1, "The Reasons Why," examines the extraordinary significance U.S. decision makers attached to events in Vietnam in the early and mid-1960s. Their belief in these events' significance appears in retrospect fatally unjustified, but at the time it virtually dictated American ground combat intervention and spawned an investment of American prestige so great as to prolong intervention long after it should have been apparent that declared U.S. objectives in Indochina were beyond affordable reach. American decision makers also initially viewed the character of the war in Vietnam in a manner that emphasized purely military responses at the expense of necessary political and economic reforms. Ironically, after the Tet Offensive, as the war's political content diminished and the contest became more and more a straight conventional military fight, U.S. will to employ force, sapped by years of false official optimism against a backdrop of returning body bags with no convincing signs of progress, ultimately diminished to the point of self-renunciation. The nature of the Vietnam War changed dramatically from 1965 to 1975, but the United States, in contrast to the Vietnamese communists, was prepared to wage only one kind of war.

Chapter 2, "Stakes, Stamina, and Fighting Power," examines the serious U.S. underestimation of the Vietnamese communists' political tenacity and military effectiveness, and overestimation of its own. Underestimation of the enemy was especially pronounced among those key officials, such as Walt Rostow, who believed that limited war was first and foremost an act of political communication, and that the application of exquisitely calibrated driblets of conventional military power could be gradually escalated until the enemy cracked. Senior air power enthusiasts, such as Seventh Air Force commander William C. Momyer and CINCPAC commander U. S. Grant Sharp, also believed that Hanoi could be cowed, albeit by a massive air campaign against both strategic and interdiction targets.

Gradualists and "sharp blow" proponents alike believed that North Vietnam had a rational breaking point based on the kind of cold cost-benefit analysis that governed the American corporate world. The MACV generally took a less optimistic view, but it too underestimated the enemy. This misjudgment applied particularly to the enemy's ability to take—and control—his own casualties, an ability that compromised the principal assumption of MACV's attrition strategy. U.S. civilian and military decision makers as a corporate body were ignorant of Vietnam's martial history and culture, and believed that there was little if anything to be learned by studying the French defeat in Indochina. Their underestimation of the Vietnamese communists had disturbing parallels in U.S. disdain for Japanese military prowess and Chinese fighting power before, respectively, Pearl Harbor and China's intervention in the Korean War.

Both the Johnson and to a lesser extent the Nixon administrations overestimated public and congressional tolerance for U.S. involvement in a protracted, bloody war that never displayed convincing and timely signs of moving toward a definitive conclusion. Popular disaffection was exacerbated by the Johnson White House's refusal early on to mobilize opinion, and its subsequent, pre-Tet Offensive public portrayal of the war as an enterprise firmly on the road to certain victory. The Nixon administration, to be sure, recognized—and acted upon—public sentiment for a U.S. withdrawal from direct participation in the ground war in Vietnam, but to the very end Nixon at least seemed to believe that sufficient public and congressional support would be available for the use of U.S. air power to counter major North Vietnamese conventional military attempts to conquer South Vietnam.

Chapter 3, "The War in the South," addresses U.S. military effectiveness as it was displayed in the MACV's conduct of the war in South Vietnam. The Vietnam War was a clash of two quite different styles of warfare representing the cultures and historical experiences of agrarian Vietnam and post–World War II America. Generally speaking, it is fair to say that U.S. military effectiveness was compromised in the pre-Tet years by the still predominantly unconventional nature of the Vietnam War, and in the post-Tet years by a steady erosion of U.S. political will to use force. Throughout the war it was plagued by the difficulty of applying traditional American military solutions to the alien political-military challenges it encountered in Indochina. Firepower-heavy U.S. conventional forces optimized to defeat Soviet tank armies on the North German Plain were in many respects ill-suited to deal with an elusive, revolutionary guerrilla enemy in Southeast Asia that presented few worthy targets for the 8 million tons of bombs U.S. forces dropped in Indochina during the war. The Pentagon fought the only war it knew how to fight, whereas its Vietnamese enemy proved far more supple in adapting to the evolving demands placed on its military power in the decade separating U.S. ground combat intervention and the fall of Saigon. Moreover, the

Pentagon permitted longstanding interservice rivalries and bureaucratic imperatives to further compromise potential U.S. military effectiveness.

Chapter 4, "The War against the North," looks at the U.S. attempt to bomb North Vietnam into impotence or submission. Only loosely related to the MACV's war in the South, the U.S. air campaign was plagued from the start by faulty premises, confused objectives, organizational weaknesses, and half-hearted execution.

Chapter 5, "Hollow Client," examines the failure to construct in South Vietnam a politically viable alternative to the potent nationalist appeal of the communist side. Perhaps such an alternative was simply not within an alien Western nation's power to create. Notwithstanding a huge U.S. political and economic investment in South Vietnam, the United States never succeeded in translating disaffection with communist rule into a willingness to fight and die for a noncommunist South Vietnam. In the end, the Republic of Vietnam, which to a large extent was a creature of the American taxpayer, commanded about as much genuine legitimacy as the now extinct German Democratic Republic halfway around the world. Whereas the American experiment in reconstructing Germany and Japan succeeded, the experiment in Vietnamese nation-building failed, and it failed in large measure because there was little to work with in Vietnam south of the Seventeenth Parallel.

Chapter 6, "The War Along the Potomac," addresses the bitter civil-military struggle within American officialdom over the Vietnam War's conduct, a struggle that continues to be waged today among the war's civilian and military veterans. The chapter begins by recapitulating in summary form the primary causes of U.S. defeat in Vietnam, and then proceeds to identify and examine the specific issues of civil-military contention and the perspectives each side brought to those issues. Particular attention is paid to restraints imposed on the military effort and the reasons they were imposed. Additionally, the intrusiveness of restraints in Vietnam is compared, for illustrative purposes, to those imposed on U.S. military operations in the Korean and Persian Gulf wars. The chapter then assesses the degree to which responsibility for defeat can be apportioned between the civilian and military decision-making authorities, with specific emphasis placed on the organizational, operational, and policy deficiencies of U.S. military performance in Vietnam within the realm of politically imposed limitations on the use of force.

The book's final chapter, "Lost Victory?," addresses the great question still begged: Could the military have delivered victory if it had been permitted to fight the war the way it wanted to? Because an affirmative answer to this question carries with it the burden of proof, I examine the principal suppositions of those who continue to argue that victory in South Vietnam was self-denied—that is, that an operationally meaningful definition could have been established; that the military was of more or less one mind about how to win the war; and that the military's preferred path to victory could indeed have provided an enduring solution to the struggle in Vietnam. How valid are these suppositions, and if they are not, was the entire American enterprise in Vietnam doomed from the start?

Abbreviations

CIDG	Civilian Irregular Defense Corps
CINCPAC	Commander in Chief, Pacific Command
CORDS	Civil Operations for Revolutionary Development Support
DPRK	Democratic People's Republic of Korea
DRV	Democratic Republic of Vietnam
FEAF	Far East Air Forces
GVN	Government of Vietnam
JCS	Joint Chiefs of Staff
MACV	Military Assistance Command, Vietnam
NLF	National Liberation Front
NVA	North Vietnamese Army; also known as PAVN
OB	Order of Battle
OSD	Office of the Secretary of Defense
PACOM	Pacific Command
PAVN	People's Army of Vietnam; also known as NVA
PROVN	Program for Pacification and Long-Term Development of South Vietnam
RVNAF	Republic of Vietnam Air Forces
SAC	Strategic Air Command
SEA	Southeast Asia
SEATO	Southeast Asia Treaty Organization
SVN	South Vietnam
USSBS	United States Strategic Bombing Survey
VC	Viet Cong

THE WRONG WAR

1. The Reasons Why

IN HIS MASTERPIECE, *On War,* Carl von Clausewitz observed that the "first, the supreme, the most far-reaching act of judgment that the statesman and commander have to make is to establish . . . the kind of war on which they are embarking; neither mistaking it for, nor trying to turn it into, something that is alien to its true nature. This is the first of all strategic questions and the most comprehensive."[1]

Unfortunately, U.S. foreign policy decision makers in the mid-1960s committed a supreme act of misjudgment by intervening directly in the Vietnam War. Intervention proved calamitous. Among other things, it violated an established strategic injunction against committing U.S. military power to a large-scale land war on the mainland of Asia. Since World War II, U.S. military leaders, including Omar Bradley, Douglas MacArthur, and Matthew Ridgway, had cautioned against ground combat involvement in wars on the Asian mainland, where, it was felt, U.S. naval and air power's effectiveness would be diluted, and where Asian foes could exploit their great superiority in manpower and bog the United States down in a protracted conflict. This strategically sound aversion underpinned the Truman administration's refusal to commit U.S. ground forces on behalf of the Nationalist Chinese government in the latter half of the 1940s as well as its opposition to MacArthur's pleas in 1951 to widen the Korean War. It also played a significant role in the Eisenhower administration's refusal in 1954 to intervene on behalf of beleaguered French forces in Indochina.

The profound misjudgment that propelled the United States into the Vietnam War was captured in two November 1961 cables from Gen. Maxwell Taylor to President Kennedy, which are reprinted in *The Pentagon Papers*.[2] Taylor, the president's special military representative and later chairman of the Joint Chiefs of Staff and then U.S. ambassador to South Vietnam, recommended the introduction of U.S. ground combat troops into Vietnam. He did so despite his own estimation: that the "strategic reserve of U.S. forces is presently so weak that we can ill afford any detachment of forces to a peripheral area of the communist bloc where they will be pinned down for an uncertain duration"; that "U.S. prestige is already engaged in SVN [South Vietnam]" and "will become more so by the sending of troops"; and that if "the first contingent is not enough to accomplish the necessary results, it will be difficult to resist the pressure to reinforce." Having offered compelling reasons to stay out of Vietnam, Taylor went on to declare that for U.S. troops "SVN is not an excessively difficult or unpleasant place to operate" and that the "risks of backing into a major Asian war by way of South Vietnam are not impressive," in part because "North Vietnam is extremely vulnerable to conventional bombing." For Taylor, the case for introducing American ground combat troops boiled down to the conclusions that "there can be no action so convincing to the people and Government of SVN and to our other friends and allies in SEA [Southeast Asia]" and that the troops would "produce the desired effect on national morale in SVN and on international opinion." Maxwell Taylor, to paraphrase 1988 Democratic Vice Presidential candidate Lloyd Bentsen's remark about Dan Quayle, may have known Matthew Ridgway (his former Army superior and decisive opponent among the Joint Chiefs of Staff of U.S. military intervention to save the French at Dien Bien Phu in 1954), but he himself certainly was no Matthew Ridgway.

To be sure, the U.S. decision in 1950 to fight in Korea seemed to violate the injunction against mainland wars. Yet that decision did not assume the possibility of decisive Chinese counterintervention, without which the war would have been successfully concluded within a matter of months. When the Chinese did come in, the Joint Chiefs of Staff sagely resisted calls from an unnerved and humiliated MacArthur for military operations against China. A wider conflict, JCS Chairman Bradley warned, would embroil the United States "in the wrong war, at the wrong place, at the wrong time, and with the wrong enemy."[3] Unlike their Vietnam War successors, the Chiefs during the Korean War supported the White House's determination to cap U.S. investment in the war; they opposed escalation on the grounds that it would endanger more important U.S. commitments elsewhere. This fundamental consensus on the conflict's proper scope (MacArthur faced a united civil-military front in Washington) accounts in no small measure for the Korean War's lack of an attendant stab-in-the-back myth. Bradley and the other Chiefs wanted stringent limits on U.S. military liability in Korea, and they supported President Truman's sacking of MacArthur as a means of enforcing those limits.

There was also a consensus on the nature of the conflict. During at least the early years of the Vietnam War there was serious dispute within both civilian and military decision-making institutions over whether the war was predominantly an internal insurgency or conventional cross-border aggression. But in the early 1950s, U.S. political and military leaders (correctly) regarded the Korean War as largely a linear, conventional fight in which territory taken and held was the proper and reliable measure of success.

Moreover, the peninsular geography and barren topography of Korea permitted a very effective use of conventional U.S. military forces, especially naval and air power. Indochina, however, was neither peninsular nor barren; on the contrary, it provided communist forces extensive staging areas and infiltration routes impervious to permanent denial by U.S. air or ground forces. It was a standing invitation to precisely the kind of war against which an older, wiser generation of U.S. military leaders had warned. Dean Rusk, who as secretary of state argued ad nauseam that the United States had to fight in Vietnam if for no other reason than because it was, in his (widely disputed) view, unalterably committed to do so under the provisions of the 1954 Southeast Asian Treaty Organization (SEATO), later confessed that "I thought the SEATO Treaty was a mistake" precisely because "[n]o one really stopped to think what an American commitment to collective security on the Asian mainland might mean."[4] This is a truly extraordinary admission; apparently Rusk, like McNamara (now known to have been disillusioned about the war by late 1965), had early and profound doubts about the efficacy of U.S. involvement in Vietnam, but nonetheless stayed in office and continued to press publicly for an ever expanding commitment of U.S. blood and treasure to the war.

U.S. policymakers also accorded to events in Indochina a strategic significance far in excess of their actual and potential consequences for U.S. security. They further misread the character of the Vietnam War in a manner that promoted conventional U.S. military responses to what was still—in 1965—essentially a revolutionary political challenge. In doing all of these things, American decison makers committed to an exceedingly difficult conflict a measure of U.S. military power and national prestige disproportionate to the actual stakes involved. This overinvestment, moreover, made it all the more difficult later on to cut U.S. losses in Vietnam; on the contrary, it encouraged a policy of gradual escalation in the vain hope that at some point the communists would desist.

Even before the Tet Offensive, defeat avoidance was becoming the predominant de facto U.S. war aim, at least as far as the civilian leadership was concerned. By 1968 Lyndon Johnson had become skeptical of prospects for a conclusive military outcome in Vietnam, though he remained unwilling to escalate the war further. The Office of the Secretary of Defense had become demoralized, though McNamara could not muster the courage to resign. In 1965, McNamara's trusted lieutenant, Assistant Secretary of Defense for International Security Affairs John McNaughton, declared in a memo that "70 percent" of the U.S. purpose in Vietnam was "to avoid a humiliating defeat";[5] in early 1966, he further concluded: "We . . . have in Vietnam the ingredients of an enormous miscalculation. . . . The reasons we *went into* Vietnam to the present depth are varied; but they are now largely academic."[6] The Chiefs themselves may have concluded that they were not going to get the additional troops and operational freedom of action in Indochina they believed necessary to win the war. That they continued to press for more of both, even after the Tet Offensive had discredited Westmoreland's attrition strategy and fatally undercut American public support for the war, suggests they were motivated less by professional military confidence than by a desire to establish a robust record of rejected pleas as ammunition in the inevitable postwar debate over responsibility for losing Vietnam.

The search for an "honorable" peace continued for four years—and over twenty-two thousand additional American combat dead—under the Nixon administration, which, because it bore no responsibility for the unpopular war it had inherited, probably could have liquidated U.S. participation in the Vietnam War at an acceptable domestic political price. (Nixon's own impeccable anticommunist credentials might have served him as well in "closing" Vietnam in 1969 as they did in "opening" China three years later.) Instead, the administration, preoccupied with salvaging American prestige, also chose to pursue a policy of defeat avoidance, though one based on the combination of a less restrained application of U.S. air power and a "Vietnamization" strategy premised on the assumption that an expanded and better equipped South Vietnamese army could somehow succeed where American arms had failed. In the end, Nixon managed to postpone for a few years Saigon's inevitable day of reckoning with Hanoi; U.S. prestige probably suffered as much as it would have if the Nixon administration had simply walked away from Vietnam the day it took office.

In retrospect it is clear, as was persuasively argued at the time by such astute observers as George Kennan, Hans Morgenthau, and Walter Lippmann, that a U.S. fight to preserve an independent, noncommunist South Vietnam was essential neither to core U.S. security interests nor to America's reputation as a guarantor of other nations' security. Kennan, testifying before the Senate Foreign Relations Committee in early 1966, asserted that, "Vietnam is not a region of major military, industrial importance. It is difficult to believe that any decisive developments of the world situation would be determined . . . by what happens on that territory. . . . even a situation in which South Vietnam was controlled exclusively by the Viet Cong . . . would not, in my opinion, present dangers great enough to justify our military intervention."[7]

The decision to commit to an open-ended war in an area peripheral to traditional American security interests actually compromised U.S.

ability to honor its commitments elsewhere, and raised serious questions among allies and foes alike about the soundness of America's strategic judgment. It confirmed the original assessment of the Joint Chiefs of Staff in the wake of the French defeat at Dien Bien Phu in May 1954: "Indochina is devoid of decisive military objectives and the allocation of more than token U.S. armed forces in Indochina would be a serious diversion of limited U.S. capabilities."[8] Henry Kissinger, looking back on the war, contends that a proper "geopolitical approach geared to an analysis of the national interest would have differentiated between what was strategically significant and what was peripheral. It would have asked why America had thought it safe to stand by in 1948, when the communists conquered the huge prize of China, yet identified its national security with a much smaller Asian country that had not been independent for 150 years and had never been independent in its current borders."[9]

Why indeed? The decision to abandon the Chinese Nationalist regime was strategically justified though politically controversial. Chiang Kai-shek's Kuomintang was hopelessly corrupt and politically bankrupt. It was unable to compete in China's vast rural areas with the popular and well-disciplined communist forces of Mao Tse-tung; by late 1947 entire Nationalist army divisions, complete with their U.S.-supplied weapons, were defecting to the communist side. Moreover, it was highly doubtful that direct U.S. military intervention, which was opposed not only by the Truman administration but also by even the harshest congressional critics of its China policy, could have preserved the Nationalist government in power. There was in any event little in the way of usable U.S. conventional military power available in the late 1940s for employment in China. The pell-mell demobilization of the U.S. military establishment after World War II and the administration's growing concern over Soviet behavior in Europe combined to make any significant Chinese diversion a reckless course of action. Truman, Secretary of State Dean Acheson, and Gen. George Marshall, who at one time or another served as secretary of state, secretary of defense, and Truman's special representative in China, simply did not believe that American interests in China were worth a war; the administration was prepared to provide indirect military assistance to Chiang as well as its good offices to broker a political settlement between the Kuomintang and the communists, but it was not prepared to shed American blood in China.

The U.S. decision to fight in South Vietnam must have perplexed Hanoi. Could a do-or-die stand really be expected from a United States that had abandoned China in 1948, had refused to save its French clients at Dien Bien Phu in 1954, had settled for a communist North Vietnam in that same year, had provided only fainthearted support to an attempted invasion of Cuba in 1961, and had agreed to Laos' neutralization in 1962? Was a United States whose leader had spent much of the 1964 presidential election campaign reassuring his own people that American boys were not going to be sent to fight and die in a war in which Asian boys should be shouldering that burden going to do exactly the opposite of what he said? Had the United States learned nothing from the French experience in Indochina? Did not the United States realize that its conventional armed forces had restricted utility in Indochina's operational and geopolitical setting?

If such was Hanoi's reasoning, it was certainly understandable. The United States might make a limited liability investment (i.e., naval, air, and advisory ground) in South Vietnam's defense, but surely it was not prepared to exhaust itself strategically for the sake of a politically weak and militarily incompetent regime in Saigon. One rarely presumes acts of foolishness on the part of one's enemies. Hanoi in 1964 had no more reason to believe that the United States was prepared to embark upon such a mindless dissipation of its power in Southeast Asia than did Westmoreland and his staff in late 1967 have reason to believe that Hanoi was about to expose the Viet Cong to certain decimation at the hands of American firepower for the sake of a misinformed and poorly coordinated general offensive. Nor could Hanoi have been expected to recognize that the political consequences in the United States of the Truman administration's "loss" of China in the late 1940s would have a significant bearing on the American approach to the Vietnam War in the mid-1960s.

The excessive significance U.S. policymakers attached to events in Indochina in the 1960s was evident both in the strength of perceived domestic political imperatives that made any consideration of abandoning South Vietnam without a fight unthinkable, and in the publicly declared reasons for intervention. Domestic political imperatives figured heavily in the U.S. decision to intervene in Vietnam. As Democrats, both Kennedy and Johnson bore the legacy of a political party whose presidents had "lost" both Eastern Europe and China to communism, had "permitted" the emergence of a nuclear-armed Soviet Union as a rival world power, and had waged a "no-win" war in Korea (i.e., denied MacArthur a conclusive victory over Red China). During the late 1940s and 1950s the Republicans, led by such redbaiters as Richard Nixon and Joseph McCarthy, indicted the Truman administration for being "soft on communism" at home and abroad. No post-McCarthy-era Democratic president could afford to give up additional real estate to communism; to do so would invite a right-wing backlash. (Only a war-hero Republican president like Eisenhower could have permitted the fall of North Vietnam.)

The argument that Kennedy, had he lived, would have steered the United States around and ultimately away from the kind of military investment his successor made in Vietnam must confront Kennedy's actual behavior as president: he approved escalation of the U.S. military advisory effort in Vietnam to direct U.S. involvement in combat operations in violation of the Geneva Accords of 1954, and he encouraged a coup against the Diem regime that dramatically elevated U.S. political responsibility for South Vietnam's fate. He did both of these things because he not only subscribed to the official rationales for a U.S. stand in Vietnam but also feared the domestic political reaction that abandonment of Vietnam would provoke. Having bungled a U.S.-sponsored invasion of communist Cuba and acceded to a neutralization scheme for Laos that many—including South Vietnam's President Ngo Dinh Diem—regarded as a sell-out to the communists, Kennedy could not afford to be seen as an appeaser in Vietnam. As he told senator and Vietnam skeptic Mike Mansfield after the Cuban Missile Crisis, "If I tried to pull out completely now from Vietnam, we would have another Red scare on our hands."[10] In July 1963 he is said to have told reporters at an off-the-record news conference: "We don't have a prayer of staying in Vietnam. . . . But I can't give up a piece of territory like that to the Communists and get the American people to reelect me."[11]

Lyndon Johnson was even more consumed by dread of a domestic political backlash. As a young senator and later majority leader in the late 1940s and 1950s, he had witnessed first-hand the brutal Republican soft-on-communism assaults on the integrity of such impeccable patriots as Marshall and Acheson during the wave of anticommunist hysteria that swept the country following Mao Tse-tung's victory in China and the Soviet Union's explosion of an atomic bomb. Moreover, he regarded anything less than a strong stand in Vietnam as a threat to his ambitious domestic political agenda. A Johnson administration perceived as not allocating sufficient resources to defeat communism in Vietnam would provide opponents of the Great Society the perfect argument against proceeding with costly social and economic reforms at home. "Conservatives in Congress," he told Doris Kearns, "would use [the war] as a weapon against the Great Society. You see, they'd never wanted to help the poor or the Negroes in the first place. But they were having a hard time figuring out how to make their opposition sound noble in a time of great prosperity. But the war. Oh, they'd use it to say they were against my programs, not because they were against the poor—why, they were just as generous and charitable as the best of Americans—but because the war had to come first."[12] Even the emergence of a strident, leftist antiwar movement didn't phase Johnson, who once cautioned Under Secretary of State George Ball to "pay no attention to what those little shits on the campuses do. The great beast is the reactionary elements in this country."[13]

Reinforcing domestic political imperatives was a genuine conviction that a U.S. stand in Vietnam was indispensable to American security and international order. Indeed, the declared rationales for U.S. intervention in Vietnam accorded little intrinsic importance to a non-communist South Vietnam, but instead conferred upon U.S. behavior there a transcendental and vital significance; the imperative of making a stand in Vietnam was regarded as far more momentous than Vietnam's actual fate. British counterinsurgency expert and occasional war advisor to the White House Sir Robert Thompson declared in 1968 that "the war will be of critical consequence to the future of the world . . . and may well prove to be as decisive as any war in this century."[14] Indeed, better even to fail in Vietnam than not intervene at all. "We cannot assert that a policy of sustained [bombing] reprisal [against North Vietnam] will succeed in changing the course of the contest in Vietnam," wrote National Security Advisor McGeorge Bundy to President Johnson in February 1965, but "even if it fails, the policy will have been worth it. At a minimum, it will damp down the charge that we did not do all we could have done, and this charge will be important in many countries, including our own."[15] A year earlier, Bundy had conjectured in a memorandum to Johnson: "Question: in terms of domestic U.S. politics, which is better: to lose now or to lose after committing 100,000 men? Tentative answer: the latter."[16] The United States must be seen to be willing to fight, whatever the result, because the stakes were so high. Even early journalistic critics of U.S. policy in Vietnam accorded critical importance to the war's outcome. "The fall of Southeast Asia," wrote Neil Sheehan in 1964, "would amount to a strategic disaster." A year later, David Halberstam concluded that South Vietnam "is perhaps only one of five or six nations that is truly vital to U.S. interests."[17]

The record shows that U.S. entry into the Vietnam War was largely the product of strategic fright occasioned by the twin convictions that the United States was losing the Cold War, especially the war with Moscow and Beijing for power and influence in the Third World, and that communist expansion anywhere in the world was strategically unacceptable. In the early 1960s, U.S. policymakers considered the decolonizing underdeveloped world a crucial battleground in an era of East-West conventional military stalemate in Europe and eroding U.S. nuclear supremacy. They were, in fact, mesmerized by the challenge of so-called "wars of national liberation," touted in major speeches by Soviet Premier Nikita S. Khrushchev in 1961 and by Chinese Defense Minister Lin Piao four years later as a cheap, low-risk, and disavowable means of furthering communist expansion in Asia and Africa. The key was what U.S. policymakers called "covert aggression," or simulation of civil war via reliance on the techniques of guerrilla rather than conventional warfare and on infiltration rather than overt cross-border attacks.

The importance of the Third World and of the national liberation war threat were assumed simply because Moscow, Beijing, and Hanoi publicly regarded them as important. Moreover, notwithstanding a very mixed record of communist guerrilla insurgencies (success in China and northern Vietnam, but failure in Greece, Malaya, and the Philippines) that suggested the overriding importance of local political and economic conditions, wars of national liberation were believed to be easily exportable, and South Vietnam to be a test case for this new and insidious communist strategy. "The war in Vietnam," said Rusk in August 1965, "is a test of a technique of aggression: what the Communists, in their upside-down language, call 'wars of national liberation.' They use the term to describe any effort by Communists, short of large-scale war, to destroy by force any non-Communist government. . . . if [this kind of aggression] against South Vietnam were permitted to succeed, the forces of militant Communism everywhere would be vastly heartened and we could expect to see so-called 'wars of liberation' in Asia, Latin America, and Africa."[18] Walt Rostow, Johnson's national security advisor and staunch proponent of intervention, defined wars of national liberation as "an international disease . . . , guerrilla war designed, initiated, supplied, and led from outside an independent nation."[19]

Policymakers thus read the war in Vietnam as but a local manifestation of an externally orchestrated conspiracy. "Our political leaders," observes Colin Powell, "led us into a war for the one-size-fits-all rationale of anticommunism, which was only a partial fit in Vietnam, where the war had its own historical roots in nationalism, anticolonialism and civil strife."[20] In reading the war as an external plot, policymakers not only overlooked the powerful indigenous roots of the war in Vietnam but also conveniently simplified the case for U.S. intervention. Public and congressional opinion could hardly be expected to support the spilling of American blood in someone else's civil war, but that opinion could be carried for intervention if what appeared to be a civil war was in fact—or at least could be convincingly portrayed as—a new form of international communist aggression. In public testimony Rusk repeatedly cast the war in Vietnam as "an act of outside aggression as though the Hanoi regime had sent an army across the 17th parallel rather than infiltrating armed forces by stealth."[21] He and others conceded (in the words of Under Secretary of State George Ball, who privately opposed intervention but publicly preached its virtues) that "if the Vietnam War were merely what the Communists say it is—an indigenous rebellion—then the United States would have no business taking sides in the conflict."[22]

Not only would a successful U.S. stand in South Vietnam take the bloom off wars of national liberation; it would also thwart implementation of China's imperial agenda in Southeast Asia. Of all the misassumptions that guided the United States to disaster in Vietnam, perhaps none was as wrong and intellectually embarrassing as the conviction that North Vietnam and its communist brethren in South Vietnam were little more than instruments of Red Chinese expansionism. This conviction reflected an utter ignorance of the history of Sino-Vietnamese relations, an insufficient awareness of events within China in the early and mid-1960s, and a willingness to take at face value much of Beijing's rhetorical posturing vis-à-vis the Soviet Union on Third World issues.

The conclusion that Hanoi was a stalking horse for Beijing in Southeast Asia rested on surface appearances rather than serious inquiry. China and North Vietnam were, after all, both communist states (and neighboring ones at that); China had indeed provided significant military assistance to the Viet Minh during the French-Indochina War (and was to provide substantial material and manpower support, though not combat troops, to Hanoi in the 1960s);[23] and both China and North Vietnam espoused wars of national liberation and world revolution. Kennedy certainly saw China's hand in the struggle in South Vietnam. Asked by David Brinkley in September 1963 if he doubted the domino theory, he replied: "No, I believe it. I think the struggle [in South Vietnam] is close enough. China is so large, looms so high just beyond the frontiers, that if South Vietnam went, it would not only give them an improved geographic position for a guerrilla assault on Malaya but would also give the impression that the wave of the future in Southeast Asia was China and the Communists. So I believe it."[24] A year later, Secretary of Defense McNamara declared that "Hanoi's victory [in South Vietnam] would be a first step toward eventual Chinese hegemony over the two Vietnams and Southeast Asia and toward exploitation of the new [wars of liberation] strategy in other parts of the world."[25] President Johnson agreed: "Over this war—and all Asia—is another reality: the deepening shadow of Communist China. The rulers in Hanoi are urged on by Peiping."[26]

These judgments reflected a Cold War mentality that regarded communism and nationalism as utterly incompatible—a view perhaps valid in theory but not in practice. In 1950, Secretary of State Dean Acheson declared that Soviet and Chinese communist diplomatic recognition of the DRV "should remove any illusions as to the 'nationalistic' nature of Ho Chi Minh's aims and reveal Ho in his true colors as the mortal enemy of native independence in Indochina."[27] Judgments like these prompted John Kenneth Galbraith to observe later that in "the conspiratorial vision of world communism that developed following World War II, one thing was axiomatic. Communism outside the Soviet Union could never successfully identify itself with nationalism. It was a foreign as well as a wicked thing which no country could have except as it might be imposed or infiltrated from abroad."[28] In 1951, astoundingly, Rusk himself characterized Mao's communist regime as "a colonial Russian government—a Slavic Manchukuo on a large scale. It is not the Government of China."[29] In fact, all of the world's most prominent communist leaders of the day—Stalin, Mao, Tito, and Ho—had successfully identified with and captured nationalist sentiment in their respective countries. Moreover, China was—and remains—Vietnam's hereditary enemy. The two thousand-year history of Vietnam is largely a history of fierce resistance to Chinese aggression. Though culturally Chinese, the Vietnamese have always feared and distrusted their giant neighbor to the north, a fear and distrust born of a thousand years of hated Chinese rule. (China occupied Vietnam from 111 B.C. to A.D. 938, and later, from 1406 to 1428.)

Communism's spread to Vietnam changed little. In 1946, Ho Chi Minh was confronted with the choice of acceding to the return of French forces to the northern half of Vietnam, which was then occupied by Nationalist Chinese troops (for the purpose of receiving the surrender of Japanese troops), or letting the Chinese stay on without a firm departure date. Ho chose the return of French colonialism rather than letting the Chinese stick around. "It is better to sniff French dung for awhile," he said, "than to eat China's all our life."[30]

In 1954 the Chinese and Russians sold out their communist comrades in Vietnam by pressuring the Viet Minh to accept a political settlement of the French-Indochina War far more favorable to Paris than the nearly hopeless French military position in Indochina warranted. Specifically, the Chinese pressured the Vietnamese communists at the Geneva Conference to make two concessions—concessions that paved the way for the establishment in the South of a rival, anticommunist regime which, with U.S. assistance, delayed Vietnam's reunification under communist auspices for another twenty-one years. The Chinese, who for their own reasons wanted an end to the French-Indochina War and were prepared to threaten their Vietnamese comrades with a cessation of military assistance to obtain it, insisted that Ho Chi Minh and his Democratic Republic of Vietnam (DRV) accept a negotiated settlement that (1) mandated a military truce but postponed a resolution of political issues until nationwide elections scheduled in 1956, and (2) delimited the DRV's southern boundary at the Seventeenth Parallel. Ho and his colleagues felt—and were—betrayed. They believed that the combination of France's political exhaustion and the Viet Minh's commanding military position (controlling at least three-quarters of Vietnam's territory and population)[31] entitled them to an immediate and comprehensive political settlement highly favorable to the communist cause. Absent such a settlement, they would accept a DRV southern boundary at least as far south as the Thirteenth Parallel, which would give the DRV both the exquisite natural port of Da Nang (Tourane) and the historical and psychological prize of Hue, the old imperial capital.[32]

Lin Piao's famous September 1965 speech, "Long Live the Victory of People's War," though interpreted by the Johnson administration as an incitement to worldwide revolution and a declaration of unqualified Chinese support for a communist victory in Vietnam, was in fact a warning to Hanoi not to expect any direct Chinese intervention on the DRV's behalf. Lin characterized Vietnam as a testing ground for both a people's war and American efforts to defeat it; but he also in effect told the Vietnamese that this was their war, stressing the necessity for self-reliance and avoidance of reckless military action. (Lin was preaching a Chinese version of the Nixon Doctrine four years before Nixon had a chance to proclaim it.) China was on the verge of starting its long march toward the disaster of the Great Cultural Revolution, a domestic political upheaval of titanic proportions prompted in part by a bitter dispute within the political leadership over whether the Soviet Union was supplanting the United States as the main threat to China's security. Under such circumstances, and with memories of the horrendous losses the Americans had inflicted on Chinese forces in Korea, Beijing had every reason to avoid war with the United States (and had, in fact, indicated to the United States that it would not intervene in the Vietnam War unless the Americans invaded North Vietnam).[33]

Nor did China have an interest in the creation of a powerful, unified and Soviet-allied Vietnam hostile to Chinese interests in Southeast Asia. Indeed, the emergence of just such a Vietnam in the 1970s (highlighted by Hanoi's formal alliance with the Soviet Union, the brutal expulsion of Chinese living in Vietnam, and Vietnam's invasion of Cambodia and defeat of the Chinese-backed Khmer Rouge there) induced the Chinese in early 1979 to launch a short but bloody invasion of Vietnam's northernmost provinces.

So much for the Vietnamese as Chinese stooges. A genuinely informed focus on containing Chinese imperialism in Southeast Asia in the 1960s would have dictated—at the very minimum—U.S. acquiescence to the establishment of a strong reunified Vietnam under any—though preferably noncommunist—auspices. The Russians, who successfully courted the DRV in the Sino-Soviet struggle for influence in Hanoi, understood this even if the United States did not. Indeed, for the Russians, the Vietnam War was a strategic windfall: it bogged American military power down in a peripheral area while at the same time providing the foundation for the DRV's ultimate recruitment as an important Soviet client in Moscow's own campaign to curb Chinese imperialism.

The failure to recognize that Vietnam was not an agent of Chinese southward expansionism but rather a potential obstacle to it stemmed from a view of communism as, at worst, a monolithic international conspiracy, and, at best, as a powerful international movement set upon global domination and capable of subordinating local nationalist impulses to the demands of ideological conformity. Indeed, U.S. policymakers were wont to equate communism in the 1950s and 1960s with fascism in the 1930s and 1940s, and any refusal to stand and fight to prevent communism's spread anywhere as tantamount to a Munich-style act of appeasement. By 1965, when the Johnson administration committed ground combat units to the Vietnam War, the U.S. doctrine of containment had been thoroughly militarized and extended beyond Europe to almost any country willing to ally itself with the United States. (As originally envisaged by George Kennan, containment entailed largely nonmilitary responses to a Soviet threat to Western Europe's industrial democracies regarded as predominantly political and psychological in nature.) Containment's universalization prompted Kennan's condemnation: "[W]e have made no mistake so fundamental in American foreign policy than concluding that a design suitable for Europe would also be suitable for those regions of the world that have just thrust off European rule, and that we failed to take into account how very different the underlying situation was in Asia and Africa."[34] Unfortunately, those responsible for America's Vietnam intervention had come to believe that communist expansion anywhere, even in strategically remote areas against unsavory noncommunist dictatorships, threatened U.S. security.

The Munich analogy and its attendant domino theory heavily influenced official American thinking. Truman, Acheson, Eisenhower, Dulles, Johnson, and Rusk all believed that the Western democracies' accession in 1938 to Hitler's territorial demands on Czechoslovakia paved the way for World War II and proved that appeasing aggression simply invited more of it. They believed that totalitarian states, be they fascist or communist, were inherently and insatiably aggressive, and that, as such, they could be stopped or contained only by a collective resort to force—or at least a demonstrated willingness to fight—on the part of their intended victims.

They further subscribed, at least with respect to post-World War II Asia, to the domino principle, which held that the loss to communism of a single Southeast Asian country, be it French Indochina before the 1954 Geneva Conference or the Republic of (South) Vietnam after the conference, would inexorably lead to communist control of the rest of Southeast Asia, including Thailand, Burma, Malaya, and Indonesia. After all, did not Hitler pursue an agenda of inexorable aggression from the Rhineland to the Austrian *Anschluss* to the Sudetenland to Czechoslovakia proper to Poland and then on to the rest of Europe?

Did not the road to Pearl Harbor and Bataan start with unchecked Japanese aggression in Manchuria?

Fear of falling dominoes was certainly pervasive among U.S. civilian and military officials working in Vietnam. Shortly after my arrival in Vietnam, I was lectured by my nominal Mekong Delta regional boss, an Air Force lieutenant colonel named Beaulieu, on just how extensive the domino effect would be if the United States gave up in Indochina. Colonel Beaulieu, whom I learned immediately after our first meeting was Elvis Presley's father-in-law (the pictures of "The Pelvis" and Priscilla ornamenting Beaulieu's office should have been a hint), declared that the dominoes extended all the way to Europe. "Once Vietnam falls," he said, "so will Southeast Asia, then India, Iran, and Turkey," though he could never define which communist powers would be involved in this great drive westward, or, for that matter, why anyone would wish to conquer and administer independent India.

The reasoning spawned by Munich was nowhere more cogently expressed than by Truman in a 1951 radio address on the Korean War and U.S. policy in the Far East. He declared that the "Communists in the Kremlin are engaged in a monstrous conspiracy to stamp out freedom all over the world," adding that, "It is easier to put out a fire in the beginning when it is small than after it has become a roaring blaze. And the best way to meet the threat of aggression is for the peace-loving nations to act together. If they don't act together, they are likely to be picked off one by one. . . . if the free countries of the world had acted together to crush the aggression of the [fascist] dictators [in the 1930s], there probably would have been no World War II. If history has taught us anything, it is that aggression anywhere in the world is a threat to peace everywhere in the world."[35] Two years later, Eisenhower, who first publicly used the term "domino" on the eve of the French collapse in Indochina, warned that "if Indochina goes, several things happen right away. The Malayan peninsula would scarcely be defensible . . . . all India would be outflanked . . . [and] how would the free world hold the rich empire of Indonesia? So you see, somewhere along the line, this must be blocked. It must be blocked now."[36] Eisenhower subsequently appealed for British help in rescuing the French: "[W]e failed to halt Hirohito, Mussolini and Hitler by not acting in unity and in time," he wrote Prime Minister Churchill in 1954. "That marked the beginning of many years of stark tragedy and desperate peril. May it not be that our nations have learned something from that lesson?"[37]

Lyndon Johnson also saw Munich lurking in Indochina: "[E]verything I knew about history told me that if I got out of Vietnam and let Ho Chi Minh run through the streets of Saigon, then I'd be doing exactly what [Neville] Chamberlain did. . . . I'd be giving a fat reward to aggression."[38] For Dean Rusk the stakes in Vietnam were nothing short of another global conflict. The "overriding problem before us in Southeast Asia was . . . how to prevent World War III. The principal lesson I learned from World War II was that if aggression is allowed to gather momentum, it can continue to build and lead to general war."[39]

I myself was directly exposed to the Munich analogy's hold on even low-level American officialdom in the summer of 1967 at the Foreign Service Institute's Vietnam Training Center, which I attended for eight months prior to my participation in the U.S. pacification effort in Vietnam under the auspices of the Civil Operations for Revolutionary Development Support (CORDS) organization. At the center, located in Arlington, Virginia, my classmates and I received intensive instruction in Vietnamese history, culture, and language as well as U.S. policy in Indochina. "What is frightening," I noted in a diary I kept throughout my Vietnam service, "are the talks given by political officers from the State Department. The theme has become routine. Inevitably, each lecture begins with Munich and ends in Vietnam without dropping a single political stitch along the way. The pre-World War II conditions and environment of Europe are unquestionably accepted as being almost entirely relevant to present-day Indochina. The sadistic Nazi jackboots of the Nuremberg rallies are the precursors of the Asian communist guerrillas. Industrial, white, advanced Europe equals backward, non-white, rural Asia; Ho equals Himmler; the Viet Cong equal the blackshirts. South Vietnam has become Czechoslovakia, and the antiwar peaceniks are equated with Neville Chamberlain's 'peace in our time.'"

The Munich analogy presupposed not only aggression pursued relentlessly on behalf of extensive, even unlimited, imperial ambitions, but also an availability of resources sufficient to act upon those ambitions. Nazi Germany and post-1945 Soviet Russia had both, though

Stalin and his successors pursued their imperial ambitions with a great deal more patience and caution than Hitler pursued his.

The Munich analogy's corollary domino principle presupposed a relative homogeneity in vulnerability to takeover (absent external assistance) of aggression's intended victims. (Dominoes' physical characteristics and obedience to the law of gravity render them all virtually identical.) Nazi Germany was a great power bent on dominating the Eurasian land mass, and until 1941 it faced no adversary capable of effectively resisting the force of German arms on the Continent; the Czech, Polish, Danish, Norwegian, Belgian, Dutch, and even French dominoes toppled quickly when tapped by Hitler's legions. Soviet Russia supplanted Germany as Eurasia's principal hegemon, and faced no opponent other than the distant United States capable of containing Moscow's ambitions. Munich did in fact harbor lessons appropriate for dealing effectively with the Soviet Union during the Cold War.

In Southeast Asia, however, Munich blinded rather than enlightened American officialdom. Policymakers' tendency to view events in Southeast Asia in the 1950s and 1960s through the prism of events in Europe in the 1930s and 1940s helped lay the foundation for the very disaster memories of which today shape U.S. policy just as profoundly as did memories of Munich in Southeast Asia. In Southeast Asia the United States was not dealing with the Soviet Union but rather a small, poor communist state. There was simply no analogy between Ho Chi Minh and Hitler, and between South Vietnam and the Sudetenland. As noted, the Asian communist dictator was not an instrument of Chinese expansionism. Nor did he harbor imperial ambitions outside of the boundaries of French Indochina, a piece of real estate of virtually no intrinsic value to the United States. North Vietnam was a small, impoverished state whose ultimate victory in Indochina toppled not a single additional Southeast Asian domino of any strategic consequence. (Hanoi's ability, having conquered South Vietnam, to dominate Cambodia and Laos was never in doubt, and after Laos's neutralization in 1962 no serious consideration was given to a direct U.S. defense of either country.) John F. Kennedy's characterization of South Vietnam as "the cornerstone of the Free World in Asia, the keystone in the arch, the finger in the dike" whose loss to communism would threaten the security of "Burma, Thailand, India, Japan [and] the Philippines"[40] was, quite simply, rubbish.

The rationale of last resort for those who plunged the United States into the Vietnam War was the perceived imperative of maintaining the integrity of U.S. defense commitments worldwide. The argument was as simple as it was specious: the United States was committed to defend South Vietnam from external aggression, and failure to honor that commitment would lessen confidence in U.S. commitments elsewhere, from Berlin to Seoul. It made little difference whether the commitment to South Vietnam's defense was wise or militarily sustainable; America's word was at stake. Dean Rusk summed up this line of reasoning in an interview with CBS Television News in 1965: "The fact is that we know we have a commitment. The South Vietnamese know we have a commitment. The Communist world knows we have a commitment. The rest of the world knows it. Now, this means that the integrity of the American commitment is at the heart of this problem. I believe that the integrity of the American commitment is the principal structure of peace throughout the world." Rusk then added that "if our allies or, more particularly, if our adversaries should discover that the American commitment is not worth anything, then the world would face dangers of which we have not yet dreamed."[41]

Was the United States obligated to do what it did in Vietnam? Johnson administration officials paraded the SEATO Treaty of 1954 ad nauseam in public speeches and congressional testimony as the legal basis of the U.S. commitment to South Vietnam's defense. Secretary of State John Foster Dulles, who regarded the extension of U.S. defense guarantees to any and all willing countries, regardless of feasibility considerations, as an effective deterrent to communist aggression, had indeed conceived the treaty as providing the legal pretext for future U.S. military intervention in Vietnam.[42] A pretext, however, is not an obligation. There was nothing in the treaty that enjoined a U.S. defense of South Vietnam; unlike the NATO treaty, which mandated immediate military reaction by the United States to an armed attack on any ally within the treaty area, SEATO required of each signatory only that it "meet the common danger in accordance with its constitutional processes." The SEATO Treaty did not preclude the United States from

entering the Vietnam War, but it certainly did not mandate intervention. It surely did not obligate an armed response to local insurgency,
even a communist one. So testified Secretary of State Dulles in support
of SEATO's ratification. "If there is a revolutionary movement in Vietnam . . . , we would consult together [with other members of SEATO].
. . . But we have no undertaking to put it down; all we have is an undertaking to consult together as to what to do about it."[43]

No other member of SEATO felt obligated by the treaty to fight in
South Vietnam, notwithstanding official U.S. portrayal of the war from
its inception as a case of international aggression as clear cut as North
Korea's invasion of South Korea and even as would be a Soviet attack
on Western Europe. (Alone among SEATO members other than the
United States, Australia contributed forces in size proportionally sig-
nificant to its total armed forces. New Zealand, Thailand, and the
Philippines all sent token contingents, the latter two countries in
exchange for substantial U.S. military assistance. South Korea, not a
SEATO member, provided substantial forces—two army divisions and
a marine brigade—but only in exchange for hefty U.S. military assis-
tance to Seoul and a pledge by the United States not to redeploy to
Vietnam either of the two U.S. divisions stationed in Korea.) "The
Asian [allies] were ready to fight to the last American," complained
Clark Clifford, McNamara's successor as secretary of defense.[44]

SEATO itself was a diplomatic bastard child, an Anglo-French sop to
Dulles at Geneva, who opposed any negotiated settlement of the French
Indochina War that would leave the communists territory and a favorable military position, and who, failing that, futilely sought the formation of a Southeast Asian alliance as a prerequisite to any such settlement.
Unlike NATO, which was a well-planned, regionally compact alliance
with an integrated military command, SEATO was a hastily cobbled
together collection of states lacking geographic integrity and any instrument of collective military action. It was a paper alliance. SEATO's most
prominent members—the United States, France, Britain, Pakistan,
Australia, and New Zealand—lay outside Southeast Asia; and of
Southeast Asia's non-Indochinese states, only two—Thailand and the
Philippines—were members; Burma, Malaysia, and Indonesia refused
to join. Even South Vietnam, Laos, and Cambodia were included in

SEATO only as so-called "protocol" states—i.e., states to which SEATO's protection was extended but which lacked any defense obligations to other SEATO members.

Leaving SEATO aside, however, by 1965 a U.S. defense commitment to Saigon of some magnitude was implicit in the mere fact that three successive American presidents and their official spokesmen had declared (however thoughtlessly) an independent, noncommunist South Vietnam to be a vital U.S. interest and accordingly had steadily increased investment in U.S. resources and prestige in South Vietnam. But this commitment was not inherently open-ended; it dictated neither large-scale U.S. ground combat intervention—and certainly not Americanization of the war—nor unconditional U.S. support of any and all political regimes in Saigon. In 1954, Eisenhower sent South Vietnamese President Ngo Dinh Diem a letter pledging U.S. support for the new government contingent on South Vietnam's ability to use U.S. economic and military assistance effectively and on Diem's implementation of political reforms.[45] In 1961, then-Vice President Lyndon Johnson, following a trip to South Vietnam, recommended a three-year military and economic aid program conditioned on South Vietnam's pledge and implementation of political reforms.[46] Moreover, until 1965 presidents Kennedy and Johnson repeatedly stressed that the war was ultimately an indigenous fight, that the United States could—and would—assist the South Vietnamese in their struggle against communism, but that they themselves would have to shoulder the blood burden of the war. "We can help them, we can give them equipment, we can send our men out there as advisers," Kennedy told Walter Cronkite in a 1963 television interview, "but they have to win it, the people of Vietnam, against the Communists."[47] Johnson in September 1964 concurred: "We are not about to send American boys nine or ten thousand miles away from home to do what Asian boys ought to be doing for themselves."[48]

The fact that within four years there were over five hundred thousand U.S. troops fighting in Vietnam simply reflects the combination of South Vietnamese military fecklessness and the Johnson administration's strategic recklessness. No treaty or presidential pronouncement morally, politically, or legally committed the United States to this kind of intervention.

Nor did America's principal allies regard the United States's stand in Vietnam as a test of Washington's willingness to honor its defense commitments to them. The credibility of the U.S. commitment to Western Europe's defense had been repeatedly and convincingly demonstrated before 1965; Berliners, Englishmen, and even Charles De Gaulle did not need reassurance in distant Southeast Asia. Nor did the United States need to reassure South Koreans, Japanese, and Taiwanese. On the contrary, most of our allies regarded—and with good reason—America's deepening immersion in the Indochinese tar pit as a threat to Washington's ability to honor its commitments to them. To sustain, without a reserve call-up, a deployment of over five hundred thousand U.S. troops in Vietnam composed largely of draftees serving only one-year tours there, the Pentagon had to strip to the bone its forces deployed to Europe and withheld in the United States as a strategic reserve. By January 1968, the month North Korea seized the USS *Pueblo* and Hanoi launched the Tet Offensive, the strategic reserve contained only one combat ready division (the Eighty-second Airborne), and U.S. forces deployed in Europe and Northeast Asia were so enervated they could not perform their assigned missions. By that time, moreover, the post-World War II U.S. Army had been largely superseded by a conscript force.

This state of strategic bankruptcy was ultimately attributable to the ludicrously excessive significance American policymakers attached to events in Indochina, a significance which in turn derived from an American foreign policy that by the mid-1950s was no longer informed by reasoned judgment based on strategic discrimination and considerations of operational feasibility, but rather by a mindless anticommunism. Yet, if policymakers were wont to misread the importance of the war in Vietnam, they were no less inclined to misconstrue the nature of that war, and they were wont to do so in part to justify U.S. intervention in the first place. In April 1965, Hans Morgenthau, who believed that the war in Vietnam was essentially a civil conflict having no enduring strategic consequences for the United States, accused the Johnson administration of drawing "a most astounding conclusion" from its losing effort in Vietnam. "The United States," he said, citing the State Department's controversial February 1965 white paper, *Aggression from the North: The*

Record of North Viet-Nam's Campaign to Conquer South Viet-Nam, "has decided to change the character of the war by a unilateral declaration from a South Vietnamese civil war to a war of 'foreign aggression.'"[49]

Perhaps no other issue has more bedeviled discussion of the Vietnam War than that of what kind of war it was. American officialdom insisted that the conflict was a case of international aggression waged conventionally, or at least subject to defeat by conventional U.S. military action. This view continues to be embraced by those who believe that the war was morally noble or at least militarily winnable. For example, Harry Summers asserts that the Vietnam War was "a conventional war" and that North Vietnam was "the source of aggression."[50] Westmoreland agrees: "South Vietnam was not conquered by the guerrilla. It was conquered by the North Vietnamese army."[51] Nixon: "We failed to understand that the war was an invasion from North Vietnam, not an insurgency in South Vietnam. North Vietnam shrewdly camouflaged its invasion to look like a civil war. But in fact the Vietnam War was the Korean War with jungles."[52]

Conversely, those who believe that the war was unwinnable, or that the United States had no business in Vietnam anyway, claim, as did contemporary critics of U.S. intervention, that the conflict was essentially a civil war among Vietnamese who had been artificially and temporarily divided by the Cold War, and that it was unconventional, even revolutionary in character. Daniel Ellsberg has called it a "war of independence and a revolution."[53] Leslie Gelb and Richard Betts have tagged Vietnam as "a civil war for national independence."[54] The British counterinsurgency warfare expert, Sir Robert Thompson, writing in 1969, characterized the war as "basically an insurgency within South Vietnam boosted by infiltration, raids and an element of invasion from North Vietnam."[55] In 1982, historian Theodore Draper, in a review of Norman Podhoretz's *Why We Were in Vietnam,* denounced the claim of foreign aggression because it "treats North Vietnam as if it were not inhabited by Vietnamese. . . . The control of the southern Vietcong by the North Vietnamese did not make either of them less Vietnamese."[56]

How could a single war have so many perceived and contradictory faces? There has never been any doubt about the nature of World Wars I and II or the Korean War. One is tempted to conclude that simply the desire to make a lost war look retrospectively noble and winnable—or ignoble and doomed from the start—is enough to father whatever characterization is most appropriate.

A more satisfying answer, though not to those who insist that the war was either a Hitlerian act of external aggression or a pristine internal insurgency, is that the war was both civil and international, and both conventional and unconventional. It was civil in that it was waged predominantly by Vietnamese (on both sides of a Seventeenth Parallel that had no legal standing as an international border) to determine the future political control of southern Vietnam. It was international because it elicited massive direct U.S. military intervention and substantial Soviet and Chinese indirect intervention. It was conventional in the way it was fought on the battlefield by the United States throughout the war and occasionally by the Vietnamese communists, especially in 1968, 1972, and 1975. It was guerrilla in the way it was waged predominantly by North Vietnam and the National Liberation Front before—and for several years after—the Tet Offensive. It was also a total war for the communist side, whereas it was a limited war for the United States. It was total war against South Vietnam in that Hanoi wished to eliminate South Vietnam as an independent and noncommunist political entity, whereas the war the DRV waged against the United States was limited in that its objective was simply to compel U.S. withdrawal.

In these and other respects the Vietnam War bears a striking resemblance to the American War for Independence and the Spanish Civil War. The former was essentially a civil war among Englishmen over the political governance of British North America, though it elicited direct French intervention on behalf of the colonists in the form of credit, arms, Admiral de Grasse's fleet, and General Rochambeau's army that proved critical to the success of the American cause. It was waged according to the standards of European military convention by the British and sometimes by Washington's Continental Army, but waged unconventionally by American militia everywhere, Tory partisan forces in the southern colonies, and the Native American allies of both sides. The Spanish Civil War of 1936–39 was no less first and foremost a civil conflict—a war among Spaniards to determine who should govern Spain, though it too provoked substantial foreign intervention (Soviet on the Republican side, German and Italian on the fascist side). As in the American War for Independence, the war in Spain was waged both conventionally and unconventionally. Interestingly, external partisans of both Franco and the Republicans tended to assign to the Spanish Civil War, as did American policymakers to the Vietnam War, far greater strategic significance than the conflict warranted. By the 1930s, events in Spain had long ceased to have much influence beyond the Pyrenees, and fascism's ultimate victory in Spain contributed little to the subsequent fortunes of Nazi Germany. Franco proved as much of a Spanish nationalist as did Ho Chi Minh a Vietnamese nationalist; he was no more willing to place his country at Hitler's disposal (despite the German dictator's enormous pressure) than was Ho Chi Minh to serve as an imperial stalking horse for China—or was George Washington to serve as an agent of French Bourbon ambitions in the New World.

The Vietnam War simply could not be neatly fitted into the category of either foreign aggression or civil war, conventional conflict or guerrilla insurgency. Even if one chooses to label, inside Vietnam, the North Vietnamese as "foreigners" (was the movement of Union armies south of the Mason-Dixon Line in 1861–65 a case of foreign aggression?), the fact remains that at least until the Tet Offensive of 1968, the enemy's order of battle inside South Vietnam was dominated by indigenous southerners relying on locally acquired weapons. According to the State Department's own 1965 white paper, which sought to prove that the war in Vietnam was nothing more than a case of aggression from North Vietnam, of the total of 95,000 to 115,000 communist insurgents believed operating inside South Vietnam, only 20,000 were characterized as communist "officers, soldiers, and technicians . . . known to have entered South Vietnam under orders from Hanoi."[57] As additional proof of external aggression the white paper went on to list Chinese, Soviet, and Czech weapons captured from the insurgents. (Sixteen helmets and an undisclosed number of socks of North Vietnamese manufacture also were listed.) Yet the number of foreign recoilless rifles, mortars, rocket launchers, rifles, pistols, and submachine guns totaled 115[58]—or an average of one weapon for every 826–1,000 estimated insurgents! In fact, communist forces in South Vietnam in 1965 were armed almost exclusively with weapons and ammunition captured, stolen, or bribed from South Vietnamese army and security forces.

It was then—and remains today—highly misleading to assume sponsorship of an insurgency on the basis of insurgent weapons' country of manufacture. (American-made 105mm artillery pieces transferred from captured Nationalist Chinese forces by communist China to the Viet Minh proved critical to General Vo Nguyen Giap's 1954 victory over the French at Dien Bien Phu.) In the Vietnam War, almost all industrially manufactured weapons were of foreign make since neither North nor South Vietnam had an indigenous arms industry. In the coastal lower Mekong Delta, where I served immediately after the Tet Offensive, the Viet Cong were equipped with weapons ranging from homemade booby traps to Chinese and Czech mortars and semiautomatic rifles. Main force VC (there were no PAVN units present) were armed with a combination of communist bloc and captured U.S. weapons, with local VC militia and self-defense forces relying almost exclusively on U.S. World War II-vintage M-1 rifles and M-2 carbines captured, stolen, or bought on the black market from South Vietnamese government forces. (The RVNAF did not begin receiving the U.S. M-16 rifle until 1969.) Also popular were World War I-vintage German Mauser bolt-action rifles, large stocks of which had been captured in Germany by Soviet forces in 1945. The Russians subsequently transferred them to the Chinese People's Liberation Army, which later turned them over to the Viet Minh during the French-Indochina War. Weapons of French and even Japanese manufacture also were discovered in VC arms caches, as were antivehicular mines, almost all of which were home-manufactured using dud U.S. bombs and artillery shells.

Not until after the Tet Offensive did North Vietnamese regulars, serving either in PAVN units or as fillers in depleted Viet Cong formations, come to dominate communist forces in the South. As late as December 1967, one month before the Tet Offensive was launched, Sir Robert Thompson estimated that North Vietnamese comprised only 60,000 of the 300,000 communist troops in the field,[59] a figure in line with an August official U.S. estimate of 55,000 out of approximately 245,000.[60]

To be sure, what began as a low-grade and militarily self-sustaining insurgency in the South had by 1975 evolved into a straightforward conventional North Vietnamese attempt to take over the remaining noncommunist areas of southern Vietnam. But the fact of communist conventionality in 1975 proves nothing about the character of the war in 1960 or 1965, and it was a grave error for American policymakers in the early to mid-1960s to dismiss the predominantly civil and unconventional nature of the conflict. The insistence by JCS Chairman Earl Wheeler and others that "the essence of the problem [in South Vietnam] is military" rather than "primarily political and economic"[61] both served the Pentagon's desire to fight the only kind of war it really knew how to fight, and encouraged an aversion to dealing with the more difficult political challenges of the war. It also promoted an underestimation of enemy tenacity and willingness to sacrifice. By refusing to recognize or admit that the Vietnam War was from its inception primarily a civil war, and not part of a larger, centrally-directed international conspiracy, policymakers assumed that North Vietnam was, like the United States, waging a limited war, and therefore that it would be prepared to settle for something less than total victory (especially if confronted by military stalemate on the ground in the South and the threat of aerial bombardment of the North). In so making this assumption, policymakers not only ignored two millennia of Vietnamese history, but also excused themselves from confronting the harsh truth that civil wars are, for their indigenous participants, total wars, and that no foreign participant in someone else's civil war can possibly have as great a stake in the conflict's outcome—and attendant willingness to sacrifice—as do the indigenous parties involved.

It was unfortunate enough that policymakers attached excessive strategic significance to the Vietnam War and that they failed to recognize the character of the conflict primarily for what it was. But by failing to understand the asymmetry of commitment between the United States and the Vietnamese communists, they paved the way for committing the most egregious error a country going to war can make: underestimating the adversary's capacity to prevail while overestimating one's own.

2. Stakes, Stamina, and Fighting Power

IN MARCH 1954, a French sergeant at Dien Bien Phu surrendered his men to a Viet Minh officer. The officer, according to an account by the astute French journalist and Vietnam expert Bernard Fall, then ordered the sergeant and his men to the rear. "The sergeant asked how they were to get across the barbed wire and minefields. 'Just walk across the bodies of our men,' the officer told him. About 800 dead and dying Viet Minh, cut down in the final assaults on [the French strongpoint] Gabrielle, lay in front of the sergeant's trench. One of them looked up at the prisoners; they saw his lips moving and they hesitated to use him as a stepping stone. 'Get going,' the Viet Minh officer said. 'You can step on him. He has done his duty for the Democratic Republic of Vietnam.'"[1]

Underestimation of the enemy and overestimation of one's own side has produced defeat and humiliation throughout the history of war. The Vietnam War was no exception. During their eight-year war in Indochina, the French repeatedly underrated the endurance and fighting skills of the Viet Minh. When the time came for its turn in Indochina, the United States, for cultural and other reasons, also underestimated the patience, tenacity, and military capacity of the Vietnamese communists while at the same time inflating its own power to prevail over what was, after all, an impoverished, preindustrial state.

As the war progressed, American officials voiced a combination of awe and unease over the enemy's staying power. In 1965, U.S. Ambassador to South Vietnam (and former Chairman of the Joint Chiefs of Staff) Maxwell Taylor marveled, "The ability of the Vietcong continuously to rebuild their units and make good their losses is one of the mysteries of this guerrilla war. We still find no plausible explanation of the continued strength of the Vietcong. . . . Not only do the Vietcong units have the recuperative power of the phoenix, but they have an amazing ability to maintain morale."[2] A year later, Secretary of Defense Robert McNamara remarked to an acquaintance that "I never thought [the war] would go like this. I didn't think these people had the capacity to fight this way. If I had thought they could take this punishment and fight this well, could enjoy fighting like this, I would have thought differently at the start."[3] Secretary of State Dean Rusk later confessed: "Hanoi's persistence was incredible. I don't understand it, even to this day."[4] Even Westmoreland conceded that U.S. leadership "underestimated the toughness of the North Vietnamese."[5] "Any American commander," he seemed to complain, "who took the same losses as General Giap would have been sacked overnight."[6]

What accounts for this dismay? In retrospect, misjudgment of the enemy seems attributable primarily to four factors: (1) failure to recognize—and therefore to understand the consequences of—the disparity of commitment to the war between the United States and the Vietnamese communists; (2) ignorance of Vietnamese history and culture; (3) arrogant confidence in American ability to determine the future of South Vietnam; and (4) a culturally rooted predisposition to focus on the quantifiable indices of military power at the expense of intangible factors at play.

Before addressing these sources of misjudgment, however, it is perhaps instructive to recall that U.S. underestimation of the enemy in Vietnam was hardly new; it represented an extension of culturally and racially based American misjudgments of the Japanese on the eve of World War II and of the Chinese on the eve of their entry into the Korean War. Both U.S. military planners and Americans in general harbored stereotypes of the Japanese up to Pearl Harbor that dismissed them as brutal albeit—by reason of their racial inferiority—physically weak (short stature and poor eyesight) and incapable of mastering advanced technology and the organizational challenges of modern warfare. Few credited the Japanese with the imagination and operational brilliance they displayed in the planning and execution of the attack on Pearl Harbor (and subsequent swift conquest of all Southeast Asia). Japan's industrial plant was, after all, tiny in comparison to that of the United States, and the Japanese armed forces had never faced battle with a first-class Western opponent. (Japan's exceptional performance in the War of 1905 was attributed mainly to Czarist Russia's logistical and operational weaknesses.)

In Korea, the Truman administration made its fateful decision to cross the 38th Parallel into North Korea in part on the basis of reassurances by Gen. Douglas MacArthur that an invasion of the North would not provoke Chinese intervention, and that if the Chinese did come in they would be crushed by U.S. air power. At the famous Wake Island conference in October 1950, MacArthur assured Truman that the chances of Chinese intervention were "[v]ery little," and that "if the Chinese tried to get down to Pyongyang," U.S. air power would inflict upon them "the greatest slaughter."[7] MacArthur estimated that the Chinese could move no more than fifty thousand to sixty thousand troops across the Yalu; in fact, they moved three hundred thousand across and inflicted upon MacArthur the longest retreat in American military history. Chinese intervention deprived the United States of a quick and absolute military victory, stalemated the Korean War, and provoked a serious crisis in American civil-military relations that influenced subsequent U.S. conduct of the Vietnam War. In defense of MacArthur, however, it must be said that to the extent his judgment of Chinese intentions in Korea was based on an assessment of Chinese military capabilities, his view was widely shared among American officialdom. In 1950, American military planners regarded China as a backward and militarily weak state whose new communist rulers were still preoccupied with consolidation of their own authority inside China and whose armies were little more than poorly-armed peasant mobs. Unfortunately, the subsequent demonstration that a properly motivated, led, and tactically instructed Asian peasantry could stay the course on the battlefield against a materially and technologically superior Western adversary seems to have been a lesson lost upon the U.S. military establishment in the fifteen years separating China's intervention in Korea and massive American ground combat intervention in Vietnam.

One of the reasons why the Chinese People's Liberation Army fought so tenaciously in Korea was that the war there directly threatened not only China's security but also the communist regime's survival. The importance of Chinese interests in neighboring Korea greatly surpassed those of the United States, a disparity reflected in China's willingness to expose itself to far greater strategic risk in Korea than that which the United States (MacArthur notwithstanding) was prepared to entertain. China simply could not tolerate the establishment of hostile U.S. military power along the Yalu River, within easy bombing range of the country's industrial heartland in Manchuria, and the transformation of the Korean peninsula into a unified, anticommunist American client state. Even more ominous to Beijing were fears, fueled in late 1950 and early 1951 by MacArthur's growing public insubordination, that the Americans were prepared to widen the war by conducting a strategic bombing campaign against targets in Manchuria, imposing a naval blockade of China's coast, and even sponsoring a return to the mainland of Formosa-based Nationalist forces.

The United States could point to no such compelling interest in Korea. Before the war both MacArthur and Secretary of State Dean Acheson had publicly excluded Korea from the U.S. defense perimeter in Asia. Nothing that transpired in distant Korea could directly threaten vital U.S. security interests, although the extension of communism to South Korea could seriously complicate preservation of Japan's security. As in the Vietnam War, the United States went to war in Korea not on behalf of compelling material interests, but rather for declared abstract principles. It interpreted the North Korean invasion, as it did subsequent Vietnamese communist aggression, as but a local manifestation of a much larger, centrally directed international conspiracy. The United States fought a war for politically limited ends with deliberately limited means; it was not prepared to entertain strategic risks in Korea— i.e., a level of war with China which would fatally compromise U.S. ability to protect more important commitments elsewhere—beyond the minimum necessary to ensure restoration of the prewar status quo.

MacArthur's public opposition to this prudent strategic restraint was the nub of the U.S. civil-military crisis of early 1951, which pitted the vain general against not just the White House but also the Joint Chiefs of Staff. Would that the Joint Chiefs of Staff during the Vietnam War have displayed the sense of strategic prudence that their predecessors did during the Korean War.

The disparity of interest between the communist side and the United States in Vietnam was substantially greater than that which separated Chinese and American stakes in Korea. In Korea, the United States faced a communist foe dominated politically and militarily by China, another outside power whose interests in Korea, while stronger than those of the United States, were nonetheless hardly identical to those of the indigenous Democratic People's Republic of Korea (DPRK), which sought total victory on the peninsula. At the Panmunjom talks in 1953, China, like the United States, accepted a compromise military-territorial settlement that their respective Korean clients regarded as an abomination. (A year later, the Chinese similarly betrayed the Viet Minh at the Geneva Conference.)

In Vietnam, on the other hand, the United States confronted a communist adversary native to the country and not subject to the kind of external discipline the Chinese had exerted over the DPRK. In the Democratic Republic of Vietnam (DRV) and National Liberation Front (NLF) the United States also faced an enemy far more militarily experienced than the DPRK in 1950—indeed, one that by 1965 had not only perfected a formidable and tested doctrine of protracted war, but also was conducting a successful campaign for the political allegiance of South Vietnam's peasantry. At no time before or during the Korean War did the DPRK manage to challenge seriously the authority of Syngman Rhee's South Korea via internal insurgency; on the contrary, Pyongyang's invasion of the South in 1950 was prompted in part by frustration at failed attempts at armed subversion of Seoul's anticommunist government—attempts that continue to this day.

The United States intervened in Korea to repel an overt conventional military invasion of the South; it intervened in Vietnam to thwart an otherwise triumphant politically based insurgency conducted largely by southern Vietnamese, albeit increasingly directed by Hanoi. The Vietnam

War was far more than simply, as Richard Nixon sought to portray it, the Korean War with jungles. Indeed, from the standpoint of latitude alone, the lush and heavily foliated topography of Vietnam provided communist forces a measure of comfortable weather, sustenance, and concealment lacking in the frigid and barren expanses of central Korea.

In Vietnam the communist side, which had assumed the mantle of long-suffering Vietnamese nationalism via its historic expulsion from Indochina of the hated French, pursued Vietnam's reunification as its primary goal—a goal it convincingly portrayed to large audiences on both sides of the Seventeenth Parallel as stymied in the South by a United States that had simply supplanted the French and was operating through a "puppet" neocolonialist regime in Saigon. This depiction of the struggle was hardly gainsaid by the Americanization of the Vietnam War in 1965 and the domination of the Saigon regime after Diem's overthrow by military officers who had served the French during the war against the Viet Minh. Secondary to reunification but nonetheless instrumental to Vietnamese communism's appeal was its promise of a social revolution in the countryside that would relieve Vietnam's largely impoverished peasantry of such burdens as landlessness and usurious interest rates. The communists, of course, had already reneged on their promise of land ownership in North Vietnam, substituting for it the savage and stupid collectivization of agriculture. But that betrayal did not diminish the potency of their rural agenda's appeal in a South Vietnam governed by a regime that went out of its way to propitiate the demands of absentee landlords, including the post-Geneva demand forcibly to restore titles to and rents from land in Viet Minh-controlled areas that had been transferred to abused and landless peasants.

The Vietnamese communists, in short, were committed to nothing less than national reunification and a revolutionary transformation of society, stakes whose realization, especially in the face of armed American opposition, required an enormous degree of patience, determination, and willingness to sacrifice—virtues that had already been displayed for all the world to see during the eight-year struggle against the French. For Hanoi and its communist brethren in the South, the Vietnam War was as total as the Civil War had been for Americans, a war which, though lacking foreign intervention, also was waged over the issues of national unity (i.e., the right of states to secede) and of relief from oppressive social institutions (i.e., slavery). The leaders of Hanoi "had fought all their lives to establish a united, communist Vietnam and to expel foreign influence," commented Henry Kissinger. "Revolutionary war was their sole profession. If America had searched the world over, it could not have found a more intractable adversary."[8] The United States, writes John Mueller in his assessment of the communist breaking point in Vietnam, "was up against an incredibly well-functioning organization, firmly disciplined, tenaciously led and largely free from corruption of self-indulgence. To an extraordinary degree, the organization was able to enforce upon itself an almost religious devotion to duty, sacrifice, loyalty, and fatalistic patience."[9] Indeed, the war in Vietnam was hardly America's first wartime brush with a totalitarian state's capacity for self-discipline and sacrifice; the surrender of both Nazi Germany and imperial Japan required their physical destruction to the point where continued resistance invited outright extermination of their peoples.

In contrast, the Vietnam War was, for the United States, a limited enterprise. Notwithstanding the great significance policymakers attached to American behavior there, Vietnam had no intrinsic value to the United States, which was not prepared to risk war with either China or Russia over Vietnam, or place itself on a wartime footing in pursuit of victory over its Vietnamese enemy. The Johnson administration, while reciting what it believed to be compelling abstract rationales for intervention, was determined to avoid disturbing America's domestic tranquillity over Vietnam. And surely, a United States that could live with a Soviet-dominated Eastern Europe, a communized China and North Vietnam, and a Cuban Soviet client just ninety miles off its own shores, could survive Vietnam's reunification under communist auspices.

Because the U.S. end in Vietnam was limited—preservation of a noncommunist South Vietnam, not the DRV's overthrow—it was pursued with restraint. This was right and proper, notwithstanding continuing arguments over the specific restrictions on the use of force that continue to this day. Limited ends mandate limits on the amount of investment made pursuant to those ends. Total wars—wars in which both sides seek the complete overthrow of the other—are historically exceptional. The United States never sought North Vietnam's destruction or the removal of its communist regime, nor was North Vietnam in a position to attack the United States or even physically eject U.S. forces from South Vietnam.

American policymakers erred not in recognizing the need for restraint, but rather in failing to recognize that while the United States was waging a limited war in Vietnam, its communist foe was waging what for all practical purposes amounted to a total war. Asymmetry of interest produced asymmetry of commitment, which in turn yielded continual American surprise and dismay at Hanoi's political stubbornness and military perseverance. "I can't believe," declared a frustrated National Security Advisor Henry Kissinger in September 1969, "that a fourth-rate power like North Vietnam doesn't have a breaking point."[10]

The disparity in commitment was nowhere more evident than in the willingness to incur casualties. The United States lost 58,000 military dead in Indochina from 1964 through 1973. American estimates of North Vietnamese Army and Viet Cong dead vary from a "reasonable [though] possibly conservative" estimate of 500,000 to 600,000,[11] to a Defense Department count of 951,000.[12] In early 1969, Vo Nguyen Giap, in an interview with Italian journalist Oriana Fallaci, admitted to communist losses of "half a million dead,"[13] and in January 1973, South Vietnamese President Nguyen Van Thieu put the number at slightly over 1 million.[14] In 1995, Hanoi itself officially admitted communist losses of 1,100,000 dead and another 300,000 missing in action,[15] almost all of whom, given the circumstances of combat, also must be presumed dead. Still another estimate claims a total of 2,747,000 PAVN and VC dead, wounded, and missing.[16]

These numbers are staggering when placed beside the population base from which they were drawn. North Vietnam entered the 1960s with a population of 16 million, and by 1965, the North Vietnamese and the NLF were exercising effective control over territory in South Vietnam containing an estimated 4 million additional people. Thus the communist side recruited its military manpower from a base of 20 million people. Even assuming a communist death toll of "only" 1 million (slightly more than the Defense Department's estimate, but nonetheless 100,000 short of Hanoi's claim—and not counting even one of the

300,000 missing as dead), it still amounts to 5 percent of the population, or a percentage that substantially exceeds the ratio of military war dead to national population of all the most bloodied major belligerents of World War I and World War II.[17] (The 600,000 total military dead in the U.S. Civil War, by far the deadliest of all of America's wars, represented but 1.9 percent of the nation's 1860 population of 31 million; the Union states' total loss of 360,000 dead constituted only 1.6 percent of their combined population of 22 million.) Thus, the communists expended the lives of no fewer than ten and perhaps as many as twenty of their own soldiers for each American life they took.

To put the magnitude of their sacrifice in even starker relief, the communist side in Indochina during the Vietnam War suffered proportional military losses equivalent for the United States in the mid-1990s of 13 million Americans killed and 3.9 million missing in action.[18] Put another way, in terms of military dead, the communist side sacrificed thirty-six times more of their own soldiers to unify Vietnam than did the Federal government to defeat the secessionist Confederate states.

American policymakers should not really have been too surprised. The Viet Minh had sacrificed 300,000 dead to expel the French from Indochina, and their losses would have been much higher had the French enjoyed anything like the Americans' advantage in firepower. The Democratic Republic of Vietnam was a poor albeit extraordinarily well-disciplined state that openly professed a warfighting doctrine combining deliberate protraction of hostilities and a willingness to pit blood against metal. Vietnamese communist commanders were indeed prepared to take losses for which American commanders would have been sacked. As early as 1946, Ho Chi Minh warned French negotiator Jean Sainteny, "If we have to fight, we will fight. You will kill ten of our men and we will kill one of yours, and in the end it will be you who will tire of it."[19]

They were also prepared to fight on more or less indefinitely, reflecting a determination and patience that, along with their acceptance of horrific casualty lists, appeared altogether irrational to those for whom cost-benefit analysis was the foundation of decision making. In 1966 North Vietnamese Premier Pham Van Dong told *New York Times* reporter Harrison Salisbury, "We are preparing for a long war. How many years would you say? Ten, twenty, what do you think about twenty?"[20] Part of the problem for American policymakers was their failure to recognize that, for the Vietnamese, U.S. entry into the Vietnam War was but another event in a centuries-old struggle to rid their country of foreign domination, be it Chinese, French, or American. The length of this struggle bred among those Vietnamese waging it a measure of patience and a capacity to roll with very unpleasant punches that ultimately frustrated the Americans in the 1960s just as it had the French in the 1950s. The "so-called American phase of the war," writes William Duiker, "was only a relatively brief if bitter interlude in a larger struggle of the Vietnamese people to free their homeland from foreign invaders and unify their country under a single independent government."[21]

U.S. behavior certainly did not convey to Hanoi an all-out determination to prevail militarily. Policymakers in Washington imposed restraints on the use of force in Indochina well in excess of those required to fulfill the limited objective of preserving a noncommunist South Vietnam. In the pre-Tet Offensive years of the war, U.S. ground forces were prohibited from entering Laos and Cambodia, both sanctuaries essential to the security of North Vietnamese forces operating in South Vietnam. The bombing of North Vietnam was pursued on a gradually escalating basis, punctuated by numerous bombing pauses (all intended to signal willingness to negotiate), and the single most important targets—North Vietnam's sea lines of communication with the Soviet Union and land lines of communication with China—were for the most part placed off limits until 1972. Only in South Vietnam, the territory of the very ally America was seeking to protect, were U.S. forces given a more or less free hand. "U.S. objectives are not to destroy or overthrow the Communist government of North Vietnam," declared McNamara in early 1966. "They are limited to the destruction of the insurrection and aggression directed by North Vietnam against the political institutions of South Vietnam."[22]

The question of whether these and other restrictions on U.S. military operations in Indochina outside South Vietnam crippled prospects for a U.S. military victory remains the subject of bitter debate and is examined later in this book. What seems beyond doubt is that they conveyed an attitude of hesitation and confusion of purpose that did not escape the attention of Hanoi's tenacious and perceptive rulers. The North Vietnamese never hesitated to violate Laotian and Cambodian territory, and undoubtedly would have sought, had they the power to do so, to shut down the American logistical arteries in South Vietnam that sustained both U.S. and South Vietnamese forces in the field. They would have loved to mine South Vietnam's ports and bomb MACV headquarters, and their one major attack on Saigon in 1968 completely changed the character of the American commitment to South Vietnam.

The unusual level of American restraint exercised in Indochina was dictated by three considerations, none of which appears convincing in retrospect: (1) fear of provoking direct Chinese intervention, (2) unwillingness to arouse public and congressional opinion, and (3) initial infatuation with, and application of, gradualist/bargaining theories of limited war.

Fear of provoking Chinese (and even Russian) intervention loomed large in Johnson administration calculations. "I was determined to minimize the risk that U.S. military action in Indochina would draw Chinese or Soviet ground or air forces into confrontation with the United States," wrote McNamara in retrospect. "President Johnson held the same view. It was a concern, among other reasons, that led us to oppose repeated recommendations over the next four years for a more rapid intensification of the air war and a more rapid expansion of the ground war."[23] The fear was fueled by a combination of memories of Chinese intervention in the Korean War in late 1950 and of belligerent Chinese rhetoric in the 1960s. China's crossing of the Yalu had abruptly denied an almost certain and complete American win in Korea, compromised U.S. military prestige, and stalemated the conflict for almost three more years, to the great domestic political distress of the Truman administration. Indeed, the Truman administration's political fortunes never recovered from the fall of China and subsequent Chinese-inflicted military standoff in Korea.

Ironically, fear of Chinese intervention in the Vietnam War was as unfounded as was earlier confidence that Beijing would not dare enter the Korean War. Precisely because the United States refrained from actions—such as an invasion of the DRV, aerial obliteration of the Red River Delta dike system, and even (until 1972) the mining of North

Vietnamese ports—that could have threatened the integrity of North Vietnam's territory and regime, Beijing itself did not feel sufficiently endangered—as it did when an imperious MacArthur's forces lapped up to the very banks of the Yalu—to commit the People's Liberation Army directly to combat in Vietnam. To be sure, China provided substantial arms and logistical support to the DRV throughout the war. To have done anything less would have compromised the legitimacy of Beijing's competition with the Soviet Union for power and influence in Indochina and the rest of the Third World. Yet, from at least 1966 onward, China was more preoccupied with the domestic turmoil sparked by the Great Cultural Revolution and by the emergence of the Soviet Union as the principal threat to its security than it ever was by U.S. military intervention in Indochina—at least as long as that intervention did not include rolling back communism in North Vietnam. As noted previously, Lin Piao's 1965 "Long Live the Victory of People's War" speech was not a warning to the United States of possible Chinese intervention in Vietnam, but rather a warning to Hanoi not to provoke escalation of the war to the point where Chinese intervention would prove necessary. The Chinese, too, had unpleasant memories of the Korean War, but unlike the United States they were not prepared to risk dissipation of their military power in Indochina in the face of a burgeoning Soviet threat elsewhere. The Chinese did not want war with the United States, and probably did not want an Indochina reunified under Hanoi's auspices—and certainly not a Hanoi prepared to enlist in the Sino-Soviet dispute as a Soviet client state. The Chinese made known their intention to stay out of the war on several occasions, but it took the arrival of the Nixon administration, specifically, Dr. Henry Kissinger, for American diplomacy to fully recognize and exploit both Sino-Soviet and Sino-Vietnamese tensions.[24]

The Johnson administration clearly exaggerated prospects for Chinese intervention and in so doing unnecessarily constrained U.S. military operations in Indochina. Actions it regarded as dangerously provocative—entering Laos and Cambodia, mining Haiphong, slamming targets inside the off-limits Hanoi "doughnut"—all were subsequently undertaken by the Nixon administration without eliciting any direct Chinese military response. Indeed, by 1972, Beijing was eager, even desperate, to reach a strategic accommodation with the United States, even at the price of encouraging Hanoi to seek client status with Moscow. The Johnson administration was nonetheless right in seeking to avoid war with China, even though it is all too easy in retrospect to argue, as I have in these pages, that a war with China over South Vietnam's fate was never really in the cards. That the Joint Chiefs of Staff discounted the risk of Chinese intervention stemmed less from a superior reading of China's intentions than it did from anguish over the restraints it caused the Johnson White House to impose on U.S. military operations. From the beginning of American involvement in the Vietnam War right on through the aftermath of the Tet Offensive, the Chiefs wanted an earlier commitment of more force than did their civilian superiors, and they regarded the White House's Chinese bugaboo as a major obstacle to the war's rapid escalation.

Also serving to lessen the scope and intensity of the U.S. military effort in Indochina, and to advertise to Hanoi a lack of willingness to sacrifice beyond whatever was necessary simply to avoid defeat, was the Johnson administration's refusal to mobilize either public opinion or the reserves. The administration sought to wage a big war without inflaming public passions; it feared that arousal of war fever would not only provide its conservative critics an irresistible opportunity to torpedo the Great Society, on the grounds that the country could afford little butter when so many guns were demanded in Indochina, but also threaten its ability to control and moderate the application of force in Indochina. These fears mandated Johnson's refusal to ask for a formal declaration of war, to declare a national emergency, to request an appropriate tax increase, to disclose the full extent of planned intervention and alterations in the missions of U.S. forces, and even to come before the nation in a prime-time television address to lay out the costs and risks of intervention. Most strategically consequential of all was Johnson's refusal, against the united counsel of both McNamara and the Chiefs, to mobilize U.S. reserve forces. In no other major war had an American president not called up the reserves; their very purpose was to provide a bridge between active-duty forces and the arrival of freshly conscripted manpower on the battlefield. The decision deprived the Pentagon of the services of a vast reservoir of mature and well-trained manpower, and compelled heavy reliance on a terribly flawed conscription system that ultimately bred a more intense and enduring domestic opposition to the war than would have a decision early on to mobilize the reserves.

Johnson and his principal Vietnam War lieutenants, especially Secretary of Defense Robert McNamara, repeatedly misled the American people and Congress (and often themselves) about what was happening in Indochina, and about prospects for American success there. The White House believed, or at least wanted to believe, that it could lead the country into a war while somehow concealing the war's reality from the electorate. It was sadly—and predictably—wrong. Dean Rusk later conceded that the administration "may have made a mistake" in "asking our countrymen to support in cold blood what our men in uniform were having to do in hot blood in Southeast Asia."[25] At the time, however, McNamara boasted that "the greatest contribution Vietnam is making—right or wrong is beside the point—is that it is developing an ability in the United States to fight a limited war . . . without arousing the public ire."[26]

Both Rusk and McNamara viewed the deliberate incitement of public bloodlust as encouraging ultimate loss of civilian control of the war to the military, with its standing demand for an ever wider and less restrained use of force. Such a development could in turn prompt uncontrollable escalation toward a third—even nuclear—world war. Indeed, key officials, most of them Kennedy appointees, including McGeorge Bundy, Walt Rostow, and John McNaughton, approached the Vietnam War enamored (at least initially) of graduated escalation, an academic theory of limited warfare in the nuclear age. It was designed to avert uncontrolled escalation via incremental increases in violence aimed primarily at demonstrating political willingness to take the next escalatory step should the enemy fail to get the previous step's intended message. The theory, propounded in the late 1950s and early 1960s by such academics as Robert Osgood and Thomas Schelling, reduced limited war essentially to coercive diplomacy,[27] though the theory's call for employing violence as a tool for reasoning violates every dictum declared by Clausewitz. Force was to be employed primarily not to destroy, but rather to communicate resolve, to signal determination to use more force if necessary. The aim was not military victory, but persuasion of the enemy to see the error of his ways and seek salvation through negotiation. "It is the *threat* of damage, or of more damage to come, that can make someone yield or comply," wrote Schelling. "It is *latent* violence that can influence someone's choice. . . . It is the expectation of *more* violence that gets the wanted behavior, if the power to hurt can get it at all."[28] Gradualism's main focus on bargaining rather than actual fighting called for tight central political control of military operations. The military, after all, was to serve mainly as an instrument of political signaling. The theory also implied disregard for public opinion; coercive diplomacy was best left to experts. Perhaps most important of all, the theory presumed a relative symmetry of stakes between the two contending parties and a concomitant cost-benefit rationality on the enemy's part. Unfortunately, gradualism enthusiasts failed to recognize the absence of these two conditions during the American chapter of the Vietnam War. Hanoi was committed to nothing less than Vietnam's forcible reunification under communist auspices (requiring eviction of the Americans from South Vietnam and the extinction of their client regime in Saigon); and Ho Chi Minh and his lieutenants could not be bought off with either limited political concessions or the lure of postwar American largesse.[29] Nor was the North Vietnamese leadership intimidated by gradualism's intended signals. If anything, gradualism signaled hesitation and disunity of purpose. Simply put, the United States wanted a negotiated settlement while Hanoi wanted victory.

The gradualism theory's influence on U.S. policymakers during the decade preceding the decision for massive ground combat intervention in 1965 is undeniable. "There was an unspoken assumption in Washington," recounted Bill Moyers after he left the Johnson White House, "that a major war was something that could be avoided if we injected just a little power at a time. There was an assumption that the people in Hanoi would interpret the beginning of the bombing and the announcement of a major buildup [in the South] as signals of resolve on our part which implied greater resistance to come if they did not change their plans. There was an assumption that they feared we *might* use the power available to us; and an assumption that they were probing to see if in fact we *would*. . . . There was a confidence that when the chips were down, the other people would fold."[30] *The Pentagon Papers'* narrative observes that in "Washington there was considerable theorizing [in the first half of the 1960s] about the best manner of persuading North Vietnam to cease aid to the NLF-VC by forceful but restrained pressures which would convey the threat of greater force if the North Vietnamese did not end their support of the insurgency in South Vietnam. . . . there was what appears now to have been an amazing level of confidence that we could induce the North Vietnamese to abandon their support of the SVN insurgency if only we could convince them that we meant business and that we would indeed bomb them if they did not stop their infiltration on men and supplies to the South."[31] Maxwell Taylor, in making the case for bombing North Vietnam in testimony before the Senate Foreign Relations Committee in late 1964, said, "I can't believe they will sacrifice their economy, that they will sacrifice the society they have constructed at great pains over the last 10 years. It just wouldn't be worth it to them. If we can get that message across and organize that scenario, I would have hopes we can come out of it."[32]

Secretary of the Army Cyrus Vance cited the influence of the Cuban Missile Crisis of 1962, which he believed vindicated gradualism's application in Vietnam: "We had seen the gradual application of force applied in the Cuban Missile Crisis, and had seen a very successful result. We believed that if this same gradual and restrained application of force were applied in . . . Vietnam, that one could expect the same kind of result; that rational people on the other side would respond to increasing military pressure and would therefore try and seek a political solution."[33] Indeed, in 1964 Walt Rostow argued against using too much force. "I am concerned," he told McNamara on the subject of bombing options against North Vietnam, "that too much thought is being given to the actual damage we do in the North, not enough thought to the signal we send."[34] In January 1965 Maxwell Taylor again counseled bombing to teach Hanoi's leaders to mend their ways. In a memorandum to President Johnson, Taylor argued that as "practical men, they cannot wish to see the fruits of ten years of labor destroyed by slowly escalating air strikes . . . without trying to find some accommodation. . . . It would be in our interest to regulate our attacks not for the purpose of doing physical destruction but for producing maximum stresses in Hanoi minds."[35] Taylor did not explain how highly restricted bombing would induce Hanoi to ask for negotiations, when the carpet bombing of Nazi Germany just two decades earlier had elicited no such request from Berlin.

Gradualism, which as practiced by the Johnson White House involved in some cases daily micromanagement of military operations, was anathema to the U.S. military leadership from the very beginning of American intervention. The JCS, CINCPAC, and MACV all opposed deliberate incremental escalation of the war, especially the air war against the North, as a violation of established principles of warfare and, as such, an affront to their legitimate professional prerogatives. The focus on political signaling not only inhibited civilian acceptance of military options that might have carried greater weight in Hanoi, but also contributed to the very lack of visible progress in the war's conduct that in the end fatally undermined American public support for the war.

Making matters worse was an arrogance bordering on contempt for military opinion by McNamara and his "whiz kids," many of them young men trained as economists and having little if any personal military experience or professional appreciation of the military's concerns. Johnson himself ridiculed military opinion. In a November 1965 meeting with the Joint Chiefs of Staff, for example, he became personally abusive. Johnson's behavior was recounted thirty years later by a young Marine Corps officer (and later professional colleague of mine) who was present as an aide to Chief of Naval Operations David MacDonald. According to Charles G. Cooper, who later retired as a lieutenant general, Johnson listened quietly while the Chiefs pressed for an expanded air war in the North and the mining of Haiphong, "but then whirled to face [the Chiefs] and exploded. . . . He screamed obscenities, he cursed them personally, he ridiculed them for coming to his office with their 'military advice.' Noting that it was he who was carrying the weight of the free world on his shoulders, he called them filthy names—sh—heads, dumbsh—s, pompous assh—s—and used 'the F-word' as an adjective more freely than a Marine at boot camp." Johnson then shifted to using "soft-spoken profanities," saying "something to the effect that they all now knew that he did not care about their military advice. Totally deprecating their abilities, he added that he did expect their help and wanted each to change places with him and assume that five incompetents had just made these 'military recommendations.' He told them that he was going to let them go through what he had to go through when idiots gave him stupid recommendations, adding that he had the whole damn world to worry about, and it was time to 'see what kind of guts you have.'"[36]

Bombing pauses initiated to induce Hanoi to the negotiating table were a particular source of military bitterness. During the Rolling Thunder campaign (February 1965 to October 1968) no fewer than seven bombing pauses were undertaken, all over the military's objections. On 31 October 1968, Johnson announced suspension of air attacks on North Vietnam for good (they were not resumed until April 1972 by the Nixon administration). In each instance the North Vietnamese took advantage of unilateral U.S. de-escalation by accelerating the flow of men and supplies southward down the Ho Chi Minh Trail and by repairing and rebuilding their ever more extensive and sophisticated air defenses. They also took advantage of such White House–imposed rules of engagement as those forbidding U.S. pilots from attacking new enemy air defense sites under construction (for fear of killing any Soviet or Chinese technicians and advisers that might be present). Indeed, Westmoreland claims that when construction of the first such sites was observed in 1965, John McNaughton dismissed a general's suggestion of attacking them, saying, "You don't think the North Vietnamese are going to use them! Putting them in is just a political ploy by the Russians to appease Hanoi."[37]

More than any other issue, incrementalism divided U.S. civilian and military leadership, and it continues to be cited by stab-in-the-back proponents as the main cause of Vietnamese communism's defeat of an otherwise unbeatable American cause in Indochina. (Civilian decision makers were divided over the desirability of a reserve call-up, which McNamara and McGeorge Bundy initially favored.)

American misjudgment of the enemy in Vietnam stemmed not just from incomprehension of the fact and consequences of the enormous disparity of stakes in the conflict between Hanoi and Washington. It was no less the product of American officialdom's pervasive ignorance of Vietnamese history and culture. Thirty years after he counseled U.S. ground combat intervention in Vietnam, McNamara finally conceded that U.S. "misjudgments of friend and foe alike reflected profound ignorance of the history, culture, and politics of the people of the area, and the personalities and habits of their leaders."[38] Thomas Schelling, a leading propounder of the limited war theory whose application in Vietnam came to grief, also has conceded "a poverty of knowledge about Vietnam." Indeed, according to Schelling, "it would have been difficult to choose any place of comparable importance about which so little was known as about Vietnam."[39]

Senior U.S. policymakers and military leaders not only knew little about Vietnam and the Vietnamese; they also didn't care to know because they didn't believe such knowledge mattered. The highly decorated Vietnam veteran and outspoken commentator David Hackworth recalls visiting the Pentagon's library during the height of the war, where he discovered dozens of French after-action reports detailing French commanders' "frustrations, failures, and lessons learned" during the French-Indochina War. Though translated into English, none had ever been checked out.[40]

So what if the Vietnamese had spent an entire millennium fighting Chinese rule? What did it matter that the Viet Minh had defeated the French? Who cared that Vietnamese communism professed an allegiance to protracted war as a matter of policy? The Chinese experience in Vietnam was ancient history. The French hadn't won a war since Napoleon, and the French in Indochina were morally and politically tainted as colonial oppressors. As for protracted war, Hanoi could impose it on the United States only if it could capture the initiative on the battlefield and thereby control its losses.

Official ignorance was one thing, but lack of curiosity was quite another. What accounted for the latter? In a word: arrogance. Virtually no one in a senior civilian or military leadership position, almost all of which were occupied by men for whom the glorious and total American victory of World War II was the great referent experience for judging the likely outcomes of subsequent conflicts, believed that a piddling little country like North Vietnam could stand up to the awesome might of the United States. A United States that had crushed Nazi Germany and imperial Japan—and that had kept the hordes of the Chinese People's Liberation Army at bay in Korea—could surely cow into submission a small, impoverished, preindustrial state on the Asian mainland's periphery. "It seemed inconceivable," wrote Chester Cooper, who served as McGeorge Bundy's assistant for Asian affairs on the National Security Council staff, "that the lightly armed and poorly equipped Communist forces could maintain their momentum against, first, increasing amounts of American assistance to the [South] Vietnamese Army, and, subsequently, American bombing and [ground] combat forces."[41] "How could the army of the most powerful nation on Earth," asked another student of the Vietnam War, "materially supported on a scale unprecedented in history, equipped with the most sophisticated technology in an age when technology had assumed the role of a god of war, fail to emerge victorious against a numerically inferior force of lightly armed irregulars?"[42]

Americans were confident in their military, and many continue to believe that the United States's defeat in Vietnam was the consequence primarily of civilian-imposed restrictions on military operations. After all, until Vietnam the United States had never lost a war—or so Americans, forgetting the War of 1812 and the British torching of Washington, believed as their country approached intervention in Vietnam. The military was no less confident in its abilities. If anything, it suffered from the disease of victory, that hubris bred by repeated success on the battlefield. As William Dupuy, a senior U.S. Army commander in Vietnam, put it, "We were arrogant because we were Americans."[43] The enemy's order of battle, his strategy, and his past military performance really didn't matter in the end because the Vietnamese communists would be subjected to the same crushing American superiority in firepower and technology that had bested Germany's and Japan's armies. If the Germans, the century's most operationally gifted military professionals, couldn't stand up to American might, what chance did a poorly armed Asian peasant army have? The North Vietnamese Army and their Viet Cong allies would be decimated just like the Chinese in Korea. "We found it difficult," wrote General William Rosson in retrospect, "to accept that the VC and NVA soldier could be content under conditions of jungle living, limited rations, few creature comforts, and the ever-present danger of artillery and air attack. We were certain that his knowledge that he was in the war for the duration—in contrast to our one-year tour of duty—was demoralizing. What we failed to appreciate . . . was that the typical VC and NVA soldier was a peasant whose pre-military lifestyle was one of hardship and privation that helped to prepare him for the rigors of field service. Moreover, we found it hard to visualize the pivotal influence in morale of the enemy's system of indoctrination and control."[44]

The French lost because their cause—restoration of colonial rule—was unjust, and because they lacked the enormous firepower and technological superiority the United States could bring to bear. Never mind France's superior knowledge of Vietnamese history, culture, geography, and style of warfare. Never mind that the quality of French soldiery in Indochina—all career professionals serving twenty-six-month tours of duty—surpassed that of the indifferently trained, short-tour conscripts the Americans would later send.

American arrogance extended well beyond the military realm. Policymakers believed the United States could not only prevail militarily in Indochina but also create an economically and politically viable Vietnamese nation-state south of the Seventeenth Parallel. In the 1960s, "nation-building" was not the pejorative term it later became. America embraced nation-building throughout the Third World as a means of countering communism's expansion. That was what such things as the Peace Corps and the Alliance for Progress were all about. Americans believed they could convert South Vietnam, as they had South Korea, into a functioning anticommunist state capable of competing effectively in the worldwide struggle to halt communism's advance. The keys to success in Vietnam were population security, land reform, sustained economic progress, and political stability—four areas in which substantial progress was in fact made by the time of the Paris peace agreement of 1973. What the United States could not accomplish, because of the very fact and scope of its sponsorship of the Republic of Vietnam in the 1950s and subsequent Americanization of the war, was to invest any of the string of regimes that paraded through Saigon with a measure of political legitimacy sufficient to attract its citizens' willingness to fight and die for the Republic. From Ngo Dinh Diem through

Nguyen Van Thieu, Saigon regimes could not shake the image—and reality—of being little more than surrogates of a racially and culturally alien power. The United States never exercised in South Vietnam the direct and absolute political and military authority it enjoyed in post–World War II Germany and Japan.

But the depth of Saigon's political disabilities was not fully comprehended in 1965. Observes Robert D. Schulzinger, in 1965, "nothing as catastrophic as the Vietnam experience had happened before in U.S. foreign policy, so why should the doomsayers be right now? The United States had succeeded in most of its overseas undertakings since 1941, so why should not the good results continue? While the experience of the previous ten years in Vietnam made policymakers pause, their successes in other places in the world in World War II and the early Cold War gave them a sense of near invincibility. Nearly all of Johnson's advisers in 1965 believed it was better to do something—almost anything—to solve a problem than to admit that American action would not make things better."[45]

Much of U.S. arrogance in Vietnam was unconscious. For example, American culture and historical experience encouraged assessments of overseas military challenges on the basis largely of their measurable indices. The American war in Vietnam was waged by managerial technocrats—civilian and military. They were products of an advanced industrial society and heirs to European military tradition. As such, they practiced an especially capital-intensive brand of conventional warfare that placed a premium on material and technological superiority. A pronounced superiority in one or both had been the key to United States strategic success beginning with the Confederacy's defeat exactly 100 years before the first American ground combat forces were sent to Vietnam.

In Vietnam the focus on the quantifiable indices of military power—and on such countable measures of the war's "progress" as sorties flown, bomb tonnages dropped, artillery shells fired, and enemy killed—probably was inevitable. The MACV selected attrition as its preferred strategy in part because it appealed to American military strength and tradition. "Attriting" the enemy—i.e., exhausting him via destruction of his field forces and war-making capacity faster than he could replace them—was the foundation of industrial warfare. Pronounced Union superiority in the measurable aspects of military power more than offset the tactical talents of Lee, Jackson, and Longstreet; by 1863, the Confederacy could no longer replace its losses, whereas the North was just beginning to mobilize its latent military power. Similarly, in World War II, U.S. war production dwarfed that of Germany and Japan combined; the operational genius of a Rommel or Yamamoto could not prevail over the flood of men, ships, planes and tanks that poured out of North America.

No American official more epitomized the managerial approach to war than Robert McNamara, the insufferably arrogant auto executive upon whom it apparently never dawned—until it was too late—that managing a large bureaucracy, be it Ford or the Pentagon, had little to do with forging success in a shooting war. Maximizing productivity at Ford taught nothing about defeating an Asian revolution. The most disastrous American public servant of the twentieth century (he combined a know-it-all assertiveness with a capacity for monumental misjudgment and a dearth of moral courage worthy of Albert Speer), McNamara transformed the office of the secretary of defense into a temple of quantitative analysis. Infatuation with the countable was established as the foundation of not only force structure and weapons choices, but also assessments of foreign military challenges and even of the Vietnam War's progress. "Numbers!" complained Chester Cooper. "There was a numbers mill in every military . . . installation in Vietnam. Numbers flowed into Saigon and from there to Washington like the Mekong River during flood season. Sometimes the numbers were plucked out of the air, sometimes the numbers were not accurate. Sometimes they were accurate but not relevant. Sometimes they were relevant but misinterpreted. . . . By 1967 the numbers may have been accurate, relevant, and correctly interpreted, but few really believed them. The 'briefees' had become numbers numb."[46]

McNamara believed that most things could be precisely measured, and that those that could not probably didn't matter much anyway. He was a forceful and innovative secretary of defense, but a fatally incompetent minister of war. In his belated, lachrymose memoirs of the war, the man David Halberstam rightly called "a fool"[47] conceded that he and other key officials not only "failed . . . to recognize the limits of modern, high-technology military equipment, forces, and doctrine in confronting unconventional, highly motivated people's movements,"[48] but also "greatly underestimated Hanoi's determination, endurance, and ability to reinforce and expand Vietcong strength in the South."[49]

The problem for McNamara and the managerial technocracy he represented was that the enemy's real strength lay beyond the accountant's ledger of raw military power. The enormous effort the U.S. intelligence community invested in postulating an accurate enemy order of battle was all to the good (though the military favored a significantly more restricted definition of the enemy than did the civilian side of the community, a dispute that was finally settled by bureaucratic fiat). Quantitative analysis is the starting point for an assessment of any military establishment; force size and level of armament are basic indicators of crude capacity for violence. But counting the countable is only a starting point; it tells little about the presence and relative power of intangible factors, or what Martin van Creveld has called "fighting power"—"the moral, intellectual, and organizational" dimensions of military power as manifested in such things as "discipline and cohesion, morale and initiative, courage and toughness, the willingness to fight and the readiness, if necessary, to die."[50]

Vietnamese communism ultimately triumphed in Indochina because it mustered and maintained a superiority in the intangibles over a period of time sufficient to cancel out the significant edge the Americans and their South Vietnamese allies enjoyed in manpower and weight of metal. Material advantage can and has been beaten by superior organization, strategy, and willingness to incur vastly disproportionate casualties. The Americans believed their advantage in firepower and technological know-how would prove decisive in Vietnam—and indeed it would have if they had faced, as they did in the Persian Gulf a quarter of a century later, a Third World enemy who could think of nothing more imaginative than to ape the industrial state model of military organization and style of warfare. George Ball was one of the few senior American officials who understood that the "quintessential advantage of the North Vietnamese and Viet Cong could not . . . be expressed in numbers or percentages. It was the incomparable benefit of superior *élan,* of an intensity of spirit compounded by the elemental revolutionary drives of nationalism and anti-colonialism."[51]

No one understood the decisiveness of the intangibles in Vietnam better than the North Vietnamese. During the war, Vo Nguyen Giap remarked that the "United States is waging war by arithmetical strategy. They ask their computers, make additions and subtractions, extract square roots, and on that they act. But arithmetical strategy doesn't work here. If it did, they would have exterminated us already. They can't get it in their heads that the war in Vietnam can be understood only by the strategy of a people's war, and that the war in Vietnam is not a question of numbers and well-equipped soldiers, that all that doesn't solve the problem."[52] After the war he told Stanley Karnow: "We were not strong enough to drive out a half-million American troops, but that wasn't our aim. Our intention was to break the will of the American Government to continue the war. Westmoreland was wrong to expect that his superior firepower would grind us down. If we had focused on the balance of forces, we would have been defeated in two hours."[53]

American officialdom overestimated public and congressional willingness to stay the course in Vietnam as much as it did the country's ability to win militarily. "As secretary of state," wrote Dean Rusk, "I made two serious mistakes with respect to Vietnam. First, I overestimated the patience of the American people, and second, I underestimated the tenacity of the North Vietnamese."[54] Accustomed to public and congressional docility, even Pavlovian obedience, when it came to taking up the cudgels against the advance of communism, and convinced, or at least hopeful, that Hanoi would fold once it recognized that it could not beat the United States, key U.S. policymakers in the mid-1960s seem never to have considered the possibility that the country could or would turn decisively against the war. The White House was politically terrified of a right-wing backlash if it failed to defeat, or at least stand up to, further communism expansion in Vietnam, though it resisted military and conservative political pressure to "take the gloves off" for fear of unwarranted escalation that could threaten domestic social reform and control of the war itself. In fact, a majority of Americans polled supported U.S. intervention in Vietnam right on through the Tet Offensive; liberal and radical antiwar sentiment, though strident, was more than counterbalanced by conservative frustration that the war was not being prosecuted forcefully enough.

Tet, however, fundamentally altered public perspectives, in large part because it undermined officialdom's inflated claims of the war's progress. At the root of public—and increasingly, congressional—dismay was a growing conviction that an open-ended investment in American blood and treasure was yielding nothing that could redeem sacrifices already made. Only belatedly did policymakers come to realize that there were limits to public patience with a war that exhibited no persuasive evidence of concrete progress toward a definable end, as well as to public tolerance for sustaining a war on behalf of seemingly nothing more than abstract objectives unaccompanied by palpable direct threats to clear-cut national interests.[55] The elevation of U.S. participation in World Wars I and II into moral crusades was firmly moored in public outrage at unprovoked German and Japanese attacks on Americans (unrestricted German submarine warfare against U.S. shipping on the high seas; the "dastardly" Japanese attack on Pearl Harbor), and a sense that a conclusive German victory in Europe in either war would fundamentally threaten the well-being of the United States. Vietnamese communism never posed a convincing threat to the United States; Indochina was a geographically, strategically, and culturally remote place which the Joint Chiefs of Staff in 1954 had correctly declared to be "devoid of decisive military objectives" and unworthy of the "allocation of more than token U.S. forces."[56] Ho Chi Minh's ambitions did not appear Hitlerian in scope, and certainly the warmaking resources Ho had at his disposal bore no resemblance to those at the German dictator's command. Moreover, notwithstanding frenetic official efforts to cast the war as a case of international aggression as infamous as Hitler's invasion of Poland, the civil and revolutionary dimensions of the conflict were manifest and undeniable. Vietnamese were killing Vietnamese to determine the future political and social order of Vietnam south of the Seventeenth Parallel. Were the issues at stake for the United States really such uninspiring abstractions as demonstrating resolve, affirming the integrity of American commitments, taming Chinese expansionism, stepping up to the plate to show the futility of wars of national liberation, and learning the proper conduct of limited war as coercive diplomacy?

The fact that the nightmare of a right-wing backlash on the order of "Who lost China?" in the 1950s never materialized in the 1970s over "Who lost Vietnam?" is attributable to the post-Tet war's utter unpopularity and seeming unwinnability (short of a politically unsustainable accelerated level of military effort). But it was also due in no small measure to the Johnson administration's refusal even to try to turn the war into a moral crusade via deliberate arousal of public passions. Norman Podhoretz believes that fear of backlash was misplaced because, "[l]ike the majority of most Americans, the hawks were unable to work up any enthusiasm for a war whose purpose had been defined in terms so bloodless that they could not justify or redeem the blood being shed for its sake, and so they were by now [in the wake of the Tet Offensive] reduced, again like the majority of Americans, to the negative demand that the United States not be defeated or humiliated."[57]

The fact that U.S. withdrawal from the Vietnam War was initiated and orchestrated by a Republican administration also stifled potential conservative reaction. No one could accuse Richard Nixon of being soft on communism, and while the deal he cut with Hanoi in Paris achieved little more than an intermission in the thirty-years war between Vietnamese communism and the West, it did provide the vehicle for an ostensibly "honorable" American departure. Henry Kissinger recounted that the "basic challenge to the new Nixon Administration was similar to De Gaulle's in Algeria: to withdraw as an expression of policy and not as a collapse."[58]

The Tet Offensive convinced both the outgoing Johnson and incoming Nixon administrations that a U.S. disengagement from Vietnam had to be effected even at the risk of jeopardizing the American cause in Indochina. Both faced not the threat of a "Who-lost-Vietnam?" orgy of political recrimination, but rather of public and congressional opinion increasingly opposed to continued U.S. participation in the Vietnam War under any conditions. Accordingly, the United States drastically lowered its basic war aim from pursuit of a military victory sufficient to compel Hanoi to cease and desist from its support of the communist war in the South, to one of ensuring a "decent interval" between U.S. military extrication and the inevitable resumption of the fighting on terms that could not possibly be as favorable to South

Vietnam's survival as those that attended the presence of five hundred thousand U.S. troops.

The Vietnamization policy provided the political and moral cover for a U.S. withdrawal dictated mainly by irresistible public and congressional insistence on quitting Vietnam. The policy's three White House conditions for implementation—level of enemy activity, South Vietnam's ability to defend itself, and progress in the Paris negotiations—were never permitted to block or seriously impede what amounted to a politically involuntary unilateral withdrawal from a war for whose negotiated settlement the United States was prepared to abandon its longstanding insistence on the reciprocal departure of North Vietnamese troops from southern Vietnam. Vietnamization was, as General Phillip Davidson succinctly put it, "essentially a 'cut and run' strategy . . . dictated . . . by the collapse of will to support the war among the decision-making elite of the United States."[59]

In the end, Nixon, if not Kissinger, seems to have persuaded himself that a combination of continued U.S. military aid and threatened resumption of U.S. bombing could preserve a noncommunist South Vietnam even after the withdrawal of U.S. ground combat forces, and he blamed Congress for gutting aid requests for Saigon and for crippling presidential exercise of U.S. military power in Southeast Asia. "Congress turned its back," he said, "on a noble cause and a brave people."[60] Congressional actions, however, simply registered the collapse of public willingness to have anything more to do with the Vietnamese tar baby. Moreover, the notion that the RVNAF, a cheap and weak copy of its American counterpart, could accomplish what the United States Army had failed to accomplish was self-delusion. The United States had Americanized the war in the first place precisely because the RVNAF was literally disintegrating in the face of the communist onslaught of late 1964 and early 1965, and having Americanized the war, the MACV did little to prepare the RVNAF for the eventual departure of U.S. forces. The MACV believed it could beat communist forces without the RVNAF's help. Even the establishment of Vietnamization as the cornerstone of U.S. policy in Vietnam failed to improve the RVNAF's long-term prospects. Aside from the venality and professional incompetence of much of its senior officer corps, the RVNAF could hardly be expected to shoulder the immense technical and logistical demands imposed upon it by the American style of warfare it was trained and equipped to wage. Though by 1975 the war had been thoroughly Vietnamized, the RVNAF had been transformed into a military force incapable of sustaining itself in combat, notwithstanding the mountains of American military equipment and ammunition that were transferred to the RVNAF between 1973 and 1975. Vietnamization, wrote a young Sen. Sam Nunn on the eve of Hanoi's final offensive, "has resulted in the Americanization of the Vietnamese" via "the dumping of massive amounts of military equipment and supplies on a South Vietnamese force that was unprepared and incapable of coping with the logistics and maintenance requirements related to that equipment."[61]

There was no more reason to have confidence in U.S. air power than in Vietnamization. Even if Congress had been prepared to approve a post-Paris U.S. reentry into the Vietnam War—which it manifestly was not—it is far from clear that any amount of U.S. bombing, absent a return of U.S. ground forces, could have thwarted Hanoi's ultimate victory in the South. At no time during the war had bombing succeeded either in shutting off the flow of supplies down the Ho Chi Minh Trail or in compelling Hanoi to negotiate a settlement on terms that precluded reasonable chances for Vietnam's subsequent forcible reunification. Linebacker II, the so-called "Christmas bombing" of targets in and around Hanoi in 1972, was launched in part to persuade Hanoi to accept settlement terms additional to those which it had already accepted the preceding October but on which the United States, because of bitter South Vietnamese objections, sought to renege.

The United States abandoned its cause in Indochina because it was strategically, politically, fiscally, and morally exhausted. Never prepared (nor should it have been) to make anything remotely approaching the proportional sacrifices in blood and treasure in Indochina that its communist enemy was willing to—and did—make, and being a democracy in which official policy fundamentally hostile to the electorate's wishes could not be indefinitely pursued, the United States withdrew from Vietnam because it had no other choice. The critical domino at stake in the Vietnam War was American public opinion, to which Hanoi seemingly paid longer and more profitable attention than did the

White House. The Johnson administration made no serious effort to galvanize public support for the war until the second half of 1967, when it sought to counter increasing popular dismay by unleashing a flood of rosy—and highly misleading—official pronouncements on the war's progress, a campaign that was fatally embarrassed by the Tet Offensive.

By the time of Nixon's inauguration in January 1969, there was little sentiment for a military victory, which most Americans no longer believed was attainable at an acceptable cost, but rather a desire for the war's termination. In fact, the United States was headed for a major debacle in Vietnam with potentially disastrous political and international repercussions. The Nixon-orchestrated U.S. invasion of Cambodia in 1970, the RVNAF "incursion" into Laos the following year, and U.S. mining of Haiphong harbor in the spring of 1972 represented attempts to cover the U.S. withdrawal and to bolster South Vietnam's post–U.S. withdrawal military position. They were acts of a fighting withdrawal, not an agenda for military victory. Hanoi was well aware of the American public mood and of the strategic intent of post-Tet U.S. military operations, although the Politburo could not resist one final attempt to settle the war by force of arms. And, as even President Thieu himself concluded, but for a massive employment of U.S. air power to crush the so-called "Easter Offensive", Hanoi probably would have toppled South Vietnam in 1972 rather than in 1975.[62]

The disintegration of American will was manifest not just in public and congressional attitudes but also in the internal near-collapse of the U.S. military in Vietnam—especially the Army—as an effective fighting force. By 1971, remaining U.S. forces in Vietnam had become thoroughly demoralized by the combination of unilateral withdrawals, manifest loss of public support for the war as well as respect for military service itself, the arrival of the 1960s American counterculture in Vietnam, rising racial tensions, and the sharply eroding quality of the officer corps. Rates of indiscipline, including open drug use, "fraggings" (attempted assassinations of unpopular officers), and "combat refusals" (i.e., mutinies) skyrocketed. One seasoned military observer was prompted to conclude: "The morale, discipline and battle worthiness of the U.S. Armed Forces are, with a few salient exceptions, lower and worse than at any time in this century and possibly in the history of the

United States. . . . Intolerably clobbered and buffeted from without and within by social turbulence, pandemic drug addiction, race war, sedition, civilian scapegoatise, draftee recalcitrance and malevolence, barracks theft and common crime, unsupported in their travail by the general government, in Congress as well as the executive branch, distrusted, disliked, and often reviled by the public, the uniformed services today are places of agony for the loyal, silent professionals who doggedly hang on and try to keep the ship afloat."[63]

Though exaggerated, this judgment underscored the imperative of ending U.S. participation in the Vietnam War as fast as possible if for no other reason than simply to preserve a minimal level of morale and cohesion within the armed forces. Secretary of Defense Melvin Laird believed that the armed forces' well-being was at stake, and he repeatedly sought—sometimes successfully—to accelerate the pace of the U.S. troop pull-out favored by Nixon and Kissinger.[64] Thus, long before the final communist triumph in Vietnam, the United States had exhausted both its will and capacity to effectively use force—or at least its army—in Indochina.

3. The War in the South

"FIGHTING THE VIET MINH," Marshal Jean Leclerc warned in 1946, "will be like ridding a dog of its fleas. We can pick them, drown them, and poison them, but they will be back in a few days."[1] The great French general also warned his civilian superiors in Paris that pursuit of a military victory in Indochina would strategically bankrupt France elsewhere, and that simple anticommunism offered no effective counter to the Viet Minh's nationalist appeal.

A decade later, Under Secretary of State George Ball warned the White House that "we have no basis for assuming that the Viet Cong will fight a war on our terms. . . . we can scarcely expect [General Giap] to accommodate us by adopting our preferred method of combat, regardless of how many troops we send. There is every reason to suppose that the Viet Cong will avoid providing good targets for our massive bombing and superior firepower."[2]

Still later, Henry Kissinger observed that, with "rare and conspicuous exceptions.., our modern generals have preferred to wear down the enemy through the weight of materiel rather than the bold stroke, through superior resources rather than superior maneuvers. In this they reflected the biases of a nonmilitary, technologically oriented society.

But wars of attrition cannot be won against an enemy who refuses to fight except on his own terms. The Vietnamese terrain, the nature of guerrilla warfare, the existence of sanctuaries, all combined to make it impossible for Westmoreland to wear down his adversary as he sought. Instead, the North Vietnamese hiding in the population and able to choose their moment for attack wore us down."[3] Kissinger's judgment was echoed by his White House boss: "Our armed forces were experts at mobilizing huge resources, orchestrating logistic support, and developing enormous firepower. In Vietnam, these skills led them to fight the war *their* way, rather than developing the new skills required to defeat the new kind of enemy they faced. They made the mistake of fighting an unconventional war with conventional tactics."[4] Indeed, in the early 1960s at least two Rand Corporation-created wargames, in which Maxwell Taylor, CIA Director John McCone, and other senior U.S. officials participated, produced a decade-long stalemate with five hundred thousand U.S. troops deployed to Indochina and an eventual collapse of public and congressional support.[5]

If the Vietnam War exhibited profound asymmetries in strategic stakes and political will between the Vietnamese communists and the United States, it also displayed equally consequential differences in styles of warfare between the two sides. In Indochina, an industrial style of warfare based on massive firepower and harnessed to a strategy aimed at an enemy's physical attrition collided with an agrarian style of warfare based on a strategy of protraction and elusivity designed to politically and psychologically exhaust an enemy. In the end, the American approach to war proved a misfit in Indochina. Preoccupation with the enemy's military destruction blocked a comprehensive understanding of the war, especially its critical political dimensions and the consequences of superior communist determination and willingness to sacrifice. It also bred an operational rigidity in the face of the war's multifaceted character. Insistence throughout the struggle in Indochina that the war was simply a case of transnational conventional military aggression did not make it so, though it certainly comforted those who wished to wage a conventional war. The MACV and, at least initially, the Office of the Secretary of Defense, deluded themselves into thinking that the kind of approach to war that had defeated like industrial adversaries in the past would of course work against a piddling, preindustrial dwarf like North Vietnam.

The professional U.S. military's conception and conduct of the war, even taking into account the strategic, operational, and tactical consequences of civilian-imposed political restrictions on the use of force in Indochina, continues to spark controversy among military as well as civilian observers. Prominent among the major contentious issues are, first, the decision in 1965 to Americanize the ground war in the South, a decision strongly urged by official military opinion but only belatedly endorsed by civilian decision makers. Though critics have condemned Americanization as both a strategically disastrous act for the United States and a fatal blow to the Republic of Vietnam's inherently tenuous claim to political legitimacy, few have been willing to address the almost certain collapse of South Vietnam in 1965 as the only realistic alternative to Americanization. On the other hand, military enthusiasts of Americanization wrongly foresaw it as the key to a conclusive military victory.

The second issue is the MACV's selection and pursuit of an attrition strategy and concomitant reliance on enemy order-of-battle assessments and body counts as indicators of success or failure. Westmoreland's adoption of attrition, though consistent with U.S. military strengths and tradition, spawned an intense controversy—among military as well as civilian opinion—that continues to this day. Clearly, attrition failed because the strategy wrongly presumed, among other things, a "reasonable" communist breaking point, an ability by U.S. forces to dictate the terms and timing of combat, and a reporting system whose integrity could be preserved against internal abuse and external deception. That attrition failed, however, does not mean that alternative strategies would have worked. Those who believe that the MACV should have pursued a population protection rather than the chosen search-and-destroy strategy would have asked the U.S. military establishment, in effect, to conduct the war in a fashion utterly foreign to its understanding of what war was all about. Some argue that the only real alternative to what they admit was a doomed attrition strategy was a combination of U.S. ground force operations against the communists' Laotian and Cambodian sanctuaries and unrestricted air attacks on

North Vietnam's external supply routes. They, however, must answer the question of why the JCS, CINCPAC, and MACV, when it became clear that civilian decision makers were not prepared to grant the military such operational latitude, could bring themselves neither to protest such civilian "interference" effectively nor to devise a winning strategy within civilian-imposed operational constraints. If a successful military strategy was impossible within the use-of-force parameters established by the White House, then those senior military officers who believed it to be impossible but who continued to serve as instruments of that policy have much to answer for.

The MACV's adoption of personnel rotation and other policies aimed at enhancing U.S. troop morale and comfort is the third issue. No commander is to be faulted for concern over the welfare of his troops, and the one-year tour of duty for Army enlisted personnel and the provision of what, under the circumstances, was an extraordinary level of creature comforts for all ranks undoubtedly made life less unpleasant for Americans in Vietnam than it otherwise would have been. Yet the abbreviated duty tours compromised the quality of U.S. tactical performance on the battlefield, and the prodigal base camps promoted rear-area bloat at the expense of maximizing combat arms productivity. If President Johnson's refusal to mobilize U.S. reserves was historically unprecedented, so too was Westmoreland's sacrifice of military efficiency for the sake of obliging personnel's peace of mind.

The fourth issue is the search by the JCS and especially CINCPAC for an alternative, indirect route to military victory via the bombing of North Vietnam. Military opinion was divided on the proposition that bombing, independent of ground combat operations inside South Vietnam, could compel Hanoi to submit to war settlement terms that would preserve South Vietnam as an independent noncommunist state. But from late 1964 on, air power enthusiasts within the Air Force, JCS, and Pacific Command (supported by such initially ardent civilians as McGeorge Bundy and Walt Rostow, and by such former military men as Maxwell Taylor) argued that North Vietnam's communist leadership could not reasonably be expected to sacrifice its own national economic accomplishments for the sake of continuing to promote a communist takeover of South Vietnam. In this, they not only misjudged the totalitarian and agrarian DRV's relative political and material imperviousness to air attack, but also ignored the history of aerial bombing as a poor tool of strategic persuasion. Ultimately, the potential effectiveness of strategic bombing depends on the vulnerabilities of the bombed, and North Vietnam was simply not vulnerable to strategic bombing at any level short of nuclear strikes or conventional mass bombing of its population centers. Furthermore, the U.S. military could not bring itself organizationally to conduct the air war against North Vietnam in a manner satisfying even minimal standards of managerial efficiency, and those conducting air operations also ultimately succumbed to the disease of measuring progress by the amount of resources invested rather than actual results achieved. At no time during the war did it dawn on U.S. military leadership that the air war might be politically counterproductive in terms of facilitating North Vietnam's war effort, handing Hanoi tremendous bargaining leverage in the form of hundreds of American prisoners of war, and contributing to the war's growing unpopularity in the arena of international public opinion.

This chapter addresses the first three of these issues, all of them prominent features of the MACV's conduct of the war in the South. The U.S. air campaign against the North is treated separately in the following chapter because it is essentially a separate war with its own set of objectives and conducted by a different command authority. Before examining the MACV's Americanization of the war and choice of strategy and personnel policies, however, a brief explanation of the contending styles of warfare the two sides brought to Vietnam is in order. The conventional warfare practiced by the United States was common within the industrialized world and rooted in the European military tradition. Its primary military goals are to seize enemy territory, to destroy enemy forces and war-making capacity, or both; success, accordingly, is measured in terms of territory taken, enemy forces disabled, and war production capacity demolished. Conventional warfare, though conducted on behalf of political objectives, makes no attempt to sway popular political loyalties in enemy or contested territory; it is a purely military undertaking dominated by operational considerations. Conventional warfare's principal means of accomplishing these objectives are a bold maneuver of some kind that attempts to surprise the enemy into defeat or ineffectiveness (e.g., the Germans' sweep through the Ardennes in 1940, MacArthur's 1950 Inchon landing, Israel's 1967 preemption of an Arab attack), or, more often, the application of massive firepower against enemy forces in the field and against military-industrial targets in the enemy's homeland (World Wars I and II), or some combination of both (U.S. conduct of the Gulf War). Conventional warfare's firepower/attrition variant, employed in Vietnam, is vitally dependent on the presence in the field and the enemy's homeland of large, detectable, and attackable targets whose destruction will render the enemy either defenseless or otherwise eager to terminate hostilities. It also presumes an ability to bring the enemy to battle on favorable terms more often and over a longer period of time than he can you.

Firepower and attrition have long been attractive to the U.S. military because they play to American material and technological superiority and offer a means of substituting machines for men on the battlefield. They delivered the most glorious triumph in U.S. military history (total victory over Nazi Germany and Imperial Japan). More recently, they have proved very effective against like conventional military establishments of other industrial states, and devastating against Third World states, like Iraq, that have sought to mimic industrial models of military organization.

But it is a style of warfare not well suited to dealing with the kind of war practiced by the Vietnamese communists in Indochina. The aim of revolutionary war, since at least the American Revolution, has been the violent seizure of political power from materially and numerically superior forces of an indigenous government or colonial regime. In more recent years, it is a style of warfare waged almost exclusively by revolutionary insurgent groups in preindustrial states against governments relying wholly or predominantly on conventional military forces. Revolutionary war is a struggle of the materially weak against the materially strong (albeit often politically weak). It commonly relies upon, but is not synonymous with, guerrilla warfare, an ancient method of combat whose tactical essence is a refusal to present decisive targets to the overwhelming firepower of conventional military opponents. Elements of this refusal include avoidance of pitched battles, camouflage and night operations, hit-and-run attacks, and use of terrain and populations as means of concealment. Revolutionary war seeks control not of territory per se, but rather of people, via methods ranging from terrorism to nonviolent political mobilization of peasant populations through such means as propaganda, land reform, and literacy campaigns. If the enemy is a foreign occupier, as were the French in Indochina until 1954, or is seen to be a creature of a foreign power, as the Vietnamese communists sought to portray the Saigon regime, revolutionary war will seek to arouse nationalist passions for liberation. The strength of the communists in Vietnam was that they were able to combine guerrilla and conventional tactics to effectively prosecute an asymmetrical strategy.

The Asian origins of the kind of revolutionary war practiced by Ho Chi Minh and Vo Nguyen Giap in Vietnam lie in Mao Tse-tung's theory and practice of revolutionary war in China in the 1930s and 1940s. Mao's great contribution to Marxist theory was to recognize that its transference from industrial Europe to preindustrial Asia required the substitution of the rural peasantry for the urban proletariat as the primary vehicle for revolution. Mao mobilized China's vast rural masses against the urban-based capitalist Nationalist Party (Guomintang) regime of Chiang Kai-shek, which it painted as not only the bulwark of an oppressive feudal social and economic order, but also a "running dog" of foreign imperial interests that had compromised China's national sovereignty.

Mao, from whose writings and experience in China the Vietnamese borrowed heavily, conceived of and waged revolutionary war in three distinct phases. The first phase, termed "contention" by Vietnamese theorists, involves construction of a political base and capacity for local self-defense in rural areas far from the easy reach of government forces. Insurgents conduct small-scale guerrilla operations, but remain on the defensive, prepared at all times to trade everything for survival. In the second phase, termed "equilibrium," insurgent forces seek to expand their political base while at the same time intensifying guerrilla operations against exposed government forces; the aims of this phase are to begin eliminating the government's presence in the countryside and to wear down the government's will and capacity to offer effective resistance—a policy, as expert Douglas Pike put it, of "vicious attrition designed to bleed and weaken the enemy."[6] The final phase calls for the insurgency's shift to conventional (or mobile) military operations—now possible because of the government's demoralization and loss of material superiority through defeat and defection—against the government's last remaining strongholds in the cities. To the last phase, which the Vietnamese labeled the "general counteroffensive," Vietnamese theorists added an accompanying "general uprising," a mass popular urban revolt both spurred by the scent of the government's impending defeat and essential to a conclusive victory. Harking back to the 1945 uprising against a return of French rule that followed Japan's surrender, confidence in a third-phase popular revolt (which was not shared by Chinese revolutionary warriors) played a major role in Vietnamese calculations behind the militarily disastrous Tet Offensive of 1968.

For both Chinese and Vietnamese communists, the key to revolutionary war's success was protraction of hostilities. Stringing out combat was an objective in and of itself because a swift victory against an enemy vastly superior in men and materiel was deemed infeasible; "protracted resistance," said Giap during the war, was "an essential strategy of a people . . . determined to defeat an enemy . . . having large and well-armed forces."[7] Ho Chi Minh assigned time a higher importance in revolutionary war than even popular support.[8] Protraction basically pitted time against enemy superiority in the quantifiable indices of military power; it also played, against the French and the Americans, to the inherent impatience of Western democracies with costly and seemingly interminable wars waged on behalf of interests ultimately regarded as less compelling than those at stake for Vietnamese communism. Ho and Giap understood that a combination of patience and an ability simply to deny decisive victory to the French and the Americans over a long enough period of time was itself sufficient to produce exactly such a victory for the communist cause. In the end, French and American political resolve to continue fighting crumbled not because of critical military reverses (even the loss of Dien Bien Phu affected only a small fraction of French military power in Indochina), but rather because of a relative Western intolerance for prolonged military stalemate.

Harrison Salisbury, during his wartime sojourn in North Vietnam, was struck by the popular commitment to see the war through to victory regardless of how long it took. "I seldom talked with any North Vietnamese without some reference coming into the conversation of the people's preparedness to fight ten, fifteen, even twenty years in order to achieve victory," Salisbury recounted. "At first I thought that such expressions might reflect government propaganda and that the individuals had been coached to talk like this. But when I found Catholic priests and Buddhists saying the same thing in much the same words as simple peasants in the villages.., I began to realize that this was a national psychology. It might have been inspired by the regime, but it certainly was entirely natural. And, I believed, it suited the North Vietnamese temperament. This spirit of stubborn determination, of fierce national patriotism, combined with a kind of teen-aged dare-deviltry, was characteristic of so many of the individuals with whom I talked."[9] Salisbury's discovery is reflective of a cyclical rather than a linear concept of time.

Only slightly less important to revolutionary war's success was a commitment to guerrilla methods of combat, at least until the material balance between insurgent and government forces had shifted decisively against the latter. Such methods, which both Viet Cong and PAVN regular forces embraced, permitted communist forces to avoid strategically decisive decimation at the hands of superior government firepower. "The first outstanding feature . . . of People's Revolutionary War, as developed by Mao Tse-tung and refined by the North Vietnamese in the two Indochina wars," wrote British counterinsurgency expert Sir Robert Thompson in 1968, "is its immunity to the direct application of mechanical and conventional power."[10] "Immunity" is perhaps an excessive characterization, since French and especially U.S. firepower superiority exacted a tremendous human toll on communist forces, especially when they exposed themselves directly to that firepower in premature attempts, as in 1951, 1968, and 1972, to move from second-phase guerrilla to third-phase conventional operations. For the most part, however, communist forces remained sufficiently elusive to control their own loss rates and thereby to sorely frustrate French and American commanders. Such frustration was evident in a senior U.S. officer's testimony in 1967 before the House Appropriations Committee:

"Do you have enough equipment?" asked Representative George Andrews.

"Yes sir."

"Do you have enough planes?"

"Yes sir."

"Do you have enough guns and ammunition?"

"Yes sir."

"Then why can you not whip that little country of North Vietnam? What do you need to do it?"

"Targets—targets."[11]

Professional military bafflement with the paucity of lucrative targets presented by both communist forces in the field and North Vietnam's homeland should have come as no surprise. Unconventional warfare is the only effective option open to the otherwise materially overpowered side; the calculated elusivity and willingness to sacrifice territory for time that the communists displayed in the presence of U.S. firepower was not at all dissimilar to that exhibited by George Washington and his Continental Army and supporting local militias in the face of superior British size and strength. After 1776, Washington "realized that the Revolution would continue as long as the Continental Army, the backbone of the Revolution, existed. . . . Washington assumed the strategic defensive and determined to win the war not by losing the Continental Army in battle, fighting only when conditions were extraordinarily advantageous," concludes an astute assessment of Washington's generalship. "He would frustrate the British by raids, continual skirmishing, and removing supplies from their vicinity, always staying just beyond the enemy's potentially lethal grasp. This strategy entailed risks. Americans might interpret it as cowardice or weakness, and since defensive war meant protracted war, they might lose heart. But Washington believed he could be active enough to prevent excessive war weariness. Prolonged resistance would also fuel opposition to the conflict in England, as well as strengthen America's hand in European diplomacy."[12] If Washington exposed the British to the challenges of military unconventionality via deliberate target deprivation, the U.S. military establishment itself subsequently faced the same challenges, from the Seminole Wars in the early decades of the nineteenth century through the Filipino Insurgency and Mexican Revolution in the first two decades of the twentieth century.

A third component of revolutionary war's success in Indochina was the communists' willingness and ability to retreat to a preceding stage of military effort in the event of serious miscalculation. This was not readily apparent to many U.S. military and civilian officials, who were inclined to believe that revolutionary war could be defeated if decisively arrested in its second, and especially third, phases. The Vietnamese communist leadership did not regard the stages as irreversible, and did not hesitate to revert to strategically defensive and less conventional operations following the three major occasions when communist forces were bloodily repulsed in moving prematurely into direct conventional confrontation (i.e., Giap's 1951 assault on fortified French positions in the Red River Delta, and Hanoi's 1968 Tet and 1972 "Easter" offensives). Deliberate de-escalation of violence was an essential means of recovering control over loss rates while at the same time prolonging hostilities.

Of course, the United States could have avoided exposing itself to the peculiar and difficult challenges of defeating a revolutionary war in a distant and alien land had it simply refrained from assuming the primary responsibility for the war's conduct. Indeed, it is now conventional wisdom to declare that Americanization of the ground war in 1965 was a mistake. In retirement, Richard Nixon, who in 1954 favored direct U.S. intervention to save the French at Dien Bien Phu, and who later asserted that "standing aside as our [French] ally went down to defeat" was "our first critical mistake" in Indochina,[13] roundly criticized the Johnson administration for "fail[ing] to understand that we could not win the war for the South Vietnamese; that in the final analysis, the South Vietnamese would have to win it for themselves." The United States, he went on to say, "bullied its way into Vietnam and tried to run the war our way instead of recognizing that our mission should have been to help the South Vietnamese build up their forces so that they could win the war."[14]

But Nixon was not president in 1965, when the United States confronted the stark choice between direct military intervention and watching the South Vietnamese lose the war without such intervention (as indeed they went on to do just a decade later). And I can find nothing in the published record indicating Nixon's expressed disapproval of the war's Americanization in 1965. One can only imagine how a White House–hungry politician who had made his political fortune redbaiting Truman administration Democrats would have reacted to a Johnson administration decision to cut U.S. losses in Vietnam in 1965—a decision, ironically, implicit in Nixon's own adoption of the war's Vietnamization just four years later.

Civilian decision makers did not happily embrace Americanization. Well into 1964 they clung to the hope that the South Vietnamese, the beneficiaries of almost a decade of generous U.S. military assistance and training, could continue to shoulder the primary responsibility for combat. Presidents Kennedy and Johnson repeatedly stated that the Vietnam War was ultimately up to Asian—not American—boys to decide. In January 1964, McNamara expressed before the House Armed Services Committee what had become the official mantra: "It is a Vietnamese war. They are going to have to assume the primary responsibility for winning it. Our policy is to limit our support to logistical and training support. . . . I don't believe that we as a nation should assume the primary responsibility for the war in South Vietnam. It is a counter-guerrilla war . . . that can only be won by the Vietnamese themselves."[15] As late as March 1965, Ambassador Maxwell Taylor, who as Chairman of the Joint Chiefs of Staff had urged commitment of token U.S. ground combat forces, now cautioned Washington that the introduction of such forces would encourage the South Vietnamese "to adopt an attitude of 'let the United States do it'" and increase U.S. "vulnerability to Communist propaganda and Third Country criticism as we appear to assume the old French role of colonizer and conqueror."[16]

U.S. military leadership, in contrast, had long been pushing for an expanded role in the war, including a sustained bombing campaign against the North and the introduction of U.S. ground combat forces in the South as needed. By mid-1964, the military seems to have had, along with such discerning field journalists as David Halberstam and Neil Sheehan, a better appreciation than its civilian superiors of just how badly the RVNAF was performing against the intensified communist offensive operations that followed the November 1963, U.S.-encouraged overthrow of the Diem regime by South Vietnam's senior military leadership. Even the legendary and outspoken army advisor John Paul Vann, who deplored his colleagues' emphasis on firepower as a substitute for what he believed were imperative counterinsurgency techniques, urged a U.S. takeover of the war because he regarded the RVNAF officer corps as congenitally incompetent.[17] No doubt also motivated by a "can do" confidence in its own ability to succeed where the RVNAF was failing, the MACV and the JCS did not, as did the White House, have to bear the political responsibility and risks attendant on the commitment of large numbers of U.S. troops to foreign combat.

U.S. military leadership in 1964–65 was professionally overconfident as well as dulled, if not oblivious, to Americanization's potentially corrosive strategic consequences for the United States and fatal impact on the Republic of Vietnam's struggle for political legitimacy. But the military can hardly be faulted for correctly concluding that the RVNAF was simply not up to the task of defeating its communist opponents. Indeed, it was perhaps the very combination of self-confidence and disdain for the RVNAF as a military ally that accounted for the MACV's relative disinterest before the Tet Offensive in preparing the South Vietnamese military for the day when U.S. forces would depart Vietnam. The MACV, CINCPAC, and the JCS all seemed to assume that U.S. forces could finish the job once and for all, and that there would be a postwar residual U.S. presence in South Vietnam, as there was in Korea, to stand guard against a re-eruption of communist aggression. The war's Americanization quickly relegated the American military advisory effort to a very distant second priority, a development reflected in the inferior status—in terms of prestige and career promotion prospects—that advisory assignments assumed vis-à-vis U.S. troop command slots. Instructing the South Vietnamese took a back seat to beating the North Vietnamese.[18] And predictably, Americanization of the war provided to the RVNAF every imaginable incentive to sit back and watch the Americans win the war.

Nor can the MACV really be faulted for offering the kind of training and weaponry it ended up providing to the RVNAF. Those who properly fault the U.S. military for failing to take advantage of the war's Americanization from 1965 to 1972 to prepare RVNAF for its ultimate day of reckoning with its communist opponents must recognize that the Pentagon was congenitally incapable of shaping the RVNAF into a genuinely effective counterinsurgency force. "U.S. military forces," observed the narrative of *The Pentagon Papers*, "were unprepared by their own experience to assist in the structuring of forces designed for other than conventional warfare. . . . This natural tendency to develop conventional forces was not only in step with the dominant trend in U.S. military strategy, it was also reinforced by . . . the generalized assumption that the ability to promote internal security was automatically provided for in the creation of forces able to promote external security."[19] It is unreasonable to expect proficiency in the art of unconventional warfare on the part of a victorious conventional military establishment, especially one convinced that a capacity to defeat Soviet armor on the North German Plain (a challenge that surely would have stymied Hanoi's revolutionary warriors) would be more than adequate to whip a ragtag body of Asian infantry. As Army Chief of Staff (1962–64) George Decker put it, "Any good soldier can handle guerrillas."[20] Critics also must recognize that the valuable instruction in waging conventional warfare the Pentagon did provide, though potentially critical to countering revolutionary war's third-phase operations, was, as has been noted, never attended by the endowment of the RVNAF with the requisite base of technical proficiency. To the very end, the RVNAF could not maintain more than a fraction of the sophisticated U.S. armaments it received.

In sum, the United States Americanized both the war and the Vietnamese armed forces, but succeeded neither in effecting a conclusive victory on its own nor in leaving behind in Vietnam a client military establishment capable of surviving without a politically unacceptable reentry of massive U.S. firepower into the Vietnam War. If, however, Americanization ultimately failed, it was almost certainly inevitable. The RVNAF was incapable of defeating the PAVN and VC, and neither the White House nor the U.S. military was prepared to entertain the only alternative to Americanization: abandoning South Vietnam without a fight.

Yet, the absence of a politically acceptable alternative to the war's Americanization in 1965 did not dictate the MACV's choice of an attrition strategy and its attendant addiction to counting both living and dead communist troops as the index of military success. In retrospect, four aspects of Westmoreland's selection and pursuit of attrition stand out.

First, it provoked intense controversy within both the civilian and military decision-making communities. Second, it rested on false assumptions regarding communist willingness and capacity to absorb huge manpower losses, and U.S. ability to gain and maintain the initiative on the battlefield. Third, attrition was politically counterproductive in both Vietnam and the United States. And finally, though alternative strategies were available within and beyond the framework of restrictions civilian authority imposed on military operations, nothing in or about attrition's failure proves that those strategies would have succeeded.

Attrition is simple in concept if not in execution. Its object is to destroy or disable enemy forces and war-making capacity at a rate faster than he can replace them. As one of Westmoreland's deputies put it: "The solution in Vietnam is more bombs, more shells, more napalm . . . till the other side cracks and gives up."[21] Presumably, the enemy would sue for peace upon or shortly after reaching what was called the "cross-over point," or the point where he could no longer make good his losses. "We'll just go on bleeding them until Hanoi wakes up to the fact that they have bled their country to the point of national disaster for generations," explained Westmoreland in 1967. "They will have to reassess their position."[22]

Westmoreland claims that attrition was mandated "by political decisions" which ruled out U.S. ground force operations against communist military sanctuaries in Laos and Cambodia,[23] an argument echoed by Gen. Dave Richard Palmer in his history of the war: "With allied ground forces restricted to the borders of South Vietnam, the only feasible strategy was to try to kill North Vietnamese and Viet Cong soldiers faster than they could be replaced."[24] Attrition, by exalting reliance on firepower, also served Westmoreland's goal of minimizing U.S. casualties among a largely conscripted U.S. infantry while maximizing the enemy's. Westmoreland further argues that while many professionals believed attrition was discredited by the trench warfare of World War I, it was suitable "against an enemy with relatively limited manpower" like the Vietnamese communists.[25]

Professional military complaints about enemy sanctuaries accompanied both the Korean and Vietnam wars, and they reflected genuine and understandable concern over operational military opportunities forsaken for overriding political considerations. In the case of the Vietnam War, there is no question that communist calculations would have been greatly complicated and their difficulties compounded if U.S. ground forces had been permitted to enter and occupy selected areas of Laos and Cambodia. But then, so, too, would have been U.S. military calculations and difficulties; a wider war would have ensued. Moreover, the prohibition on U.S. ground force movements beyond South Vietnam did not extend to air power. PAVN sanctuaries in Laos alone received a total of 3 million tons of U.S. bombs, or more tonnage than Anglo-American bomber forces dropped on Germany and Japan in World War II; lines of communication and other military targets in North Vietnam received another 1 million tons, with yet another five hundred thousand tons allocated to Cambodia (three times the U.S. tonnage dropped on Japan).[26] Particularly awesome was the employment of Strategic Air Command B-52s against the Ho Chi Minh Trail, especially against suspected storage and staging areas; no other American weapon seemed to unnerve communist forces more than the B-52. Former NLF Minister of Justice Truong Nhu Tang remembers that, "for all the privations and hardships, nothing the guerrillas had to endure compared with the stark terrorization of the B-52 bombardments. . . . It was not just that things were destroyed; in some awesome way they . . . ceased to exist. . . . One lost control of bodily functions as the mind screamed incomprehensible orders to get out."[27] Additionally, it is far from self-evident that the presence of U.S. ground forces in Laos, Cambodia, and southern North Vietnam could have effectively interdicted the flow of communist supplies into South Vietnam. U.S. forces were unable to prevent those supplies from moving *within* South Vietnam, where the MACV had relatively unrestricted operational latitude. Finally, it should be noted that the United States also enjoyed important military sanctuaries, though admittedly more because of North Vietnamese incapacity than unwillingness to deny them. Such sanctuaries included Guam, Thailand, and "Yankee Station" in the Gulf of Tonkin, all of which served as secure bases from which the bombing and surveillance of North Vietnam was conducted for eight years.

Communist sanctuaries or no communist sanctuaries, alternatives to attrition, though rejected, were available. The first alternative, favored by much of the professional military establishment and conservative opinion in the United States, was, of course, the war's escalation via some combination of U.S. ground force operations against the communists' Laotian and Cambodian sanctuaries, and a more or less unrestricted bombing campaign against North Vietnam. Those who pushed for this alternative regarded the Vietnam War as predominantly a conventional military challenge, and North Vietnam as the source of hostilities in the South. Some, like Westmoreland, were skeptical of bombing's decisiveness and focused on ground operations beyond South Vietnam's borders, while others, including the Air Force and the Navy-dominated Pacific Command, saw the air war against the North as the path to victory and even as a substitute for substantial U.S. ground combat. Proponents of an expanded war, some of whom (like Westmoreland) regarded escalation as the only alternative to attrition, were understandably frustrated throughout the war by what they believed were unnecessary constraints on the military's freedom of action in Indochina.

The second alternative entailed pursuit of a different, nonescalatory strategy inside South Vietnam. Proponents of what was first called the enclave—and later population protection or pacification—strategy rejected attrition as unnecessarily bloody, politically counterproductive, dangerously open-ended, and even downright stupid. "[O]ne thing should be made absolutely clear: attrition is not a strategy," wrote Gen. Dave Richard Palmer, who served as a colonel in Vietnam with the Second Armored Division. "It is irrefutable proof of the absence of any strategy. Any commander who resorts to attrition admits his failure to conceive of an alternative. He turns from warfare as an art and accepts it on the most non-professional terms imaginable. He uses blood instead of brains. Saying that political considerations forced the employment of attrition warfare does not alter the hard truth that the United States was strategically bankrupt in Vietnam."[28] Douglas Kinnard, in his seminal post-Vietnam War survey of general officer opinion on the war's conduct, discovered "a noticeable lack of enthusiasm, to put it mildly, by Westmoreland's generals for his tactics and by implication for his strategy in the war."[29] Population protectionists included Sir Robert Thompson, Maxwell Taylor, John Paul Vann, retired generals James

Gavin and Matthew Ridgway, Assistant Secretary of State Roger Hilsman, the commandant of the marine corps, and senior marine corps officers in Vietnam. Even Army Chief of Staff Harold K. Johnson and Creighton Abrams, Westmoreland's successor, are now known to have been highly skeptical of attrition and privately predisposed toward the enclave alternative.[30]

Population protectionists saw the war, at least until the Tet Offensive and subsequent U.S. abandonment of military victory, as primarily a civil conflict to be ultimately decided by the contest for the political control of South Vietnam's rural inhabitants. Rather than tear up the countryside in what in what they believed to be a fruitless attempt to search out and destroy communist main force units operating in the Central Highlands and strategic approaches to Saigon, population protectionists called for what amounted to discrete counterinsurgency warfare. They would start with the establishment of relatively secure enclaves in the heavily populated Mekong Delta and coastal plains, thereby isolating the enemy from local logistical and intelligence support and providing havens for government-sponsored social and economic reconstruction.

Pacification as an alternative to search and destroy was rejected by Westmoreland because in his view it ceded the initiative to the enemy. The enclave strategy "would position American troops in what would be in effect a series of unconnected beachheads, their backs to the sea, essentially in a defensive posture," he wrote after the war. "That would leave the decision of when and where to strike to the enemy. . . ."[31] Westmoreland went on to assert that, "I elected to fight a so-called big-unit war not because of any Napoleonic impulse to maneuver units and hark to the sound of cannon but because of the basic fact that the enemy had committed big units and I ignored them at my peril."[32]

What was really at issue was a fundamental dispute over the nature of the war and America's proper role in it. Attritionists sought a conventional solution to what they viewed as a military problem that only U.S. forces could handle. Pacificationists sought an unconventional solution to a problem they believed was as much political as military; they also sought to limit U.S. military liability by assigning primary responsibility for dealing with the PAVN beyond the enclaves to

U.S.-firepower-assisted South Vietnamese ground forces. Enclave proponents, who believed that the United States could prevail in Vietnam simply by denying the communists victory in the South, had greater confidence in the RVNAF's potential than did attritionists, and some, like Taylor, believed that bombing the North could compel Hanoi to abandon its support of the southern insurgency. They also feared, and rightly so, that attrition promoted an escalatory American commitment because it sought a decisive military victory over an enemy who had the manpower to stalemate the war by matching each increase in U.S. troop deployments to Vietnam. Attrition was a prescription for what enclave supporters wanted to avoid more than anything, other than outright defeat: the war's Americanization. "The acceptance of the search and destroy strategy and the eclipse of the denial of victory idea associated with the enclave strategy," concludes *The Pentagon Papers* narrative, "left the U.S. commitment to Vietnam open-ended. Written all over the search and destroy strategy was a total loss of confidence in the RVNAF and a concomitant willingness on the part of the U.S. to take over the war effort."[33]

Westmoreland's selection of the firepower/attrition approach to defeating the communists was challenged, albeit unsuccessfully, by some within the Pentagon. Though Robert Buzzanco's claim that "a virtual civil war occurred as many ranking officers virulently attacked" Westmoreland's strategy may be a bit overstated,[34] opposition was strong if not publicly outspoken. In July of 1965, for example, Gen. Harold K. Johnson, following a briefing by Bernard Fall in which the French Indochina expert challenged the Army's demographic assumptions underlying attrition, commissioned a study—Program for Pacification and Long-Term Development of South Vietnam, or PROVN—which, among other things, called for search and destroy's replacement by a population protection strategy.[35] PROVN not only recommended the establishment of an integrated U.S. civil-military effort, but also declared: "Rural Construction must be designated unequivocally as the major U.S./GVN effort. It will require the commitment of a preponderance of RVNAF and GVN paramilitary forces, together with adequate U.S. support and coordination and assistance. Without question, village and hamlet security must be achieved throughout Vietnam. . . .

R[ural]C[construction] is the principal means available to broaden the allied base, provide security, develop political and military leadership, and provide necessary social reform to the people."[36] By the time the study was completed in March 1966, however, Westmoreland was pursuing attrition, and General Johnson did not feel it appropriate to override his field commander's choice of strategy.

The army chief of staff's acquiescence to attrition came despite some evidence that pacification was succeeding in the two areas of Vietnam where U.S. military authorities had adopted it. In the early 1960s, Army Special Forces teams operating under the control of the Central Intelligence Agency pacified selected montagnard tribes in the Central Highlands to the point of erasing communist political influence among the tribes and enlisting able-bodied tribesmen into Special Forces-created Civilian Irregular Defense Groups. The CIDGs provided effective protection to montagnard villages while supplying their American advisors valuable intelligence on enemy troop movements. This pacification effort continued to produce impressive results until control of Special Forces and CIDGs was transferred to the MACV, which was hostile to CIA control of any Army units and unwilling to challenge Vietnamese prejudice against both montagnards and U.S. efforts to enlist them, however effectively, in the war against communism.

An even more ambitious American experiment with pacification was conducted by the marine corps in South Vietnam's northernmost provinces. Beginning in 1965, to the MACV's growing irritation, marine corps units in the I Corps region began conducting classic pacification operations organized around Combined Action Platoons, each containing fifteen marines and thirty-four South Vietnamese soldiers local to the area, that would move into contested villages and hamlets and live there continuously until effective security and rural construction initiatives were established. Profiting from its long history of involvement in distant small wars and pacification campaigns, the marine corps relegated destruction of communist main forces to secondary priority. At the February 1966 conference of U.S. and South Vietnamese leaders in Honolulu, Ambassador Henry Cabot Lodge summed up the argument for assigning pacification priority over search and destroy: "We can beat up North Vietnamese regiments in the high plateau for the next twenty years and it will not end the war—unless we and the Vietnamese are able to build simple but solid political institutions under which a proper police can function and a climate created in which economic and social revolution, in freedom, are possible."[37] Sir Robert Thompson declared the marines' use of Combined Action Platoons to be "quite the best idea I have seen in Vietnam, and it worked superbly."[38]

The controversial question of whether a pacification strategy could have succeeded is discussed below. What is not in dispute is attrition's failure and the reasons why. Attrition was doomed because it rested on three false premises: that there was a communist breaking point within reach of U.S. firepower; that the United States could acquire and maintain the initiative on the battlefield; and that attrition's progress could be accurately measured by keeping a reliable count of Vietnamese communists, both dead and alive. The presumption of an attainable breaking point was based on the conviction that the United States could kill more communist soldiers than Hanoi and the NLF could replace, and that once this cross-over point had been reached, Hanoi would begin to consider suspension of significant sponsorship of the war in the South. In fact, U.S. firepower, lavishly employed though it was, never came close to competing with either the communist birth rate or Hanoi's willingness to expend entire generations of young men on behalf of Vietnam's forcible reunification under communist auspices. At the height of the war in 1968, the DRV and NLF-controlled areas in South Vietnam had an estimated total military manpower pool of 2.3 million (only about half of whom were soldiers), with 250,000 new males annually becoming available for military service in North Vietnam alone. Even assuming a communist loss rate as high as the first half of 1968—during the Tet Offensive and its aftermath—it would have taken the MACV thirteen years to have exhausted this manpower pool.[39] As Thompson bluntly observed, to neutralize Westmoreland's attrition strategy, "all the people of North Vietnam had to do between 1965 and 1968 was to exist and to breed," and the "United States Air Force could interrupt neither of those activities."[40] "Despite considerable progress in the Vietnam conflict during the past year," concluded a 1968 report by the Systems Analysis division of the OSD that addressed, among other things, attrition's presumption of a reachable communist breaking point, "an end to the conflict is not in sight and major unresolved problems remain. North Vietnam still believes it can win in the long run, in the name of nationalism if not communism. It has been fighting for over 25 years against the Japanese, French, and Americans and appears prepared to fight indefinitely. . . . Hanoi is willing to wait. We have hurt them some, and we can even hurt them some more, but not so badly as to destroy their society or their hope for regaining in the future the material things they sacrifice today."[41] Indeed, throughout the war, the CIA repeatedly concluded that the North Vietnamese manpower base was adequate to support the losses the PAVN incurred.

Ironically, Westmoreland had selected search and destroy over pacification in part because he believed the former would afford the United States the battlefield initiative whereas the latter would not. In fact, communist forces assumed the initiative early and maintained it during most of the war. The MACV and other studies revealed that the PAVN and VC, not the searching and destroying Americans, initiated 80 to 90 percent of all firefights, most of which were brief (lasting only minutes in some cases), hit-and-run affairs, with communist forces routinely breaking contact to escape the full weight of certain if delayed U.S. artillery and air responses.[42] Only rarely did communist forces stand and fight, and when they did they usually came out the worse for it. What was more important was that they determined when and where they would fight and under what circumstances combat would take place. Possession of the initiative allowed the PAVN and VC to control their own casualties, at least to the point of avoiding Westmoreland's cross-over point. It also rendered the rate of communist attrition relatively immune to U.S. force levels in Vietnam; the increasing numbers of troops MACV requested from 1964 on through the Tet Offensive did not result in commensurately higher enemy body counts. By late 1967, however, MACV analysts seem to have convinced themselves that search and destroy operations had firmly placed the initiative in American hands (even though the scale of such operations usually produced little in the way of justifiable enemy kills), that indeed the cross-over point had actually been reached.[43] The MACV clearly misread the relative lull

in communist offensive operations during the six months preceding
the Tet Offensive as proof that attrition was working, when in truth the
lull reflected simply a husbanding of resources in preparation for the
great offensive to come. Even the MACV's decimation of VC (if not
PAVN) forces during Tet did not break the communists. For the next
three years they retreated to second-phase guerrilla operations, licking
their wounds while a politically and strategically exhausted United
States undertook a unilateral withdrawal of its forces from Vietnam. To
be sure, the Tet Offensive, subsequent U.S–South Vietnamese accel-
eration of rural pacification efforts, and the MACV's abandonment
(under Creighton Abrams) of search and destroy in favor of population protection fatally undermined the communist political base in the
South, propelling Hanoi toward increasing reliance on conventional
military and diplomatic means to achieve reunification. But revolutionary war's very flexibility encouraged such a shift, especially at a time
when U.S. resolve in Vietnam was visibly faltering and Hanoi began
receiving potentially decisive quantities of advanced Soviet conventional weaponry.

Attrition also failed because of lack of consensus over just exactly
who the enemy was, and because of grave distortions in calculating—
and reporting—enemy losses. Predictably, the MACV and the JCS,
because they viewed the war as a straight, soldier-to-soldier military contest, fixed on a narrow definition of the enemy's order of battle (OB)
that excluded local VC self-defense militia and other part-time paramilitary forces. To have accepted such forces in enemy OB calculations
would have been to embrace not only a much broader and more complicated definition of the Vietnam War and solutions to it, but also an
enemy of such considerably larger size as to unnerve civilian decision
makers accustomed to MACV-supplied estimates. Thus arose, in August
1967, the great order-of-battle dispute between the MACV and the CIA,
which was finally resolved in the MACV's favor by CIA Director Richard
Helms' bureaucratic fiat.[44] The starting point of the MACV's conclusion in mid-1967 that the cross-over point had been reached was its
exclusion of VC irregular forces, which kept the enemy's total OB
strength (PAVN and main force and local VC regulars) at no more than
300,000. CIA experts and other skeptics of the MACV's conduct of the

war, who saw the struggle in its political as well as its military dimensions and who recognized PAVN and VC main force logistical and intelligence dependence on the very categories of communist irregulars the MACV wished to exclude, postulated an enemy order of battle approaching 600,000. They and others continued to argue that the VC irregulars should have been counted because they performed such vital functions as local self-defense, providing intelligence to PAVN and main force VC units, and—not least—planting mines and booby traps. These accounted for at least one-fifth of all U.S. casualties,[45] and "because of their randomness" and cheapness (most were made from dud U.S. munitions), were "more economically effective in inflicting casualties while creating mental and emotional stress in the process."[46] The MACV's critics also wonder how live VC irregulars missed the count in the OB but made it into the MACV's body count when they were killed. "The Saigon brass in their plush villas didn't believe that a VC youth of twelve who mined jungle paths and scouted for main force troops, or a fifty-year-old woman who tended VC wounded, should be counted as combat or support troops," wrote combat veteran and later *Newsweek* commentator David Hackworth. "They didn't understand they were as much a part of the VC army as any of the half-dozen aides who kept Westmoreland's villa operating efficiently. The paradox was that though the generals insisted those non-regulars be arbitrarily dropped from the OB, when killed, they were included in the body count."[47]

The CIA ultimately deferred to the military because the MACV had more bureaucratic clout—it was, after all, running the war—and because, as JCS Chairman Wheeler told Westmoreland, acceptance of the CIA count, especially if leaked to the press, "would, literally, blow the lid off Washington. . . . I cannot go to the President and tell him that contrary to my reports and those of the other chiefs as to the progress of the war . . . the situation is such that we are not sure who has the initiative in South Vietnam."[48] CIA analyst George Carver had cabled Helms from Saigon that "General Westmoreland . . . has given instructions tantamount to direct order that VC strength total will not exceed 300,000 ceiling. Rationale seems to be that any higher figure will not be sufficiently optimistic and would generate unacceptable level of criticism from the press."[49]

Adulteration of the enemy body count was even more pronounced than efforts to insure that the enemy's OB stayed within the parameters of MACV's confidence in attrition's ultimate success. To be sure, the war's very nature made an accurate tally of enemy losses inherently difficult. The communists worked hard to blur the distinction between combatant and non-combatant in the Vietnamese countryside, and both the PAVN and the VC made every effort to remove their dead from the battlefield. The rugged and thickly foliated terrain of much of South Vietnam made it even more difficult to discover dead enemy soldiers than to detect live ones. Kills inflicted by U.S. and South Vietnamese air and artillery strikes were often uncountable, and there was no way of estimating the number of communist soldiers who were felled by disease, accident, and other noncombat misfortunes. A cynical enemy's deliberate use of innocent populations from which to attack U.S. units and upon which to draw U.S. fire, also encouraged American commanders to lump together all of the resulting dead Vietnamese as "enemy" bodies, notwithstanding the persistence throughout the war of an unusual disparity between the number of enemy killed and the number of his weapons captured. (The disparity admitted three possible explanations: many of the dead were noncombatants; the enemy was very good at recovering his lost weapons; or many PAVN and VC troops went into battle unarmed.)

But distortion of body counts was not simply a function of the war's political and military messiness. Precisely because OB estimates and body counts became the indices of attrition's success or failure, amassing kills became the standard of career success for U.S. commanders, and therefore an often irresistible temptation to abuse in both the infliction and reporting of enemy casualties. Even McNamara, who more than any other individual promoted worship of numbers as a substitute for seasoned judgment, conceded that many of the very same quantitative measurements of the war's progress upon which he insisted, including the "infamous . . . body counts," were "misleading or erroneous."[50] Army historian and Vietnam veteran Shelby Stanton is more brutal in his assessment: "While casualty counts are valid measurements in war, in Vietnam they unfortunately became more than yardsticks used to gauge the battlefield. Rather than means of determination, they became ends in themselves. The process became so ghoulish that individual canteens were accepted as authorized substitutes if bodies were too dismembered to estimate properly. Guidelines were even issued by MACV on factoring additional dead based on standard percentages by type of encounter and terrain. This appalling practice produced body counts that went largely unquestioned, and were readily rewarded by promotions, medals, and time off from field duty."[51]

If attrition's premises doomed it from the start, its implementation also worked against the creation of a politically viable noncommunist South Vietnam, which was, after all, the root American objective in Indochina. To the extent that the pre-Tet Offensive conflict in the South was a civil war—a struggle for the hearts and minds, or at least control, of the peasantry—pursuit of attrition was counterproductive in two ways. First, it drew U.S. military attention away from the "other war" of pacification and counterinsurgency. Second, its heavy and all too often indiscriminate employment of firepower bred immense anger and hostility among rural Vietnamese toward American forces in the field (whose American cultural values the peasantry also found highly offensive), and by extension, the Saigon regime on whose behalf U.S. forces acted. Westmoreland's preoccupation with defeating PAVN regulars along the Demilitarized Zone, the South Vietnamese-Laotian border, and the strategic approaches to Saigon, together with his conviction that pacification was a secondary task best left to America's Vietnamese ally, propelled the U.S. military effort geographically and functionally away from what enclave strategy proponents regarded as the war's center of gravity. Indeed, the available evidence strongly suggests that Hanoi conducted PAVN operations during the critical year preceding the Tet Offensive with the aim of luring the MACV's attention and forces away from easy reach of South Vietnam's cities and provincial capitals, and that Westmoreland took the bait at places like Con Thien, Dak To, and most spectacularly, Khe Sanh, because he misread PAVN sieges of these remote U.S. strongholds in the latter half of 1967 and early 1968 as the loci of the communists' main effort. Most impartial observers believe that Khe Sanh was a feint to draw MACV's attention and resources away from the cities and towns that were the Tet Offensive's real targets.[52] The fact that the subsequent communist assault on those cities and towns—which caught some U.S. forces potentially available for Saigon's defense dangerously out of position, and which Westmoreland initially judged to be an attempt to divert U.S. forces from Khe Sanh's defense[53]—was bloodily repulsed does not excuse the pre-Tet MACV from pursuing a strategy that was inappropriate for the predominate nature of the war at hand.

That strategy's enshrinement of firepower as the best means of "attriting" the enemy while at the same time substituting metal for American blood, coupled with such programs as the chemical defoliation of crops and natural vegetation in contested areas, significantly depopulated much of South Vietnam's countryside in a manner that deprived the PAVN and main force VC units of local sustenance. But it also utterly alienated from Saigon those terrorized and driven into the cities. U.S. forces employed munitions on a scale as if they were confronting Soviet Guards tank divisions in Central Europe rather than elusive Asian infantry that rarely presented lucrative targets. Indeed, the evidence, including widespread declarations of free-fire zones in "enemy"-controlled regions, strongly suggests that firepower was deliberately employed to depopulate—by death or abandonment—entire areas of rural South Vietnam. During the war, at least 50 percent of South Vietnam's peasantry was involuntarily urbanized by combat in the countryside, forced into cities and larger towns where most found only squalor and occasional employment (often at U.S. bases and their surrounding bars, whorehouses, tattoo parlors, and other gyp-joints).[54] Between 1964 and 1974, South Vietnam's urban population grew from 15 to 65 percent of the country's total, and by 1968 refugees alone accounted for 5 million of South Vietnam's total population of 17 million.[55] Some observers welcomed these demographic trends. "The Maoist inspired rural revolution is undercut by the American-sponsored urban revolution," wrote Harvard political scientist Sam Huntington, who went on to declaim that the "urban slum, which seems so horrible to middle-class Americans, often becomes for the poor peasant a gateway to a new and better life."[56] Indeed, CIA Director Richard Helms as well as analysts at the Rand Corporation, looked upon MACV's success in "generating" refugees as a positive development.[57] This demographic revolution, however, not only placed ultimately intolerable burdens upon South Vietnam's economy, but also created a vast urban underclass which, if not revolutionary in its political disposition, was estranged from the American-sponsored noncommunist political order. "The peasantry did not require," writes Gabriel Kolko in his massive history of the socioeconomic and political dimensions of the war, "a sophisticated understanding of the world to see who was using the most munitions to endanger its existence, drafting the most sons, and profoundly undermining a traditional rural order with its enormous challenges and intrusions. The minimum consequence of this widespread attitude was a hatred of Americans and of those who acted on their behalf, and this primal opinion precluded success for the . . . pacification and political program."[58]

Lack of what John Paul Vann cautioned must be "the utmost discrimination in killing"[59] actually encouraged communist units to bait U.S. forces into bombing and shelling villages from which they would snipe at passing U.S. patrols or helicopters. It "staggers the belief," commented Sir Robert Thompson in 1968, "that American helicopters were under instruction, and for all I know still are, to fire on any village which fires on them in the course of their flight (I am not referring here to an opposed landing but to a few passing shots). This return fire reinforces every word the Viet Cong say, with the result that American intentions cease to be credible."[60] As early as 1961 Bernard Fall warned that "the use of massive bomb attacks and napalm drops on villages is not only militarily stupid, but is inhuman and is likely to backfire very badly on the psychological level."[61] In 1968 in the Mekong Delta province of Ba Xuyen, I myself witnessed the complete destruction of an economically thriving district town by U.S. airstrikes. The strikes were ordered in response to VC occupation of the town after its ostensible RVNAF "defenders" fled without firing a shot (a deal obviously had been cut in advance). On another occasion, I was present when U.S. helicopter gunships attacked and destroyed, apparently for sport, a herd of domesticated water buffalo, the most prized of all possessions among Vietnam's rice-growing peasants. The herd was being tended by several small boys, some of whom also appeared to be hit.[62] On still another occasion, during the so-called mini-Tet Offensive of May 1968, I watched U.S. fighter bombers destroy much of Cholon, Saigon's Chinese section, because

RVNAF forces on the ground had received sniper fire from a local factory building. The factory and entire residential blocks around it were flattened in a crescendo of iron bombs, napalm, and helicopter gunship rocket barrages. A couple of my colleagues and I drove through the devastation shortly afterwards. "As we drove quickly through the charred ruins," my diary recounts, "even the few children remaining refused to wave at us as they almost always did in other circumstances, and when we stopped to photograph something, they did not approach but yelled at us instead, 'Number ten! Number ten!,' a pidgin English slang term of denunciation. I wondered if we weren't creating more Viet Cong than we were killing." In the battle for hearts and minds, the Americans disarmed themselves by the lavish use of firepower—especially air power—in South Vietnam.

A major part of the problem was a gross excess of firepower chasing a paucity of targets, and service bureaucratic imperatives to expend the surplus one way or the other. An excellent example of this at the local level was the so-called Phantom program that arrived in my (second) province of Bac Lieu in October 1968.

Bac Lieu was a small, out-of-the-way province at the southern end of the Mekong Delta. It was too rich in foodstuffs and too far south of the major combat areas to warrant more than peripheral military attention by either side. In 1968 there were no PAVN troops in the province, only an estimated three thousand full-time hard-core Viet Cong, or about 1 percent of the total population. (Against this threat were arrayed over twenty thousand men in various components of the South Vietnamese armed forces in the province.) There was not much in the way of fighting beyond occasional VC attacks on isolated outposts and mortaring of the provincial capital of Bac Lieu City. Both the GVN province chief and the American province senior advisor seemed acutely aware of the dangers inherent in the indiscriminate use of firepower in such a productive and heavily populated province. The GVN province chief had refused to permit B-52 strikes and the American province senior advisor had repeatedly denied U.S. Navy requests to shell the province from offshore. He had also forbidden the use of .50-caliber machine guns because their range and velocity made them too destructive in a province that was as flat as a pancake.

Air power in Bac Lieu was confined mainly to logistical support: the helicoptering of troops and ammunition to outposts, and the airlifting of critical supplies to those hamlets inaccessible by road or canal. The only aircraft permanently stationed at Bac Lieu's small dirt airstrip were five or six light, single-engine planes used for aerial observation. Air strikes were possible, but only on request. Within thirty minutes of first contact with VC units, American helicopter gunships and fighter-bombers would fly in from the large air base at IV Corps military head-quarters in Can Tho, several provinces away. Outside of actual support for the relatively rare nonperfunctory ground combat operations con-ducted by South Vietnamese forces, the only air strikes ever called in were occasional sorties over the province's three small and virtually unpopulated free-fire zones.

This atmosphere of modest restraint soon changed, however. There had always been considerable resistance within the American advisory team to any restrictions on firepower. Civilians and military men could be found on either side of the issue, but most of the opposition to restrictions came from those officers for whom Vietnam provided the first and last chance to see real combat. Some found the idea of restraint incompatible with war. Others appeared troubled by the sug-gestion that military effectiveness encompassed elements other than firepower. All opponents of restraint seemed oblivious even to friendly arguments. The moral argument, that unrestricted use of air power would result in unnecessary killing of innocent civilians, ran into the general rejoinder that "war is hell" and the specific argument that "there are no innocent civilians in Vietnam." The political argument, that such destruction would serve only to generate more recruits for the Viet Cong, confronted the firm conviction, à la Sam Huntington, that aerial terror would drive the rural population into government-controlled areas, thus denying the enemy his source of manpower. The military argument, that there were no targets in Bac Lieu warranting big air strikes, was simply dismissed.

The supporters of unfettered air power were understandably pleased when IV Corps headquarters announced in October that every province in the Delta would begin receiving helicopter gunships on a regular basis. Twice a week (for Bac Lieu, Mondays and Thursdays), each province would get a Phantom mission composed of two or three Cobra assault helicopters accompanied by an older Huey helicopter which, as the command ship, would direct the strikes. Since the missions were scheduled independently of any military operations in the province, their aim clearly was not to support troops on the ground (unless they happened to need such support on Mondays and Thursdays). They were "tasked" instead to destroy enemy personnel and installations, to interdict known and suspected enemy lines of supply, and to harass and terrorize the Viet Cong. The Cobras were very lethal, each one carrying two pods containing a total of fifty-two 3.75-inch rockets and mounting an electrically operated modern-day version of the Gatling gun capable of spewing out 100 rounds per second. Some had rapid-fire grenade launchers.

U.S. and Vietnamese provincial authorities reluctantly accepted the Phantom program under strong pressure from Can Tho and Saigon, which in turn were driven by bureaucratic imperatives. It seems that the Cobras, which were new-model helicopters making their first appearance in Vietnam, were not being fully utilized in the relatively quiescent Mekong Delta—and underutilized firepower was often taken by the chain of command as evidence of mismanagement or, worse, insufficient aggressiveness. To avoid such judgments as well as to hold on to Phantom program resources (which might really be needed some day), Phantom supporters needed to get the helicopters fully engaged— piling up achievements even in a place, like Bac Lieu, where there was no need for additional firepower.

The results of the Phantom Program were never in serious doubt. Rarely having any real targets to shoot at, the Cobras would, upon arrival in Bac Lieu, head for the province's small free-fire zones and have at it against what few VC remained there. Predictably, as I learned from subsequent sessions with Viet Cong defectors, the enemy learned that Phantom strikes occurred only on Mondays and Thursdays; they remained well hidden or simply out of the way on those days. The Viet Cong appeared to have advance warning of even the few unscheduled missions. Moreover, Phantom strikes soon began straying beyond the free-fire zones, without the restraint and close monitoring traditionally imposed by provincial authorities on the employment of air power outside the zones. By the end of 1968, the strikes were killing and wounding increasing numbers of people known to be "friendlies"; growing numbers of peasants, many of them women and children living in relatively secure areas, began arriving at the provincial hospital with wounds caused by Phantom attacks (a fact established by cross-checking the type of wound, victim testimony, and Phantom program flight logs). Protests by me and several of my colleagues on the provincial advisory team elicited two responses. First, as one of my superiors explained, "But the Phantoms are not under provincial command. Only Can Tho has jurisdiction, and there is nothing we can do." Second, as I was assured by a Cobra pilot, "We don't shoot individuals on the ground unless they run away when we approach. People that run must be Viet Cong. Why would they run unless they had something to hide?"

The program was still being conducted when I left Bac Lieu in August 1969. The program had, after all, doubled the province's "enemy" body count demanded by the insatiable MACV computers

Fully one-half of the total of 8 million tons of bombs dropped and almost all of the millions of tons of artillery shells fired by U.S. forces in Indochina were expended inside South Vietnam, the ostensible object of U.S. protection. Bomb tonnage alone was almost double the total dropped by Anglo-American bomber forces during World War II— against extensive arrays of military-industrial targets critical to German and Japanese war-making capacity, not against mostly random targets in rural areas populated by people whose political allegiance the United States sought to sway. Extravagant employment of firepower in circumstances where friend and foe were often indistinguishable alienated much of not only South Vietnam's peasantry but also domestic and international opinion, thus undermining political support for the war's prosecution. Photographs of terrified children fleeing napalm strikes and statements by American officers in the field that this or that hamlet or town had to be destroyed in order to "save it" played directly into the hands of communist propagandists, who throughout the war appreciated public opinion as a key factor in the war's outcome. Ironically, the absence of U.S. firepower in 1975 doomed the RVNAF in the face of the PAVN's final onslaught, but by then the war had become pretty much a conventional military fight in which, as we shall see, control of what remained of South Vietnam's peasantry no longer really mattered. Such was not the case, however, during the Vietnam War's pre-Tet Offensive phase, which, notwithstanding official rhetoric at the time (and subsequent declarations by such influential commentators as Harry Summers Jr.), to the contrary, was predominantly a southern-based and -manned, albeit northern-backed, insurgency whose success rested in large measure on the ability to control South Vietnam's rural population.

Would the U.S. cause have fared better had Westmoreland in 1965 selected, instead of attrition, either a wider-war strategy or a population control strategy? Political decision makers, of course, denied the U.S. military the authority to widen the war by carrying it on the ground into Laos and Cambodia (and into North Vietnamese territory just north of the Demilitarized Zone) and by opening up all key North Vietnamese military and supporting logistical targets to air attack. Thus, unlike a population control strategy, whose requirements were compatible with politically imposed restraints on U.S. military operations, a wider war was not within MACV's prerogative to order up. Because of this, and because it is the wider-war strategy that commands the attention of those who continue to argue that the United States could have prevailed in the Vietnam War but for civilian meddling in the military's business (and a biased media and perfidious antiwar movement), discussion of this issue is reserved for a later chapter.

Addressed here is the issue of whether pursuit of a pacification-first strategy from 1965 on would have produced a viable South Vietnam. Andrew Krepinevich and others have eloquently argued that attrition as practiced by the MACV was inappropriate for the insurgency at hand, and that from the beginning the MACV should have pursued—as indeed it did after the Tet Offensive—the population control alternative. While I accept their critique of attrition, I am not persuaded that U.S. forces could have successfully pacified South Vietnam's rural population. Even if they had, I do not think that it would have changed the war's outcome. In my view, the U.S. military establishment in 1965 was culturally, structurally, and doctrinally incapable of conducting a winning—and enduring—pacification program; as a Caucasian, Western, conventional military establishment lacking (except for the marines) the necessary experience in, and the patience to perform, the

delicate and complex political-military tasks of effective imperial polic-
ing, the American armed forces were military misfits in Indochina. During the Kennedy years, U.S. military leadership stoutly and successfully
resisted White House pressures to get into the counterinsurgency business as both incompatible with its main mission—defeating like conventional military challenges—and irrelevant (or at least unnecessary)
to beating insurgents, since overwhelming conventional military power
would be sufficient to do that. I believe it would have been as fruitless
to expect the utterly conventional and self-satisfied U.S. Army of 1965
to perform effective counterinsurgency operations as to expect the
PAVN to whip American armor in the Hof Corridor. "White-faced soldier armed, equipped and trained as he is not suitable guerrilla fighter
for Asian forests and jungles," cryptically cabled Ambassador Taylor to
Washington in early 1965. "French tried to adapt their forces to this mission and failed. I doubt that U.S. forces could do much better."[63] This
assessment was endorsed after the war by former CIA Director (and
Vietnam station chief) William Colby, who observed, "The Pentagon
had to fight the only war it knew how to fight and there was no organization in the American structure that could fight any other."[64]

The institutional challenge was but one of several that pacification
proponents sidestepped during the war and even to this day. Effective
counterinsurgency requires infinite patience and restraint as well as the
creation and maintenance of a viable indigenous political alternative
to the insurgency's program. The successes of the CIA and Special
Forces among the montagnards and of the Marine Combined Action
Platoons in I Corps, though exceptional, were quite limited in time and
place. To have duplicated them on a countrywide basis not only would
have required the MACV's adoption of a strategy it refused to pursue
as long as it believed a conclusive military decision was within reach; it
also would have required both White House and MACV acceptance of
a long war of time-consuming paramilitary, nation-building operations
in which conventional military forces would play but a secondary role.
The full-blown conventional solution favored by the military and reluctantly endorsed by a Lyndon Johnson innately suspicious of professional military judgment and eager to bring the Great Society to America promised—even if it did not deliver—a more rapid end to the war,

which both Johnson and Westmoreland sought, though for different reasons. However, even had the MACV exhibited the desire, patience, skill, imagination, and institutional flexibility to pursue a counterinsurgency strategy from the outset, pacification's ultimate success still would have rested on the GVN's ability to deliver social and economic reform at the village level and the requisite security to protect the beneficiaries of reform. This would have entailed, among other things, early and bold GVN cooption of much of the communists' revolutionary agenda, transformation of the RVNAF from an unmotivated horde of chicken-stealers into a competent, protective, peasant-friendly force, and GVN insistence on keeping Americans and their highly destructive style of warfare at arm's length. But such a South Vietnamese ally was never really in the cards; indeed, had one been in the early 1960s, the war's Americanization would not have been necessary. The Marines' CAP teams "were quite successful at 'winning the hearts and minds' of the local villagers," concedes Harry Summers, in a judgment shared by *The Pentagon Papers* narrative. "But the U.S. tactical successes there were at the expense of its strategic purpose. While the CAP concept rested on the premise that eventually village security would be turned over to local South Vietnamese authorities, that never happened. The South Vietnamese government lacked the resources and . . . the will to assume such responsibilities. Thus, the very effectiveness of the CAP teams highlighted the weaknesses and deficiencies of South Vietnamese officialdom, and weakened the ties between the villages and their government."[65]

The inescapable fact of the matter is that the United States never had much to work with in Saigon in terms of a politically competitive and militarily able ally—a fact evident at least a decade before the GVN's final collapse in 1975. In South Vietnam, U.S. military operations, however successful they may have been at times, could never make good the absence of a legitimate and competent South Vietnamese political authority, a situation made all the worse by the U.S.-encouraged overthrow of Ngo Dinh Diem in 1963 and the Americanization of the war two years later. Even had the United States retained an air and ground combat presence in Vietnam after 1973, as it did in Korea after 1953, the GVN would have remained a costly and permanent military ward of the United States, a strategic drain on American power in an area peripheral to core U.S. security interests. The Americans might provide temporary security to some of South Vietnam's villages, but they could not become, or—try as they might, create indigenous—effective government in that country. Eric Bergerud, in his remarkably perceptive study of the Vietnam War in Hau Nghia province, concludes that "because of unalterable structural characteristics in both the South Vietnamese government and the U.S. Armed Forces, the number of actual options available to Americans in Vietnam was very low. Rather, I am impressed with the enormous difficulties that stood in the way of pursuing any greatly different policy, military or political, that could have spared us defeat in Vietnam."[66] Once the war was Americanized, there was no realistic short-or long-term alternative in Saigon other than abject dependence on the United States.

The supreme irony is that control of South Vietnam's rural population made no difference in the war's outcome. Even a complete elimination of the communist political base in the country would not have deprived Hanoi of a capacity to launch—or afforded the GVN a capacity to resist—the decisive communist conventional invasion of 1975. Only the Americans could have defeated that invasion, but they had long since returned the war to their Vietnamese clients. Indeed, it was precisely the erosion of that base in the South in the years following the Tet Offensive that compelled Hanoi to "go conventional." The combination of massive, irreplaceable Viet Cong losses during Tet and U.S.-firepower-induced depopulation of much of South Vietnam's countryside drained the communists' revolutionary war of much of its political content and appeal. Tet also prompted MACV, now under Creighton Abrams (who, unlike Westmoreland, viewed the war's political and military ingredients as inseparable), to refocus U.S. military strategy away from search and destroy toward population control, a change mandated in any event by communist abandonment of emphasis on large-unit operations in favor of lower-level protracted war operations aimed at maximizing U.S. casualties. These events, coupled with the GVN's belated implementation of genuine land reform and its draconian assault on the Viet Cong's political infrastructure (under the auspices of the controversial Phoenix program), dramatically reduced that portion of South Vietnam's dwindling rural population under communist control. By 1972, the United States and its Vietnamese ally had more or less won the "other war" via a combination of sheer weight of resources and Tet-induced communist losses and reversion to a strategic defensive posture characterized by emphasis on low-risk guerrilla rocket and sapper attacks as a means of remaining in play while preparing for decisive phase-three operations. The communists went on to win the war militarily in spite of their political defeat in the South not because they believed they could beat the United States conventionally. They knew from the start they could not, and knew the Americans knew they could not. Rather, they correctly identified American political resolve as the critical domino of the war. In all likelihood, even the MACV's wholehearted embrace of a population control strategy in 1965 would have made little difference in the war's outcome, although it might have compelled the communists to "go conventional" much earlier than they did—before the United States abandoned its pursuit of military victory. That the MACV wrongly chose attrition does not make right the counterinsurgency alternative, although that alternative was certainly more relevant than attrition to the predominantly insurgent character of the war until the Tet Offensive. If adoption of attrition against communist military forces was boneheaded, a pacification-first strategy vis-à-vis South Vietnam's peasantry was, if more sensible, ultimately irrelevant. Timothy Lomperis believes the communists betrayed their own revolutionary ideals by settling for a conventional military victory, notwithstanding such a victory's prominent place in both communist Chinese and Vietnamese revolutionary war doctrine.[67]

Regardless of the strategy selected, however, the MACV almost certainly would have gone on to conduct the war, as indeed it did, in a most wasteful manner. If attrition emphasized the extravagant substitution of materiel for American blood, it did not dictate MACV employment of its available manpower in a way that gravely compromised its potential productivity. Indeed, it is difficult in retrospect to avoid the conclusion that Westmoreland's constant requests for more troops stemmed in large measure from the poor use to which he put the ones he already had. The MACV's personnel rotation policies and logistical improvidence seriously compromised potential U.S. military effectiveness in

Vietnam by severely constraining the number of troops actually available for combat operations and by imperiling the quality of the tactical performance of those in combat.

To be sure, the Johnson White House bears much of the blame for the grave military manpower crisis that confronted the United States in 1968. The Texas-born president's unprecedented refusal to mobilize the reserves, and consequent early and heavy reliance on a grossly inequitable conscription system that permitted many of "the best and brightest" young men to escape service in Vietnam, contributed substantially to a dangerous depletion of the U.S. strategic reserve by 1968 as well as to a marked decline in the quality of U.S. military manpower. The Vietnam War was the first major conflict in U.S. history that was waged without a reserve mobilization, even though in 1965 the Army National Guard and Reserve alone boasted a combined paid strength of 695,000—or over two-thirds the strength of the active-duty army.[68] Johnson's refusal to mobilize the reserves, the most significant and enduring source of civil-military tension during the war, compelled the army simultaneously to raid U.S. force deployments elsewhere and to drop entrance standards for draft-age men much lower and earlier than would have been the case had the reserves been mobilized. By 1968, the U.S. Army had but two-thirds of one division—the Eighty-second Airborne—remaining in the strategic reserve, and had gutted its NATO deployments. The Vietnam War "destroyed the U.S. 7th Army in Germany without firing a shot," observes Bruce Palmer. "It destroyed that army because we were so strategically out of balance we used the 7th Army as a replacement [pool] for Vietnam."[69] By mid-1968, only thirty-nine out of 465 U.S. military units in Europe were rated as ready in terms of personnel strength.[70] The absence of reservists also left the Pentagon no choice but to recruit substandard men like William L. Calley and to compress training schedules to feed the MACV's constant demands for more troops. The gross inequities of the Selective Service System also worked to depress the quality of U.S. soldiery in Vietnam by permitting the escape from military service, or at least service in Vietnam, of the well-to-do and college students like Dan Quayle, Bill Clinton, Newt Gingrich, and Phil Gramm. Eighty percent of the enlisted men who served in the war were from working-class backgrounds; many of them had never finished high school.[71] The war was fought largely by working-class nineteen-year-old draftees and draft-induced volunteers.

But the MACV made the manpower crunch much worse than it otherwise would have been. Indeed, Andrew Krepinevich correctly comments that "the Army in Vietnam instituted a personnel policy about as detrimental" to the war effort "as if it had set out with the worst intentions in mind."[72] By establishing a one-year tour of duty for enlisted men and even shorter tours for officers (six months for battalion commanders, three months for company commanders), Westmoreland gravely compromised small-unit cohesion in combat. The constant rotation of officers and men in and out of Vietnam bred units of what were essentially strangers, men unfamiliar with and often distrustful of their comrades in arms. Such abbreviated tours of duty also compromised the ability of officers and men alike to accumulate and sustain the knowledge of and skill in fighting the peculiar war in which the Americans found themselves in Vietnam. "In and out like clockwork . . . just long enough to figure out what they didn't know," observes David Hackworth of U.S. battalion and company commanders.[73] The set tours also engendered a preoccupation with surviving until the date of departure; while a great many American officers and men in Vietnam never had sufficient time to learn the ropes of their professional responsibilities, they could without exception, drunk or sober, tell anyone who asked exactly how many days they had left "in country."

Westmoreland claims that he instituted short tours of duty because he believed the war would be long and therefore potentially injurious to troop morale and health.[74] But this claim does not jibe with the unprecedented haste with which the MACV rotated officers in and out of combat command slots, a practice which was in fact aimed at exposing to combat as many officers as possible in preparation for future wars. "In the early stages of American involvement in Vietnam," writes one bitter Army critic, "Westmoreland was faced with an officer corps a large part of which had never been 'blooded' in combat. Convinced that the American expeditionary force would not be needed very long, Westmoreland set command tours at six months. . . . Its effect on units and men was disastrous, for it hurt morale, eroded discipline, and gave officers little opportunity to develop the qualities of leadership so desperately needed in Vietnam."[75] Moreover, whatever positive impact the one-year tour had on enlisted morale was probably more than offset by the penalties soldiers paid on the battlefield due to their lack of combat experience relative to the enemy, whose soldiers served, as did American infantrymen in World War II, for the war's duration. As noted, even the French, who fought their war in Indochina entirely with professional soldiers, mandated twenty-six-month tours of duty for both troops and officers (a significant percentage of whom signed up for additional tours). Lt. Gen. Harold G. Moore and Joseph L. Galloway condemned the six-month limit on battalion and brigade command as pure "ticket punching: A career officer had to have troop command for promotion. The six-month tour meant that twice as many officers got that important punch in. . . . The soldiers paid the price."[76] So, eventually, did the Army as well.

Westmoreland's concern for morale and choice of firepower/attrition as the way to win the war also fostered extraordinarily high ratios of support to combat troops, which further undermined the potential military productivity of the more than half-million troops he was ultimately granted to fight the war. To sustain the kind of capital-intensive war Westmoreland wanted to wage in so remote and logistically primitive a country as Vietnam in 1965, the MACV made an enormous investment in infrastructure and in the maintenance and servicing of U.S. combat forces. Westmoreland was also determined to provide American troops in Vietnam as high a level of creature comforts as possible. The result was a bloated U.S. military enterprise in which, by 1968, no more than 80,000—or 15 percent—of the 536,000 U.S. military personnel serving in Vietnam were actually available for sustained ground combat operations;[77] indeed, less than 10 percent of the total of 2.8 million Americans who served in what was first and foremost an infantry war served in line infantry units.[78] Given the high fat content of U.S. forces and the relatively low tail-to-teeth ratio on the communist side, the MACV was probably outnumbered in effective fighting soldiers.

To be sure, expeditionary conventional military enterprises display high ratios of support to combat troops. In Vietnam the United States built from scratch 7 jet-capable and 75 smaller tactical airfields, 6 deep water ports, 26 hospitals, and 24 permanent base facilities, many of them essentially small cities.[79] But military expeditions do not mandate the dumping of "stacks of paper plates, hot meals, ice cream, and mountains of beer and soft drinks in the forward areas," and an "insistence upon large and luxurious base camps with snack shops and swimming pools," all of which "greatly eroded the soldier's willingness to forego such comforts in extended field operations."[80] The huge base at Long Binh occupied twenty-five square miles and boasted movie theaters, slot machines, steam baths, restaurant complexes, lawns, and flower beds; it also employed twenty thousand Vietnamese, some of whom were undoubtedly communist agents.[81]

The dissipation of U.S. manpower in Vietnam stood in stark contrast to the far leaner communist forces, which relied more on stealth than firepower, and upon hundreds of thousands of peasant coolies to perform logistical tasks. Bruce Palmer, one of Westmoreland's deputies, believes the base camp idea was even worse than the one-year tour for enlisted men: "The manpower it soaked up was appalling, not to mention the waste of material resources and the handicap of having to defend and take care of these albatrosses."[82] The lavish bases also provided opponents of Westmoreland's constant demands for more troops a potent argument: why should more troops be sent when most of those already there are lolling around in base camps?

The MACV's management of U.S. military manpower in Vietnam removed from combat far more American soldiers than did communist metal on the battlefield. Westmoreland's administrative practices succeeded in "attriting" U.S. forces more effectively than his attrition strategy did the PAVN and the VC.

4. The War against the North

THE AERIAL BOMBARDMENT of North Vietnam and its military sanctuaries in Laos and Cambodia was conducted primarily by the U.S. Pacific Command (PACOM) in Hawaii. It constituted a more or less separate war from the one Westmoreland pursued from his MACV headquarters in Saigon against the PAVN and VC in South Vietnam. Sustained bombing of the DRV and of the so-called "Ho Chi Minh Trail" was initiated in February 1965 against a backdrop of what appeared to be an irresistible communist drive for victory in the South, and it continued with periodic, politically motivated unilateral suspensions through December 1972. Rationales for bombing varied. Initially, bombing was pursued primarily as a means of boosting GVN morale and as a possible substitute for the commitment of substantial U.S. ground combat forces to South Vietnam. It was also hoped that bombing would coerce Hanoi into ceasing its sponsorship of the war in the South by communicating U.S. resolve and willingness to escalate, and that, at a minimum, it would, in conjunction with U.S. ground combat operations in the South, impose intolerable costs on North Vietnam's attempts to sustain the communist challenge in the South via infiltration.

Bombing achieved none of its intended objectives, though it did produce some unintended consequences. Massive U.S. ground combat intervention was required to forestall a communist victory in 1965 and reassure America's Vietnamese clients in Saigon. Bombing certainly and significantly raised the price of infiltration to Hanoi, but did not weaken the communist leadership's determination to see the war through to victory. On the contrary, Hanoi responded to U.S. escalation of the air and ground war in 1965 with a counterescalation strategy entailing increased infiltration backed by a growing reliance on Soviet and Chinese military assistance, which Moscow and Beijing readily supplied. Bombing also afforded the communist regime the opportunity to strengthen its political discipline of the North Vietnamese war effort, and to play, with considerable success, the role of David to the American Goliath to the galleries of both U.S. and international public opinion. Finally, the air war against the North consumed enormous material resources while at the same time providing Hanoi a stable of captured American airmen whom it did not hesitate to abuse physically and politically. Sir Robert Thompson has concluded that the "bombing of the North was probably the greatest of the strategic errors of the war,"[1] while Henry Kissinger believes that the bombing campaign was "powerful enough to mobilize world opinion against us but too half-hearted and gradual to be decisive."[2]

During the war, I, together with many of my colleagues serving in the pacification effort on the ground in South Vietnam, questioned the utility of the bombing. In a diary entry for 16 April 1968, I concluded: "Once again, the American myth of air power has proven fallacious. Air power alone has never been decisive in any war. We have always been attracted to it because it is cheap, dramatic, and we have a lot of it. The bombing of the North has failed to achieve its stated purposes. It has not diminished the flow of men and arms to the South. It has had no appreciable effect on the morale of the Saigon regime or the South Vietnamese armed forces. And it has not brought Hanoi to the conference table. Hanoi has conceded nothing since the partial bombing pause [announced by the Johnson White House in the immediate wake of the Tet Offensive]; Hanoi has only agreed to discuss the complete cessation of the bombing without any guarantee of a quid pro quo on its side. A halt in the bombing would have no measurable effect on the war itself any more than a continuation would."

Controversy surrounded the air war against the North from its inception. Opinion among U.S. decision makers, both military and civilian, was divided over bombing's potential decisiveness. Leaders like former Strategic Air Command chief Gen. Curtis LeMay, Air Force Chief of Staff Gen. John P. McConnell, and Seventh Air Force commander Gen. William Momyer, as well as navy proponents of carrier-based aviation like PACOM chief Adm. U.S. Grant Sharp, and such civilian air power enthusiasts as Walt Rostow, McGeorge Bundy's successor as head of the National Security Council Staff, all regarded air power, properly employed, as a war-winning weapon, and certainly a preferable alternative to slogging it out with PAVN and the VC on the ground.[3] Indeed, LeMay was convinced that strategic bombing of the DRV offered a swift and effective substitute for a U.S. ground war in the South. "We should stop swatting flies and go after the manure pile," he once told a State Department official.[4]

Even today, air power's alleged misuse in Indochina forms the core argument of those who fervently contend that the United States could have won in Vietnam but for perfidious civilian meddling in the military's proper professional business. "My regret is that we didn't win the war," complained a retiring Momyer in 1969. "We had the force, skill, and intelligence, but our civilian betters wouldn't turn us loose. Surely our Air Force has lived up to all expectations within the restraints that have been put upon it. If there is one lesson to come out of this war, it must be a reaffirmation of the axiom—don't get in a fight unless you are prepared to do whatever is necessary to win."[5] In his own assessment, Admiral Sharp expressed his disgust that "Our air power did not fail us; it was the [civilian] decision-makers. . . . Just as I believe unequivocally that the civilian authority is supreme under our Constitution, so I hold it reasonable that, once committed [to war], the political leadership should seek, and in the main, heed the advice of the military professionals in the conduct of military operations."[6]

A different judgment of air power's utility against North Vietnam— that it was at best a useful assist to the ground war in the South and at worst an irrelevant, counterproductive delusion—was harbored within the ranks of the army's leadership (including Westmoreland and Chief of Staff Harold K. Johnson), which remains to this day suspicious of claims of air power's decisiveness. This skepticism was shared by such civilians as Secretary of State Dean Rusk, Under Secretary of State George Ball, Sir Robert Thompson, and the legions of CIA analysts and other experts who maintained throughout the war that North Vietnam was a poor candidate for coercion via strategic bombardment. Thompson expressed the view in 1969 that the bombing campaign against the DRV "enabled the North to organize the whole country on a war footing with the full support of all the people. The psychological and political advantages far outweighed any physical damage that might be done to a comparatively primitive economy."[7] Ball, who had been a codirector of the United States Strategic Bombing Survey conducted at the end of World War II, believed that the decision in 1965 to initiate a sustained air war against the North was driven by an unwillingness to cut U.S. losses in South Vietnam. "As though to demonstrate how harassed but ingenious men can turn logic upside down," he said, "my colleagues interpreted the crumbling of the South Vietnamese Government, the increasing success of the Viet Cong guerrillas, and a series of defeats of South Vietnamese units in the field not as some might expect—persuasive evidence that we should cut our own losses and get out—but rather as proving that we must promptly begin bombing to stiffen the resolve of the South Vietnamese Government. It was classical bureaucratic causistry. A faulty rationalization was improvised to obscure the painful reality that America could arrest the galloping deterioration of its position only by the surgery of extrication. Dropping bombs was a pain-killing exercise that saved my colleagues from having to face the hard decision to withdraw."[8]

The debate over bombing's potential decisiveness in Vietnam continues as part of a larger argument in the United States over the role of air power in war that began after World War I and stretched right on through the aftermath of the Persian Gulf War, which some air power proponents hailed as a conclusive if belated vindication of air power's ability to win wars almost single-handedly if furnished the proper technologies and unsullied by political intrusion upon the planning and conduct of operations.[9] The claim is made that what worked in the

Persian Gulf in 1991 would have worked in Indochina in the mid-1960s but for interference by ignorant, weak-kneed civilian authority. LeMay spoke for many true believers in 1986 when he said that the United States could have won the Vietnam War "[i]n any two-week period you want to mention" with an unrestricted B-52 campaign against North Vietnam.[10] In that same year, the magazine of the Air Force Association editorialized about the meaning of North Vietnam's quick return to the bargaining table in late1972 following Nixon's "Christmas bombing" of targets in and around Hanoi (also known by its code name, Linebacker II): "In mid-1964, air force and navy airmen began fighting for approval of a large-scale air campaign against strategic targets in North Vietnam in order to end the war quickly. But timorous military amateurs who were setting policy in Washington both feared unlikely Chinese intervention and believed that [air] support of ground forces was the way to victory. It was not until eight years, thousands of lives, and billions of dollars later that a major air campaign in the North—Linebacker II—was approved, leading to a cease fire in eleven days."[11]

Irresolute execution attributable mainly to civilian authority did indeed contribute significantly to the failure of the air campaign against the North to live up to the expectations of its most devout enthusiasts. But equally and perhaps even more culpable were the campaign's organizational mismanagement, confused objectives, and—above all—faulty premises, for which U.S. military leadership bears much responsibility. The campaign also exacted a stiff price in lost planes and air crews, many of them captured and employed as negotiating leverage. The bombing appears also, certainly in retrospect, to have been politically counterproductive.

Before examining these sources of air power's indecisiveness in Vietnam, however, it is useful to review briefly the unusual appeal of air power in the United States and its role in American strategy. Americans, more than any other people, have been inclined to regard air power as a technological substitute for relatively casualty-intense ground combat. Americans have always sought to substitute machines for men in war. Even before World War II U.S. air power proponents, in uniform and out, had fixed upon the idea that strategic bombardment—massive aerial bombing of an enemy state's industrial production base and transportation network—could provide a swift means of victory, obviating the need to slog it out with his ground and naval forces. From the outset, the war could be taken directly to the enemy's homeland, over the heads of his forward surface forces. William "Billy" Mitchell, America's most famous air power prophet, asserted in the 1920s that the "missions of armies and navies are very greatly changed from what they were. No longer will the tedious and expensive process of wearing down the enemy's land forces by continuous attacks be resorted to." Mitchell believed that "air forces will strike immediately at the enemy's manufacturing and food centers, railways, bridges, canals and harbors. The saving of lives, man power and expenditures will be tremendous to the winning side."[12] In 1943, air power polemicist Alexander P. De Seversky posed the question: "Why need we adhere to the ancient pattern of warfare when air power offers a simpler and far more effective strategy, and one in which America's potential—in resources, personnel, and productive genius—is so clearly superior to the enemy's that it guarantees complete victory?"[13] Indeed, the U.S. Army Air Forces entered World War II persuaded that strategic bombing offered a means independent of ground and naval action of winning wars, specifically, of destroying Germany's economic capacity and political will to make war. Faith in victory through strategic bombardment continued to dominate air force thinking right on through the Vietnam War, notwithstanding persuasive contrary evidence that strategic bombing played only a supporting role in Germany and Japan's defeat in the 1940s and was decisive in Korea only as a means of preserving a military stalemate on the ground. The famous United States Strategic Bombing Survey (USSBS) conducted in 1945 by such subsequently influential policymakers as George Ball, John Kenneth Galbraith, and Paul Nitze revealed that U.S. air war planners had significantly underestimated Germany's economic capacity and adaptability as well as German cities' "surprising resiliency and extraordinary ability to recover from the effects of ruinous attacks."[14] On the matter of enemy civilian morale and government ability to continue to exact enormous sacrifice under the most trying of conditions, the USSBS concluded that morale had never cracked, and that the "power of a police state over its people cannot be underestimated."[15] Planners also had gravely underestimated the effectiveness of German air defenses and the costs in planes downed and crews lost that those defenses imposed on the Allied war effort. At its peak, the Anglo-American Combined Bomber Offensive against Germany consumed the services of 1,325,000 men assigned to combat commands and more than 28,000 bombers and supporting tactical aircraft; losses included almost 160,000 pilots and air crew and more than 40,000 aircraft destroyed.

During the Korean War, U.S. Far East Air Forces (FEAF), which were given virtually free reign in bombing targets inside North Korea and communist-held territory in South Korea, quickly destroyed all of North Korea's modest industrial and military infrastructure. However, FEAF failed, despite determined efforts (and MacArthur's reassurances to President Truman), to prevent infiltration of massive Chinese forces across the Yalu River. Dropping on relatively puny Korean targets in three years almost one-quarter of all the Anglo-American bomb tonnage expended on Nazi targets in Europe in five years, FEAF sustained losses of 1,041 aircraft,[16] Moreover, one-third of those aircraft were downed during Operation Strangle of 1951–52, an unsuccessful FEAF attempt to compel a withdrawal of Chinese forces from Korea by interdicting their supply lines to Manchuria.[17] (A previous Operation Strangle, conducted against the supply lines of German forces in Italy during World War II, also failed to isolate them to the point of compelling their withdrawal or surrender.) MacArthur and others subsequently claimed that White House prohibition of FEAF bombardment of Chinese military-industrial targets and supply lines in Manchuria deprived the United States of a conclusive military victory in the Korean War. But such a move would have meant a full-scale war with China (and possibly Russia) at a time when U.S. conventional military power was still recovering from a half-decade of severe budgetary neglect and offered no more than a token defense of NATO; both Truman and the Joint Chiefs of Staff, who in the early 1950s exhibited a far greater measure of strategic wisdom than did their successors in the mid-1960s, denied requests to expand the Korean War. Both agrarian China and its elusive, logistically austere military forces and supply lines also offered very little in the way of decisive targets of the kind presented by industrial Germany and its conventional military forces in World War II. Certainly with respect to strategic bombing, it is difficult to conclude that what proved indecisive against so modern an opponent as Germany would somehow work against backward China and its predominantly light-infantry People's Liberation Army.

Confidence within the air force and among the navy's carrier admirals in strategic bombing's decisiveness was certainly not dampened in the latter half of the 1950s by the arrival of nuclear weapons in large numbers and the elevation of the air force's Strategic Air Command (SAC) as the cutting edge of U.S. air power and nuclear deterrence. Indeed, the SAC-dominated air force entered the Vietnam War with a huge fleet of B-52s as well as tactical aircraft also designed primarily for the delivery of nuclear munitions (reflecting that service's complete "Massive Retaliationization" during the two Eisenhower administrations). The air force, by its own admission, concedes that its post-Korean War operational doctrine "focused almost completely on the World War II experience, leaving out experiences learned in the Korean War."[18] The unsuitability of the air force's tactical aircraft for extended conventional combat—the F-100, F-101, F-104, and F-105 were designed primarily for either air-to-air combat or the delivery of nuclear bombs in a high-intensity combat environment against the Soviet Union and its Warsaw Pact allies—not only reduced U.S. air power's productivity in Vietnam. It also compelled the air force to adapt for its own use the navy's more suitable F-4 and A-7 fighter-bomber designs. Preoccupation with a nuclear World War III at the expense of far more likely conventional wars of the Korean and Vietnam variety also retarded development of such critical technologies as fixed-wing "gunships," electronic countermeasures systems, and guided munitions. "Since the close of the Korean War," admits Momyer, U.S. tactical air power's capacity for non-nuclear conflict had steadily "deteriorated."[19] "These choices, made by professional airmen," writes air power commentator Kenneth P. Werrell, "account in large measure for the high cost and ineffectiveness of the bombing effort in the Vietnam air war."[20]

There is no question that the potential effectiveness of the U.S. air campaign against the North was inhibited by excessive civilian micromanagement and by an infatuation, at least initially, with gradualist theories of limited war based on highly questionable intellectual and political premises. "Civilian officials . . . confused the performance of an act with its effect," correctly notes historian Donald J. Mrozek, "and they behaved as if the psychological impact of an air action could be devastating even when the action itself was not."[21] As one navy pilot put it in retrospect, "At times it seemed as if we were trying to see how much ordnance we could drop on North Vietnam without disturbing the country's way of life."[22] LeMay, who believed that the United States could have won the war if he—and not McNamara—had been permitted to select the targets in Indochina,[23] argued that once the decision to use military force had been made, it should have been employed without hesitation or restraint. "You can't get a little bit pregnant," he said. "Once you get into this, you're into it. And if you haven't got the guts to see it through to the end, you shouldn't get into it to start with."[24] Momyer also denounced gradualism: "Rather than shocking [Hanoi's] leaders and disrupting their war machinery with a concentrated, strategic air offensive, we . . . merely alerted them to start work on what would become a superb air defense system."[25]

The spectacle of the president of the United States approving (and disapproving), on a weekly and sometimes daily basis, virtually every target in North Vietnam proposed by professional air war planners testified to Lyndon Johnson's consuming fear of a repetition in Vietnam of China's surprise entry into the Korean War. It also reflected his contempt for professional military judgment and his conviction that nothing short of the closest and most constant oversight of his generals would preserve civilian control of the war's direction. Johnson was innately suspicious of military men and extremely reluctant to delegate significant authority to anyone, be it a legislator in Congress or a military commander in the field. Though utterly ignorant of the military art, he nonetheless micromanaged the conduct of the U.S. air war against North Vietnam (though not the ground war in the South nor the massive air assets devoted to it) in a manner that conveyed to Hanoi an accurate reflection of his own doubts and indecision when it came to using the one military tool available for direct employment against the DRV (which the Johnson administration, after all, believed was the source of the very aggression in Indochina that elicited and justified direct U.S. military intervention). Neither the Johnson White House nor the McNamara OSD seemed to appreciate air power's brutal bluntness, which did not lend itself to fine-tuning for the purpose of subtle political signaling, especially to an enemy for whom the very idea of limited war and graduated violence was utterly alien. Indeed, the administration seemed not to understand that its obvious reliance on air power as a substitute for an invasion—or at least threatened invasion— of the North (which had no qualms about sending the flower of its youth to fight and die in the South) conveyed a measure of strategic vacillation that no subsequent display of affinity for bombing pauses and restricted rules of engagement could match. From the very beginning, bombing was probably seen in Hanoi and perhaps elsewhere in Asia for what it was: a desperate means of limiting U.S. military liability on the ground. The use of air power alone was not a convincing demonstration of America's determination. And, to be sure, the U.S. commitment of ground forces in the South in 1965 dismayed Hanoi, but the Johnson administration's public disavowal of an invasion of North Vietnam and its inability to block burgeoning communist infiltration down the Ho Chi Minh Trail served to reassure Hanoi that its behavior would not elicit a strategically decisive American response.

If civilian-imposed restrictions on what U.S. air power could attack in North Vietnam were perceived by air war planners as onerous, restrictions on how targets could be attacked were considered even more so. Rules of engagement dictated by civilians were in many cases unnecessary, excessively detailed, and stifling of initiative and innovation. Often, they resulted in otherwise avoidable losses of American lives. For example, for fear of endangering the lives of "civilian" workmen and Soviet technical advisors, U.S. pilots over North Vietnam were prohibited from attacking surface-to-air missile sites under construction; the sites could be attacked only when they were "ready and operational and demonstrated that readiness by shooting at us."[26] For the same reasons, time-tested and effective aerial bombing profiles against bridges were discarded in favor of perpendicular approaches that minimized the chances of hitting the target but maximized aircraft exposure to hostile fire.[27] And again, out of concern for "civilians," certain types of munitions, such as cluster bomb units and napalm, that were liberally employed in South Vietnam—causing considerable collateral damage among the very people on whose behalf U.S. military intervention was being conducted—were prohibited north of the Seventeenth Parallel. Attack profiles and bombing tactics were devised to assure accuracy, often at the pilot's expense, so as to ensure minimal collateral damage to civilian structures.

Perhaps most grating of all were White House-imposed bombing pauses. There were a total of seven during the Rolling Thunder campaign, which began in February 1965 and ended with a bombing halt in October 1968. These interruptions in the bombing were undertaken as signals both to Hanoi and to domestic and international public opinion of America's willingness to negotiate an end to the war, even though until the Tet Offensive both sides were pursuing military victory and were accordingly unprepared to make any meaningful concessions that might have produced fruitful negotiations. The pauses were anathema to many professional military men, who convincingly argued that such unilateral demonstrations of restraint did little more than advertise U.S. political irresolution and afford Hanoi opportunities to repair bomb damage and shove ever more men and supplies down the Ho Chi Minh Trail.

Yet the military itself, especially the air force, bears significant responsibility for shackling air power's potential in Vietnam. Micromanagement was not a disease to which only civilian decision makers fell victim. Former F-105 pilot Jack Broughton is but one of many Vietnam-experienced air commanders who have cited the deleterious effects in Vietnam of modern communications technology upon the spirit, initiative, and innovativeness the military has traditionally encouraged in subordinate commanders on the spot. Complaining that the military chain of command "would not listen to those who were doing the fighting in Vietnam," Broughton contends that in the interim between Korea and Southeast Asia, improved information transmission technologies ended up "saturating communications channels" to the point where it made "the highest commanders think they were in the cockpit or at the head of the platoon," even though "[f]our-star generals . . . make poor combat pilots or riflemen."[28] Access to real-time information in Vietnam, Broughton argues, "begat an increased desire for control, which justified more headquarters with larger staffs, who created new reports requiring further detailed analyses, which required additional information."[29]

Moreover, despite air force's rhetorical allegiance to the principle of air power's indivisibility and Korean War experience of divided command in the air, parochial service interests were permitted to prevail in Indochina. In the Vietnam War, the Nebraska-headquartered Strategic Air Command retained operational authority over all B-52 bombers, including the timing and target selection of all B-52 missions in Indochina, which created tension with the Thailand-headquartered U.S. Seventh Air Force, which was responsible for most of the air force's share of the air war over both North and South Vietnam. (The Seventh also was granted control over U.S. Navy operations in South Laos and South Vietnam, but not North Vietnam.) Additionally, all marine corps aviation in South Vietnam remained (until 1968) under the authority of the Third Marine Amphibious Force Commander. (The MACV demanded—and finally received—control of marine aviation in South Vietnam. Westmoreland has recounted that it was "the issue—the one issue—that arose during my service in Vietnam to prompt me to consider resigning. I was unable to accept that parochial considerations might take precedence over my command responsibilities and prudent use of assigned resources.")[30] The navy's air campaign against North Vietnam was directed by the Hawaii-headquartered U.S. Pacific Command, to which both the air force's Pacific Air Force and the navy's Pacific Fleet reported.

No less convoluted was the target request and approval process. The MACV requests were submitted to the CINPAC and then routed on to the JCS, which in turn submitted them to the OSD for submission to the president. Approvals (and rejections) were sent back down from the White House to the OSD to the CINPAC and finally the MACV.

Compounding this bureaucratic sclerosis was the division of targets in North Vietnam into seven different "Route Packages," three farmed out to the air force and four to the navy. Targets in the Hanoi area, northwestern rail lines, and the area just north of the Seventeenth Parallel were assigned to the Seventh Air Force. Targets in the Haiphong area and the northeastern part of the country were assigned to the Seventh Fleet. The MACV had no authority whatsoever in the air war against North Vietnam except for the area just north of the Demilitarized Zone, which it shared with the Seventh Air Force. Nor did the

MACV have operational control of the numerous C-130 cargo planes that operated in South Vietnam but were based outside the country; they were controlled by the Pacific Air Force. And, as noted, neither the MACV nor the U.S. Pacific Command exercised any operational authority over the SAC's B-52s. Even the air force itself violated the principle of unity of command; General Momyer's proposal that B-52 targeting and operations be placed under his authority as Seventh Air Force commander was rejected by both the SAC and the air force chief of staff.[31] Momyer complained that the route package system "compartmentalized our air power and reduced its capabilities. . . . and inevitably prevented a unified concentrated air effort."[32]

The "bizarre way the air campaign was organized throughout the war," correctly observes Henry Kissinger, "told more about the Pentagon bureaucracy than about military realities; indeed, it showed that Washington's organizational requirements overrode strategy." The situation was one of "institutionalized schizophrenia."[33] (It should be noted that the elusive goal of a single-commander air war was finally realized only in the Persian Gulf War and largely as the result of organizational reforms—mandated by the Defense Reorganization Act of 1986—imposed by a determined Congress on a kicking and screaming Pentagon.)

Professional military mismanagement of the air war against the North reflected to some extent an absence of consensus on just what the air campaign's objectives were. Rolling Thunder initially was seen by many as a means of boosting GVN morale in the South and as a tool of coercive diplomacy against the North. "The air war against the North was launched in the hope that it would strengthen GVN confidence and cohesion, and that it would deter or restrain the DRV from continuing its support of the revolutionary war in the South," recounts *The Pentagon Papers* narrative. "There was hope also that a quite modest bombing effort would be sufficient; that the demonstration of U.S. determination and the potential risks and costs to the North implicit in the early air strikes would provide the U.S. with substantial bargaining leverage."[34] Indeed, bombing as a vehicle for displaying U.S. will loomed very large in early 1965, when it became obvious to Hanoi and Washington alike that a communist takeover of South Vietnam was imminent absent some dramatic U.S. escalation of the fighting. "The prospect in Vietnam is grim," wrote McGeorge Bundy in a key memorandum to President Johnson in February in which he urged the sustained bombing of North Vietnam. "The energy and persistence of the Viet Cong are astounding. They can appear anywhere and almost at any time. They have accepted extraordinary losses and they come back for more. They show skill in their sneak attacks and ferocity when cornered. . . . There is one grave weakness in our posture in Vietnam that is within our power to fix—and that is the widespread belief that we do not have the will and force and patience and determination to take the necessary action to stay the course."[35]

By the end of the year, however, it had become clear that the bombing had neither intimidated Hanoi nor contributed anything to political stability in Saigon. Indeed, Hanoi's response to Rolling Thunder's initiation and the subsequent dispatch of substantial U.S. ground combat forces to South Vietnam was a massive hike in infiltration and increased demands upon its amenable Soviet and Chinese patrons for arms and technical assistance, including the construction of what soon became the most formidable air defense system U.S. pilots ever encountered—before or since. However, while North Vietnamese behavior in 1965 thoroughly discredited the gradualist, coercive theory of limited war, and caused McNamara for the first time to suspect that the Vietnam War might not be militarily winnable, the bombing continued for another three years, though with significant political restrictions. Bombing was offered as a means of raising the cost to Hanoi of its sponsorship of the war in the South and of assisting U.S. ground operations in the South by reducing as much as possible communist traffic along the Ho Chi Minh Trail. Die-hard strategic bombardment proponents continued to hold out for a more or less unrestricted air war against North Vietnam's industry, military infrastructure, and port facilities, which they believed could compel Hanoi to negotiate an end to the war on terms favorable to American interests; throughout the remainder of Johnson's presidency, the Joint Chiefs of Staff repeatedly pressed the White House for fewer bombing restrictions, and though some restrictions were lifted over time, their elimination always fell short of granting the military the operational latitude that victory-through-air-power proponents regarded as essential to victory.

The root of the air war's strategic indecisiveness, however, lay in the political and economic character of North Vietnam itself. Totalitarian regimes have shown themselves to be remarkably resistant to overthrow or intimidation via external military action short of the outright physical destruction of their armed forces or occupation of their territory. Intense strategic bombardment alone did not produce Germany's or Japan's decision to capitulate in 1945 or Iraq's decision to abandon Kuwait in 1991. If Hanoi did indeed have a political "breaking point" during the Vietnam War, it was probably reachable only through an invasion of the country, or perhaps a bombing campaign aimed at the destruction of North Vietnam's agriculture or the North Vietnamese people themselves. Neither of these options, however, could pass the tests of political and moral acceptability in a war which, for the United States, if not North Vietnam, was limited in terms of both political objectives pursued and military means employed. There is no doubt that the United States could have bombed the North Vietnamese back to the Stone Age, but there is also little doubt that such a campaign would have been exceedingly difficult if not impossible to justify morally or militarily.

As a preindustrial state, moreover, North Vietnam had little in the way of economic or military infrastructure targets whose destruction might cripple its capacity to make war. North Vietnam manufactured virtually nothing of military value on its own, relying instead on Soviet, Chinese, and other external supply sources. Decisive targets were as scarce north of the Seventeenth Parallel as they were in South Vietnam. Indeed, theories of strategic bombing's decisiveness presume like industrial adversaries presenting a large array of detectable and attackable economic and conventional military targets essential to a capacity to sustain combat. Agrarian North Vietnam's very economic primitiveness—reinforced by Hanoi's absolute police power over the country's inhabitants—made it an unsuitable candidate for victory through air power. Moreover, Hanoi could—and did—more than cover the damage and losses it incurred in the U.S. air campaign through increased Soviet and Chinese assistance, while at the same time imposing on the United States increasing losses in planes and air crews.

Two investigations of bombing's effectiveness completed in August 1966 and December 1967 for the office of the secretary of defense by a panel of scientists assembled by the Jason Division of the Institute for Defense Analyses concluded that the air war was largely irrelevant. "Although political constraints seem clearly to have reduced the effectiveness of the bombing program, its limited effect on Hanoi's ability to provide such support [for the communist war in the South] cannot be explained solely on that basis," stated the 1966 study report. "The countermeasures introduced by Hanoi effectively reduced the impact of U.S. bombing. More fundamentally, however, North Vietnam has basically a subsistence agricultural economy that presents a difficult and unrewarding target system for attack."[36] The second Jason study, which took yet another look at the bombing, concluded that "U.S. bombing of North Vietnam has had no measurable effect on Hanoi's ability to mount and support military operations in the South."[37] The study further judged that "the expectation that bombing would erode the determination of Hanoi and its people clearly overestimated the persuasive and disruptive effects of the bombing and correspondingly, underestimated the tenacity and recuperative abilities of the North Vietnamese. . . . a direct, frontal attack on a society tends to strengthen the social fabric of the nation, to increase popular support for the existing government, to improve the determination of both the leadership and the populace to fight back, to induce a variety of protective measures that reduce the society's vulnerability to future attack and to develop an increased capacity for quick repairs and restoration of essential functions."[38] An unrelated but complementary study of the economic effects of the bombing was completed in early 1968 by the OSD's Systems Analysis Division. This study concluded that North Vietnam's bombing-inflicted losses since Rolling Thunder began were offset by more than four times the total of $1.6 billion in military and economic assistance Hanoi received from its allies. The study also concluded that North Vietnam's population growth, workers released by Rolling Thunder's destruction of North Vietnam's industry, and China's provision of tens of thousands of logistical troops, together more than offset the estimated 750,000 North Vietnamese diverted to the tasks of bomb damage repair, casualty replacement, construction, transportation, and air defense.[39] The Jason and Systems Analysis studies, in short, rediscovered what the United States Strategic Bombing

Survey had discovered in 1945: that strategic bombardment, unaccompanied by effective surface military action, is a poor instrument of political coercion against a totalitarian state, and that the economic recuperative powers of such a state, especially one rich in manpower and generous allies, are not to be underestimated.

McNamara himself, though initially an ardent Rolling Thunder enthusiast, argued before the Senate Armed Services Committee in the famous August 1967 Stennis hearings on the employment of air power in Vietnam, that the North Vietnamese people "are accustomed to discipline and are no strangers to death," and are "accustomed to few of the modern comforts and conveniences that most of us in the Western World take for granted. They are not dependent on the continued functioning of great cities for their welfare. They can be fed at something approaching the standard to which they are accustomed without reliance on truck and rail transportation or on food processing facilities." McNamara went on to assert that the U.S. air campaign "has rendered inoperative about 85 percent of the country's electric generating capacity," which, he said, before the bombing represented but one-fifth of the power produced by the single Potomac Electric Power Company plant in Alexandria, Virginia, and that "sufficient electricity for war-related activities and for essential services can be provided by the some 2,000 diesel-driven generating sets which are in operation."[40]

Food and people were probably the only two targets with which U.S. air attacks might have truly crippled Hanoi's capacity to sustain major war. But genocidal, Dresden-style saturation bombing of North Vietnam's population centers would have been contrary to air force doctrine, morally repugnant to most Americans and international opinion, and incompatible with limited U.S. war aims in Indochina. For the same reasons, systematic destruction on North Vietnam's Red River Delta dike and irrigation system was never seriously considered.

The air war against the Ho Chi Minh Trail proved no less indecisive because the war, at least until the Tet Offensive, remained one largely of guerrilla combat conducted primarily by inhabitants of South Vietnam relying on local logistical support. Though the logistical dependence on North Vietnam of the war in the South steadily increased in the face of rising U.S.-firepower-inflicted losses in men and materiel, it never reached the point where it could be effectively stanched by U.S. air attack. Like Chinese infantry in Korea, Viet Cong and even PAVN units were materially very austere by American standards. Communist forces in the South, by one estimate, never exceeded a dependence on food, fuel, and ammunition from the North of more than 380 tons a day—in contrast to the 750–2,000 tons a day a single U.S. infantry division consumed."[41]

Defense analyst and historian Earl H. Tilford Jr. believes that Rolling Thunder failed for two reasons. "First, in their pride American civilian and military planners did not, probably could not, imagine that North Vietnam could endure aerial attacks. . . . Second, military leaders failed to develop and propose a strategy appropriate to the war at hand. Bombing strategic targets in the North and the unconventional war going on in the South had little direct interconnection."[42]

If anything, the evidence suggests that bombing's unintended consequences played a greater role in the war's outcome than did its declared rationales. World War II provided ample testimony that bombing someone else's homeland tends to anger both its inhabitants and government, affording the latter an increased claim on the former's willingness to sacrifice; the inspirational force of Churchill's call for "blood, toil, tears, and sweat" in May 1940 was immeasurably enhanced by nightly German bombing attacks on London and other British cities. Similarly, the U.S. bombing of North Vietnam made it much easier for Hanoi's communist leaders to place the entire country on a wartime footing. The legendary Edward Lansdale observed that the very "presence of U.S. aircraft over North Vietnam gave visible veracity to the Politburo's claims that it was leading the people of Vietnam in a struggle against an invading foreign power."[43] *The Pentagon Papers* narrative concludes that the "bombing clearly strengthened popular support of the regime by engendering patriotic and nationalistic enthusiasm to resist the attacks," and also "strengthened . . . Hanoi's political relations with its allies."[44] The bombing of the North also served to justify Hanoi's dispatch of ever more troops to the South, and provided a major source of propaganda-assisted sympathy for the regime both inside the United States and abroad. "[T]aking all factors into consideration—the groundswell of world opinion against the United States, the intense antagonisms the bombing had produced within the United States, the remarkable welding together of the North Vietnamese people under the impact of the bombs," wrote Harrison Salisbury in 1967, "the air program had been counterproductive. It had cost us far more than we had originally estimated (or even now would admit). It had not produced military, political or psychological results to justify its continuance."[45] On the contrary, observed Herman Kahn in 1968, the bombing helped create "empathy and support for the heroic little man in black pajamas and antagonism toward the white man in the B-52."[46]

Cost, indeed, was prominent among bombing's major downsides. During the period 1965–68, U.S. air operations throughout Indochina consumed 47 percent of all U.S. war expenditures,[47] and by one unchallenged estimate, the $600 million worth of damage inflicted by Rolling Thunder on North Vietnam was dwarfed by $6 billion in replacement costs for the 990 U.S. aircraft lost in the campaign.[48] Between 1962 and 1973, theaterwide U.S. aircraft losses, including helicopters, totaled 8,588, including 2,257 planes and 2,700 airmen killed in action.[49] Airmen moreover accounted for the great majority of U.S. military captives in North Vietnam and over 80 percent of the 2,255 personnel still carried as missing in action.[50] Additionally, while Hanoi deserves the strongest censure for its brutal mistreatment of American prisoners of war, it bears no responsibility for the Nixon administration's cynical fusing of POWs and MIAs, and its subsequent elevation of the POW-MIA issue to a level of importance that afforded Hanoi a measure of bargaining leverage it otherwise would not have had. The air war against the North failed to break North Vietnam's will to fight, but it did provide Hanoi a growing population of American hostages which it exploited skillfully at the negotiating table, in part because at times the Nixon administration appeared to attach greater importance to the fate of American POWs than it did to the outcome of the war itself.

The question remains whether the air war against the North could have been decisive had the U.S. Pacific Command been permitted to conduct the relatively unrestricted, "sharp blow" campaign it favored from the beginning. True believers point to the haste with which Hanoi returned to the Paris talks in the wake of the potent, Nixon-ordered, eleven-day "Christmas bombing" of heretofore restricted targets in the great Hanoi-Haiphong area. There is no question that the short Line-backer II campaign, which followed Linebacker I's unprecedented mining of North Vietnamese ports, made a much greater impact upon Hanoi's war-sustaining capacity and diplomatic strategy than did the more restricted operations of Rolling Thunder. But to claim that what seems to have worked in 1972 would have worked in 1965, and thereby would have spared the United States seven years of agonizing military stalemate in Indochina, is to ignore critical differences in the strategic circumstances of 1965 and 1972.

In 1965, the war in the South was still largely a guerrilla conflict only marginally dependent on North Vietnamese manpower and material assistance; by 1972, it had become, as exemplified by Hanoi's launching of its "Easter Offensive," a largely orthodox fight in which U.S. air power could—and did—deliver punishing blows to the PAVN's road-bound conventional forces, which were attempting to take and hold territory. U.S. war aims also were different. In 1965 the United States sought a military victory encompassing, among other things, the destruction or complete withdrawal of PAVN forces from South Vietnamese territory; by the end of 1972, the United States, having long since abandoned the search for a conclusive military decision, was unilaterally withdrawing its forces from South Vietnam and desperately seeking a diplomatic settlement that would provide a "decent interval" between its departure and the inevitable resumption of hostilities on terms that could be favorable only to Hanoi. The Nixon administration had dropped long-standing U.S. insistence that the PAVN also leave South Vietnam, thus ensuring communist retention of a decisive military advantage in the coming struggle. "In December 1972, with most of the North's military and political objectives won," observes Tilford, "it made good sense for Hanoi to sign a peace agreement, one which President Nguyen Van Thieu of South Vietnam found absolutely abhorrent."[51]

Indeed, Thieu—not Hanoi—was the real target of Linebacker II. The North Vietnamese had already, in October, agreed to the basic terms of what became the January 1973 Paris peace agreement. Thieu, however, had rejected them—for the very reasons Hanoi had accepted them—in the face of enormous White House pressure to sign. Accordingly, the Nixon White House sought to renegotiate the terms in a manner more accommodating to Saigon, while at the same time demonstrating to Thieu that it was willing to use strong force against Hanoi if the communists violated the accords.[52] Presidential historian Stephen E. Ambrose notes that "it was the Americans—in response to demands from Thieu—who backed off the October agreements, not the North Vietnamese. But Nixon could not have Kissinger straightforwardly tell the American people his administration was bombing Hanoi to convince Thieu to sign."[53] Moreover, "something had to be done to convince Thieu that, whatever the formal wording of the cease-fire agreement, he could count on Nixon to come to the defense of South Vietnam if the [PAVN] broke the cease-fire."[54] It was Washington, not Hanoi, that returned to the terms of the October agreements, to which Thieu also finally acceded, but only after Nixon threatened to sign what amounted to a separate peace with North Vietnam. Claims that Linebacker II forced Hanoi to accept a settlement satisfactory to the United States "do not hold up to close scrutiny," concludes Vietnam War historian George C. Herring.[55] It was Thieu who was compelled to accept an agreement unsatisfactory to South Vietnam. As Tilford so eloquently put it, "Air power, marvelous in its flexibility, had succeeded in bombing a United States ally into accepting its own surrender."[56] Further, it is to be noted in passing that Linebacker II not only cost the United States fifteen downed B-52s, ninety-one airmen missing in action, and thirty-one captured; it also provoked a torrent of both domestic and international outrage and condemnation, driving Nixon's public approval rating down to an unprecedented 29 percent.[57]

One can never be certain how Hanoi would have responded in 1965 to a U.S. air campaign that was unrestricted relative to the one that was actually launched in that year. But, given North Vietnam's political and economic composition, it is hard to resist *The Pentagon Papers'* conclusion that the "idea that destroying, or threatening to destroy, North Vietnam's industry would pressure Hanoi into calling it quits seems, in retrospect, a colossal misjudgment."[58] The fact that civilian decision makers mishandled the employment of air power against North Vietnam does not mean that the full-blown campaign consistently recommended by the military would have produced a satisfying end to the Vietnam War.[59]

5. Hollow Client

DISCUSSION OF AMERICA'S DEFEAT in Vietnam continues to center on the military dimensions of the conflict. In fact, no U.S. military strategy in Indochina could have guaranteed the survival of an independent noncommunist South Vietnam absent the establishment in the South of a politically viable alternative to communist rule. Such an alternative, in turn, had to be sufficiently attractive to command a willingness not only of most South Vietnamese to sacrifice on the GVN's behalf, but also of the American public and Congress to support continued U.S. assistance after the Paris peace accords, including, if necessary, the reentry of American air power to punish major communist violations of the cease-fire.

To be sure, by 1973 the Vietnam War had evolved almost entirely into a test of military strength in which the nominal allegiance of South Vietnam's war-weary population counted for little. But Hanoi's prospects for the swift and conclusive victory it finally achieved in 1975 still hinged upon both an ineffective RVNAF (however well-armed by the Americans) and a U.S. refusal to enter the war. When the 1975 offensive came, however, the GVN, notwithstanding twenty years of generous U.S. assistance, proved a house of cards. Like France in 1940, South Vietnam thirty-five years later was politically and militarily bankrupt. Alone among America's threatened Cold War allies in Asia after 1949, South Vietnam fell to communism. Lacking the genuine democratic institutions of its great American patron or the totalitarian political and social controls of the DRV (or even the firm autocratic rule of Syngman Rhee's Republic of Korea), the Republic of Vietnam by 1975 consisted of little more than a professionally feckless oligarchy of corrupt senior military officers masquerading as a sovereign state. (Rhee and his successors had an enormous political advantage over South Vietnam's leaders: they faced no North Korean equivalent of Ho Chi Minh. Kim Il Sung, having spent much of World War II as an officer in a multinational unit in the Soviet army, was installed in Pyongyang by Soviet occupation forces after the war; accordingly, he had no independent nationalist credentials.) The RVNAF never evolved, as did its South Korean counterpart, into a fighting force capable of assuming the primary burden of ground combat against its communist enemy. Gen. Cao Van Vien, the RVNAF Chief of Staff, describes a domino doomed to fall by 1975: "South Vietnam was approaching political and economic bankruptcy. National unity no longer existed; no one was able to rally the people behind the national cause. Riddled by corruption and sometimes ineptitude and dereliction, the government hardly responded to the needs of a public which had gradually lost confidence in it. Despite rosy plans and projects, the national economy continued its course downward, and appeared doomed short of a miracle. Under these conditions, the South Vietnamese social fabric gradually disintegrated, influenced in part by mistrust, divisiveness, uncertainty, and defeatism until the whole nation appeared to resemble a rotten fruit ready to fall at the first passing breeze."[1]

What happened in 1975 would have happened in 1965 but for the war's hurried Americanization. South Vietnam in 1965 had no more political or military staying power than it did a decade later. It succeeded neither in creating a legitimate and attractive alternative to Ho Chi Minh's DRV, which early on seized and retained all the keys to Vietnamese nationalism, nor in fashioning a professionally effective military establishment capable of sustaining the war's Vietnamization. Saigon officialdom—aloof, city-bred, largely Catholic, and tainted by association with foreign intruders—could never genuinely identify with the interests and aspirations of South Vietnam's mostly peasant population.

Ironically, South Vietnam's first president, Ngo Dinh Diem, had respectable nationalist credentials, certainly compared to his regime's successors: military cabals that paraded as governments in Saigon for the remainder of the Republic of Vietnam's brief life. Diem, born and trained a mandarin, not only hated the French (he started out serving the colonial regime, but he broke with it over France's refusal to entertain any plan for Vietnam's real independence). He also deeply distrusted the Americans; indeed, before his assassination in a 1963 U.S.-encouraged coup, Diem resisted expansion of the U.S. military advisory presence in South Vietnam (whose exact strength and growth the Kennedy White House kept secret from its erstwhile ally).[2] There is also strong evidence to suggest that Diem—and certainly his powerful and opium-addicted brother, Ngo Dinh Nhu—was prepared to seek accommodation with Hanoi as an alternative to increased American influence in his country. Paul Kattenburg may be correct in his judgment that Diem, for all his shortcomings, proved "the only leadership figure to appear between 1945 and 1975 in Saigon even remotely capable of thinking disinterestedly of his country and its future, of building a political structure and challenging Communist leadership on something approaching legitimate grounds."[3] But Diem's nationalism was hardly competitive with that of Ho Chi Minh. He did serve the French for twelve years, as well as the Japanese occupation regime during World War II, and he could not have come to power in 1955 or stayed there without major and unstinting covert and overt American support. His regime moreover served the interests of all those Vietnamese who most profited from the colonial order—the Catholics, big landlords, and the French-trained South Vietnamese officer corps. Diem's nationalism, such as it was, did not save him or the American cause in Vietnam because the reclusive, Frenchified, dictatorial, mandarin-era-nostalgic, Catholic celibate trusted no one outside his immediate family, and had absolutely nothing in common with—or any understanding of—the agrarian misery and aspirations of the vast majority of his countrymen and the degree to which they were vulnerable to the NLF's revolutionary appeal. Diem "had the extravagant expectations of a Rousseau, and he acted with the zeal of a Spanish Inquisitor," judged *The Penta-gon Papers*. "Despite extensive travel and education in the West, and despite his revolutionary mien, he remained what he had been raised: a mandarin of Imperial Hue, steeped in filial piety, devoted to Viet-nam's past, modern only to the extent of an intense, conservative Catholicism. The political apparatus he created to extend his power and implement his programs reflected his background and experience: a rigidly organized, over-centralized family oligarchy."[4] U.S. ambassador Henry Cabot Lodge called the Ngo family "essentially a medieval, Ori-ental despotism of the classic family type, who understood few, if any, of the arts of popular government. They cannot talk to the people; they cannot cultivate the press; they cannot delegate authority or inspire trust; they cannot comprehend the idea of government as a servant of the people. They are interested in physical security and survival against any threat whatsoever, Communist or non-Communist."[5]

The insurgency that began the so-called Second Indochina War, into whose maw the United States recklessly plunged, originated in South Vietnamese peasant grievances against the Diem regime that were as morally and politically legitimate as the grievances of those who fought to overthrow British rule in North America in the last quarter of the eighteenth century. That the communist leadership in Hanoi aided and abetted that insurgency, and later betrayed South Vietnam's peas-antry (as it had North Vietnam's in the 1950s), does not absolve the American-backed Diem regime from behaving in a manner seemingly calculated to alienate and embitter the country's peasantry. In terms of its impact on the war in the South, the NLF's greatest ally from 1955 to 1963 was not Hanoi, but Saigon. Again, *The Pentagon Papers*: "Peas-ant resentment against Diem was extensive and well founded. More-over, it is clear that dislike of the Diem government was coupled with resentment toward Americans. For many Vietnamese peasants, the War of Resistance against the French-Bao Dai rule never ended; France was merely replaced by the U.S., and Bao Dai's mantle was transferred to Ngo Dinh Diem. The Viet Cong's opprobrious catchword '*My-Diem*' (America-Diem) thus recaptured the nationalist mystique of the First Indochina War. . . . But Viet Cong slogans aside, in the eyes of many Viet-namese of no particular persuasion, the United States was reprehensible as a modernizing force in a thoroughly traditional society, as the provider of arms and money for a detested government, and as an alien, disruptive influence . . . "[6]

Sources of peasant anger abounded, though they seemed a mystery to Diem, who viewed the insurgency from its inception as a case of exported violence having no indigenous political roots. Diem was his own worst enemy. In a country whose predominant religious persuasion was a combination of Buddhism, animism, and ancestor worship, Diem accorded preferential treatment to his Catholic coreligionists (many of them refugees from the North) in land redistribution, relief and assistance, government employment, military promotions, and commercial licenses. (It was his regime's persecution of Buddhist clergy that triggered his downfall.) In a country with a longstanding tradition of village autonomy in village affairs, Diem abolished village elections, replacing elected village councils with Saigon-appointed outsider village chiefs, many of them Catholic. (In contrast, the Viet Cong were locally recruited, and thereby "able to identify directly with the rural population and exploit bonds of family and friendship."[7] The insurgents' familiarity with local conditions also made their intelligence-gathering greatly superior to that of the GVN in the countryside.) In a country in which the Viet Minh during the First Indochina War had redistributed vast amounts of absentee landlord-owned land to peasants, Diem employed the RVNAF to restore forcibly landlord titles and authority, and in so doing "destroyed at a blow the dignity and livelihood of several hundred thousand peasants. . . . He might have attempted to use American aid to compensate owners and capitalize on peasant goodwill; instead, he courted the large landholders. Farmers who had been working land they considered theirs, often for years, now faced demands for back rent and exorbitant new rates. It was an economic disaster for them."[8] In a country where peasants remained tied to their sacred ancestral burial plots and rarely ventured beyond the villages in which they lived, Diem brutally uprooted millions, herding them into so-called strategic hamlets that were often constructed by their own forced labor. Diem also eliminated any pretense of the rule of law by decreeing the establishment of ad hoc military tribunals that could jail or execute anyone suspected of treason, the definition of which was ambiguous enough to ensnare virtually anyone the Ngos did not like. Further, Diem presided over the creation of a South Vietnamese officer corps in which personal loyalty, not professional competence, was the basis of promotion; ironically, key members of this "loyal" officer corps, with the encouragement of the American embassy in Saigon, overthrew and murdered Diem and his brother Nhu. Finally, Diem, despite his anti-French reputation, failed to erect a regime that, in the eyes of his countrymen, appeared as anything essentially less alien and autocratic. Eric M. Bergerud has observed that, to the peasantry, the GVN "represented a continuation of the political and social structure established over the years by the French colonial administration. South Vietnam's urban elite possessed the outward manifestations of a foreign culture and often professed an alien faith."[9]

Small wonder that South Vietnam's peasantry provided the communists, who did not hesitate to assassinate the more odious (as well as the relatively few incorruptible and effective) GVN officials in the countryside, a rich recruiting base and source of intelligence. Diem's initial success in reversing the Republic of Vietnam's slide toward anarchy, impressive and commendable though it was, was more than offset by his creation of an unenlightened dictatorship that was utterly oblivious to the revolutionary impulses afoot in his country. Neither the insurgency's indigenous base nor its popularity in the rural areas can be denied. In 1955, the influential columnist Joseph Alsop, later to become one of America's most fervid Vietnam War hawks, penned for the *New Yorker* the following assessment of his tour of communist-occupied areas of Vietnam: "I could hardly imagine a Communist government that was also a popular government and almost a democratic government. But this is just the sort of government the palm-hut state actually was. . . . The Viet Minh could not possibly have carried on the resistance for one year, let alone nine years, without the people's strong, united support."[10] Six years later, Vice President Lyndon Johnson, just returned from a whirlwind trip to South Vietnam that prompted him to proclaim Diem the "Churchill of Asia," revealed in a confidential report to President Kennedy a much more skeptical view of Diem's performance, tempered by a sense of strategic priorities that somehow abandoned him as president just four years later. "If the Vietnamese government backed by a three-year liberal aid program cannot do the job," he cautioned, "then we had better remember the experience of the French who wound up with several hundred thousand men in Vietnam. . . . Before we take any such plunge we had better be sure we are prepared to become bogged down chasing irregulars and guerrillas over the rice fields and jungles of Southeast Asia while our principal enemies China and the Soviet Union stand outside the fray and husband their strength."[11]

Diem looks better in hindsight than he did at the end of his rule, in large measure because of the relative political chaos and governmental incompetence that followed his downfall. Many U.S. officials associated with American policy in Vietnam, including Johnson, Edward Lansdale, William Colby, and Sir Robert Thompson, at the time or later regarded U.S. encouragement of the coup that removed Diem to be a great mistake. Interestingly, most senior U.S. military officials involved in advising the RVNAF opposed Diem's overthrow, perhaps because they, more than any other Americans on the ground in Vietnam, had a clear understanding of just how professionally mediocre and politically inept the RVNAF's senior leadership really was. Certainly, those U.S. officials—Lodge, Harriman, Hilsman—who pushed most for getting rid of Diem seemed to assume that whoever came after him could not possibly be as much of an obstacle to the prosecution of the war as Diem and his brother had been.

They also seem not to have fully understood that American complicity in Diem's overthrow would lock the United States into a measure of subsequent responsibility for South Vietnam's fate from which no president could easily walk away. This was Kennedy's most damning Vietnam policy legacy to Lyndon Johnson. Diem, for all his disastrous deficiencies, proved far more willing than any of his successors to defy the United States. He was defiant in part because he more than any of them, except for perhaps Nguyen Van Thieu, understood that the United States, when push came to shove, was unwilling to employ its vast potential leverage over Saigon because in the final analysis the United States attached greater importance to the war against the communists than did its Vietnamese clients. The South Vietnamese, beginning with Diem, recognized that the ultimate U.S. sanction available to discipline Saigon was the threat of total withdrawal, a threat that no

U.S. administration was prepared to make, much less carry out. (Nixon's pre-Paris accords threat to Thieu to sign what amounted to a separate peace with Hanoi came after the departure of all U.S. combat forces from Vietnam.) "The United States would support Diem unstintingly and expect, in return, meaningful reforms and improvements within [the] GVN," observes *The Pentagon Papers*. "But it was caught in a dilemma when the expected reforms did not take place. To continue to support Diem without reforms meant quite simply that he, not we, would determine the course of the counterinsurgent effort and that the steps he took to assure his continuance in power would continue to take priority over all else. To deny him support in a variety of ways would erode his power without any viable alternative in sight."[12]

Those who still believe that the United States should have adopted the policy of "sink or swim with Ngo Dinh Diem" (the phrase coined by legendary *New York Times* Vietnam correspondent Homer Bigart in the early 1960s)[13] ignore the fact that the Diem regime was almost certainly not salvageable following its initiation and handling of the Buddhist crisis of the spring of 1963. That Diem's successors failed to save South Vietnam does not mean that Diem would have succeeded had he not been overthrown. It is important to remember that by mid-1963 the Diem regime had alienated virtually all classes and elements of Vietnamese society (including the military) as well as the government and public opinion of its chief foreign patron, and that it had taken to such things as gunning down Buddhist monks and jailing the schoolchildren of its own military officers and civil servants.[14] Under such conditions, and with a politically paralyzed RVNAF beginning to crumble in the field against a mounting communist assault, Diem almost certainly would have been overthrown in 1963 or 1964 with or without American encouragement. Indeed, Hanoi was a more or less passive bystander as the Diem regime tottered toward its overthrow. "That Diem, who had the communists on the run from at least 1955 to almost the end of the decade, should have faced defeat at their hands by early 1961 is inexplicable in terms of the Communists' own strength," concluded Theodore Draper after Diem's assassination. "It is understandable only in terms of the inner degeneration of Diem's regime. . . . The fatal disease was political, not military."[15]

The military rule that followed Diem did eventually succeed in obtaining a measure of governmental stability in Saigon without excessive reliance on the nastier features of the Diem dictatorship, But, in contrast to Diem, it had not even a shred of a claim to political legitimacy. U.S. complicity in the 1963 coup and the subsequent Americanization of the war made it virtually impossible for any post-Diem government in Saigon to cast itself as much more than an almost wholly-owned subsidiary of U.S. anticommunism, and the dim prospects for creating a politically viable regime were hardly enhanced by such ludicrous displays as that of Premier Nguyen Cao Ky swaggering around in his U.S. Air Force-copy flight suit with his like-dressed and Western-coifed wife in tow.

Moreover, from the Republic of Vietnam's inception in 1955 until its ignoble collapse twenty years later, its leadership failed to create a military establishment of sufficient integrity and competence to give as good as it got against the PAVN and Viet Cong. If the RVNAF and its supporting Regional and Popular forces enjoyed a pronounced numerical and firepower advantage over their communist adversaries, they also suffered—before, during, and after the war's Americanization—a decisive inferiority in the intangibles that make up genuine fighting power. With some notable exceptions, RVNAF units were poorly led and motivated, and in great contrast to both communist and U.S. fighting forces, did not seek contact with the enemy. They were also, again with notable exceptions, corrupt—from the chicken-stealing private to the national-treasury-looting general—and, by most accounts, thoroughly penetrated by communist agents. A 1967 State Department assessment of the RVNAF concluded that it suffered from poor leadership, poor morale, poor relations with the population, and "low operational capabilities including poor coordination, tactical rigidity, overdependence on air and artillery support arising in part from inadequate firepower, overdependence on vehicular convoy, unwillingness to remain in the field at night or over adequately long periods, and lack of aggressiveness."[16]

The conventionality of the RVNAF's force structure, widely criticized as unsuited for the challenge posed by communist revolutionary war, probably did not really matter in the long run; the effectiveness of any

force structure ultimately hinges upon the professional ability of its officer corps to lead and upon the willingness of its soldiery to be led, and
the RVNAF proved fatally deficient in both respects. The RVNAF was
as incapable of dealing with the communists' conventional offensive of
1975 as it was the communist insurgency of the early 1960s. The Nixon
administration's policy of Vietnamization rang hollow from the start
because it rested on the absurd premise that the RVNAF could succeed
where U.S. military power had failed. Insightful observers, including
members of Congress, were not fooled by what appeared to be a smoke-
screen for a U.S. bug-out, albeit a slow one. Sen. John Stennis, among
others, warned in 1969 that the United States "would be badly mistaken
if we think that we can depend too much on the South Vietnamese winning this war. I don't believe they will be able to do it and I believe
Hanoi knows this better than we do. . . . We'll have to stay there for
ten years at best."[17]

The sources of the RVNAF's professional incapacity were evident to
most close observers of South Vietnam's armed forces. The first was a
highly politicized and venal officer corps. Both Diem and his successors elevated loyalty over professional competence as the wheel of promotion and other rewards; they also organized and deployed the
RVNAF to maximize insulation from attempted coups, even though the
resulting force dispositions compromised the RVNAF's potential military effectiveness against the communist enemy. If professional medi-
ocrity and (all too often) incompetence were hallmarks of the officer
corps, so too was corruption, particularly among senior officers. Stealing was obscenely profitable in a relatively small and poor country sud-
denly flooded with American wealth, and it was certainly easier and
much safer than fighting the enemy, which, after all, the Americans in
1965 had volunteered to take care of anyway. The professional attractiveness of combat command that was paramount in other armies was
notable for its absence in the RVNAF, where the lure of stealing was
well-nigh irresistible. Why risk one's life in battle when one could
acquire money and position in a rear-echelon staff job? Small wonder
that the National Military Academy in Dalat (South Vietnam's West
Point) graduated officers that wanted staff rather than line assignments; in one 1966 class, every graduating infantry officer expressed

preference for assignment to a division headquarters rather than an infantry company.[18]

Corruption of officers (as well as GVN civilian personnel) assumed several major forms, some of them common in the Third World. Simple bribery for favors rendered, including "protection" provided, was especially rampant. Black market operations trafficking in U.S. goods stolen or otherwise illegally obtained from vast U.S. and GVN warehouses was also a major feature of RVNAF corruption. There was virtually nothing that could not be had for the right price in Saigon's teeming black market, including U.S. arms, ammunition, military radios, and medicines. Communist purchasing agents plied the market in Saigon and the other major cities, especially for items, such as medicines, that communist field forces could not readily supply themselves from their own or captured stocks. The buying and selling of promotions and especially administrative positions, such as that of the country's forty-four province chiefdoms (all of them held by military officers), formed yet another source of graft. An ambitious and politically acceptable colonel could pay to become a province chief, a position financed in turn by the systematic selling of subordinate district chiefdoms and the shakedown of local merchants. In my (second) province of Bac Lieu, vast quantities of surplus rice moved freely to province markets and beyond only after wholesalers paid off provincial authorities who controlled Bac Lieu's main canals and other waterways along which the rice moved in sampans and barges. Still another common practice was the commanders' collection of pay for so-called "ghost" or "roll-call" soldiers—soldiers deceased, AWOL, or granted permanent leave but for a few obligatory roll calls. Given the RVNAF's high desertion rates, a commander could pocket anywhere from 25 to 50 percent of his unit's nominal-strength payroll.

Corruption was not the exception, but rather the rule in South Vietnam. A postwar survey of exiled South Vietnamese military officers and civilian leaders revealed that "corruption was considered more than a problem that could have been solved by the firing of a few generals or civilians. It was regarded by many of the respondents as a fundamental ill that was largely responsible for the ultimate collapse of South Vietnam."[19] U.S. Army colonel Stuart A. Herrington argues that "any attempt to discipline those South Vietnamese officers who were involved in corruption would have required a purge that would have decimated the officer corps. . . . To have attempted to cut out the cancer would have killed the patient."[20] U.S. military and civilian personnel advising their Vietnamese counterparts at the various levels of the RVNAF and GVN found corruption impossible to eliminate for reasons other than its pervasiveness. Attempts to apply direct threats, such as the withholding of further U.S. aid, were only infrequently undertaken for fear either of undermining the GVN's war efforts or of provoking charges of U.S. intrusion upon the GVN's sovereign prerogatives. A determined advisor could labor for months, even years, building and documenting a case against a corrupt province chief or military commander, only to succeed in having the culprit transferred to another province or command. Advisors certainly did not advance their careers by attempting to overthrow their Vietnamese counterparts, and at no time was evidence of official Vietnamese venality, especially if it managed to reach the press, welcomed by high American officialdom.

American frustration with the scope and persistence of Vietnamese corruption and incompetence hardly advanced the U.S. cause in Vietnam; on the contrary, it bred bitter contempt for the Vietnamese ally as well as grudging respect for the enemy, whose military forces and civil administrators displayed significantly greater tenacity, integrity, and professional competence. Distinctions were quickly drawn by U.S. military men between "our gooks" and "Victor Charlie" or "Mr. Charles"—terms of respect for the Viet Cong. Indeed, "Why can't *our* Vietnamese fight like *their* Vietnamese?" was a question widely pondered throughout the U.S. advisory community, and the manifest answer to that question— that "our" Vietnamese lacked the will, initiative, and leadership to best the highly disciplined and motivated PAVN and VC—only increased American demoralization and cynicism. Even among the most idealistic of my CORDS colleagues in Vietnam, confidence in American "can do" and "nation building" invariably suffered when exposed to the reality of the client the United States was fighting for in Vietnam.

The ultimate corruption—and testimony to Vietnamization's innate futility—was spiritual: the RVNAF's unwillingness to seek or risk battle with the communists. Whereas U.S. forces actively searched for the enemy and occasionally caught him, RVNAF commanders always seemed far more interested in avoiding a firefight, even one on favorable terms. They probably recognized the communists' pronounced superiority in fighting power, and after 1965 hoped, and probably believed, that the Americans would win the war for them. Even when it became apparent that the Americans were going to leave without having done so, the GVN made no attempt to endow its officer corps or soldiery with the ingredients necessary to become militarily competitive with its communist enemy. RVNAF field operations were often designed to avoid contact with the enemy. Sweeps of contested territory typically were launched well after sunrise (and terminated well before dark), and knowingly telegraphed in advance by deliberately lax security and noisy preparation; forces moved slowly and hugged roads and other lines of communication; and on those rare occasions where contact with the enemy was made, the tendency was toward immediate withdrawal behind a curtain of artillery fire and air strikes.

Lack of aggressiveness stemmed not just from a highly politicized senior officer corps, the recruitment and promotion of junior officers based more on economic and family status than on ability and motivation, and a chronic shortage of experienced NCOs. Lack of trust between officers and men, which ironically began to corrode the U.S. Army's effectiveness in Vietnam in the years following the Tet Offensive, was an inherent feature of the RVNAF. South Vietnam's soldiery was drawn from the country's peasantry, whereas its officer corps was recruited almost entirely from among the urban educated and socially-advantaged strata of South Vietnamese society. John Paul Vann regarded these class differences as unbridgeable and, as such, a powerful argument for U.S. assumption of the war's control, including direct command of the RVNAF.[21] The differences were all too often reflected in officer contempt for the common soldier (similar to the class arrogance and callousness that separated officer from enlisted man in the pre-1914 British army), to which the latter predictably responded with fear and distrust. At no time during the Vietnam War did South Vietnam's senior military leadership see fit to provide its troops even minimally adequate pay, dependent housing, medical care, and rotation out of isolated and vulnerable outpost duty. Open physical abuse of enlisted men and even junior officers for sins real and imagined was not uncommon; during my eleven-month tour of duty in Bac Lieu, I witnessed several such beatings, including one brutally administered by an ivory-swagger-stick-wielding battalion commander upon a cringing first lieutenant (who shortly thereafter deserted, perhaps to seek revenge in the Viet Cong).

The RVNAF's high rates of desertion and missing in action (once out of battlefield sight of their officers, many soldiers simply laid low until the shooting stopped and then ran away) came as no surprise, nor did the soldiers' propensity to supplement their meager pay through theft of chickens and other items of value taken from the villages they entered by day but abandoned before dark. Unable to provide genuine protection to South Vietnam's rural population, the RVNAF's poorly trained and disciplined soldiery was unable to refrain from predatory behavior toward that population. Unlike the communist enemy it faced, the RVNAF lacked the one thing that could have compensated for the perennial poverty, homesickness, and fear of death common to soldiers on both sides: superb discipline and a powerful and unifying patriotism capable of eliciting a willingness to sacrifice one's life on behalf of a larger cause. "The South Vietnamese soldier, in the end," concludes Guenter Lewy, "did not feel he was part of a political community worth the supreme sacrifice; he saw no reason to die for the GVN. The country lacked political leadership which could inspire a sense of trust, purpose, and self-confidence."[22]

When the end came in 1975, it very much resembled, as noted, the collapse of the French Third Republic in 1940. Like the Third Republic, the GVN had ceased to command any positive loyalty on the part of its citizens, and its military forces disintegrated not for lack of arms and ammunition but because of professional incompetence and in some cases moral cowardice in the face of a determined and gifted enemy that recognized that no amount of military wherewithal could offset an advanced state of political putrefaction. Thieu's decision to delay abandoning the Central Highlands until they were in the process of being overrun by the PAVN was but the straw that broke the camel's back. The RVNAF "did not collapse in its foxholes, or for lack of supplies," writes Arnold R. Isaacs. "It disintegrated when its senior officers—the class of South Vietnamese society that had virtually monopolized the political and material rewards of the American alliance—deserted it. Material shortages . . . may explain the decision to give up the central highlands. But they cannot explain why, once that decision was made, ranking commanders fled before their troops."[23] It is ironic that the Frenchified South Vietnamese elite ended up emulating the very French defeat that in 1940 opened up Indochina to effective imperial Japanese control. But in its essence, 1975 was little more than a replay of 1965—without the benefit of an American presence. Of the RVNAF in the twilight years of the Diem regime, Ronald Spector has observed, "The central fact [was] that the ineffectiveness of the Vietnamese Army was not something that could have been dealt with simply through finding a more effective training program. Much more basic were the problems of corruption, incompetence, low morale, poor leadership, and lack of security. . . . But since weapons and training were far more amenable to influence than the political and social problems [being exploited by the communists], American leaders continued to concentrate on the former and neglect the latter."[24]

The question remains whether a direct U.S. assumption of civil and military authority in Vietnam would have made any difference in the long run. There was certainly precedent, and seemingly encouraging precedent, for doing so. In postwar Japan and western Germany the United States exercised absolute civil and military power, which it used to rebuild both countries as prosperous democracies; in neither case, of course, did it face a violent challenge to its authority. In Korea in 1950 the United States entered a war in which it wielded operational control over all South Korean forces, including the authority to dismiss corrupt or incompetent Korean commanders. Additionally, in a process known as encadrement, thousands of specially selected Korean soldiers were attached to American and allied combat units for the purposes of improving their quality and keeping those units up to strength. The United States also enjoyed in Korea a United Nations mandate for repelling what indisputably was conventional aggression. This mandate conferred international political legitimacy upon both the anticommunist war effort (attracting national military contingents and other contributions from dozens of United Nations members) as well as the Rhee government itself. This legitimacy in turn was enhanced by Kim

Il Sung's lack of legitimate nationalist credentials and by Korean anti-communism's lack of any taint of association with a former colonial exploiter. South Korean forces initially performed badly because of poor leadership and even poorer arms, but ended the war fighting with a level of skill and determination that reflected not only the experience of direct U.S. command, but also the virulent and pervasive anticommunism south of the Thirty-eighth Parallel (that persists to this day), in sharp contrast to the relatively tepid anticommunism south of the Seventeenth Parallel in Vietnam in the following two decades. In Vietnam, anticommunism was always burdened by its initial association with detested French rule and by its antipathy to the powerful Vietnamese nationalist sentiment mobilized by Ho Chi Minh against both the French and their American successors.

The simple truth is that, politically, the Americans had very little to work with in the South after the Geneva Conference, and that the more responsibility they assumed for the anticommunist struggle—out of frustration with their client's incapacity—the more they compromised the Republic of Vietnam's claim even to a pretense of national legitimacy. Ngo Dinh Diem, to his credit, resisted the war's Americanization because he understood the fatal impact it would have on that legitimacy. Unfortunately, not even Diem himself, who commanded far more respect (if not admiration) in both his own country and the United States than any of his successors, could fashion a viable Vietnamese alternative to the war's Americanization. Ironically, even Americanization did not bring the kind of direct U.S. control of at least the RVNAF that in Korea had served the United States and South Korean army so well. The pretense of GVN sovereignty was maintained, with Westmoreland rejecting early on proposals for encadrement (made by both McNamara and President Johnson),[25] and even the idea of a combined command for fear it might offend the nationalist sensitivities of his Vietnamese counterparts. Thus, even though by 1968 the scope of U.S. military participation in the Vietnam War and the volume of U.S. military and economic assistance had for all practical purposes reduced the power relationship between Washington and Saigon to that of a ventriloquist to his dummy, the United States refused to pull all the necessary strings. It preferred to suffer all the political and propaganda disadvantages of being tarred as a neocolonial power, while denying itself the full benefits that its domination of the GVN might have afforded the anticommunist war effort. The point here is not that a completely U.S. controlled war would have produced victory, but rather that the United States refused to exert the measure of discipline over its client commensurate with the actual leverage it enjoyed. Diem might have balked (perhaps even cutting a deal with Hanoi), but Thieu's capitulation in the face of Nixon's threat to sign a separate peace with Hanoi suggests that none of Diem's successors, of whom Thieu was by far the ablest and most politically secure, could have resisted a U.S. diktat.

If the GVN was little more than a creature of U.S. Cold War diplomacy and the American taxpayer's largesse, its ranks were also thoroughly infiltrated by communist double agents. By one estimate, some twenty thousand active communist spies served in the South Vietnamese military, police, and other organs of government,[26] alerting their compatriots to GVN decisions and RVNAF operations. In stark contrast to the near-absolute impenetrability of totalitarian North Vietnam, communist "cadres and sympathizers had infiltrated the GVN at every level," observes Eric Bergerud. "Though it is impossible to document, it is wise to assume that every major offensive operation by [the RVNAF] and most of those undertaken by U.S. forces were compromised to some degree."[27] Lack of RVNAF security undoubtedly was one of the reasons—albeit unexpressed—that the MACV opposed formation of a MACV-RVNAF combined command, although the MACV did not seem unduly concerned by the high risk of communist penetration inherent in U.S. base camp reliance on hordes of Vietnamese workers ranging from gardeners to bargirls to servants to construction workers. (Every communist agent operating inside the GVN or in GVN-controlled areas could be counted upon to have impeccable government-issued identity cards and other obligatory papers.)

The most telling manifestation of the GVN's fecklessness was its inability in the years following the Tet Offensive to convert substantial and unexpected progress in rural pacification into a measure of popular loyalty to the anticommunist political order in the South sufficient to enable the GVN effectively to assume at least the primary burden of the ground war (which was, after all, Vietnamization's objective as well as a strategic imperative for the GVN if it was to survive the Americans' departure). The communist insurgency and its popularity suffered grievous and irreparable damage during and after the Tet Offensive. The combination of U.S.–firepower-induced depopulation of much of the countryside and Tet's decimation of the southern communist cadre was followed by genuine, if long overdue, GVN-sponsored land reform and improvements in local security in much of the Mekong Delta. (By 1971, for example, one could safely drive down the entire length of the Delta, from Saigon to Camau, without encountering a single mine or sniper shot.) But peasant appreciation of land reform and greater security, and relief over the recession of the Viet Cong, who were increasingly detested because their very presence attracted artillery fire and air strikes, never crossed the line into active resistance to the communist revolution, whose Marxist-Leninist agenda was always well-cloaked by its deliberate appeal to Vietnamese nationalism. In many cases, such as the CORDS pacification initiatives, the Marine Corps' Combined Action Platoons, and the Special Forces' work with the montagnards, the Americans could effectively perform counterrevolutionary tasks for the GVN, but the Americans could never become the GVN, which remained fatally out of touch with its own people. And though U.S. military power could hold the line against communist military forces, it could provide no political compensation. As Henry Kissinger noted in 1969, "We are so powerful that Hanoi is simply unable to defeat us militarily. By its own efforts, Hanoi cannot force the withdrawal of American forces from South Vietnam. . . . Unfortunately, our military strength has no political corollary; we have been unable so far to create a political structure that could survive military opposition from Hanoi after we withdraw."[28] Nor did the Nixon administration succeed in creating such a political structure by the time it withdrew the last U.S. combat troops from South Vietnam.

George C. Herring has concluded that, "Originally created by the French, the Saigon regime could never overcome its origins as a puppet government. Political fragmentation, the lack of able and far-sighted leaders, and a tired and corrupt elite which could not adjust to the revolution that swept Vietnam after 1945 afforded a perilously weak basis for nationhood. Given these harsh realities, the American effort to create a bastion of anticommunism south of the seventeenth parallel was probably doomed from the start."[29] Gabriel Kolko goes even further: "The history of Vietnam after 1954 was only incidentally that of a civil war, for the artificiality and fragility of the anti-Communist social order precluded a serious conflict between the Revolution and its opponents. The process of conflict after 1954 was essentially a struggle between a radicalized Vietnamese patriotism, embodied in the Communist Party, and the United States and its wholly dependent local allies."[30]

6. The War along the Potomac

Preceding chapters have identified and examined what I believe are the four root causes of U.S. defeat in the Vietnam War. To recapitulate, those causes are as follows.

First, the United States misinterpreted both the significance and the nature of the struggle in Vietnam. Beginning with the outbreak of the Korean War in 1950, American decision makers credited events in Indochina with a strategic import vastly in excess of their actual significance to U.S. security interests. They misinterpreted what was predominantly an indigenous revolutionary struggle against foreign domination in a place of marginal importance as an extension of a centrally-directed international conspiratorial grab for a strategic bellwether. Had the United States seen the struggle in Vietnam for what it was, it would either have eschewed intervention entirely or, at most, limited its military liability in the conflict to naval and air support.

The second source of U.S. defeat was an underestimation of the enemy's tenacity and fighting power, an underestimation born not only of ignorance of Vietnamese history and culture but also of the failure to realize that Hanoi did not regard the war, as did the United States, as limited in means and objective. An understanding of Victnam's history and recognition that the Vietnamese communists were waging a total war might either have dissuaded the United States from intervention, or encouraged, once the decision to intervene was made, an earlier and sharper application of force.

The third primary cause of U.S. defeat was converse to the second: overestimation of U.S. political stamina and military effectiveness. In 1965, sustained public and congressional support—or at least passive acquiescence—was assumed for almost any war to contain communism's spread, and the Johnson White House made no systematic effort to mobilize opinion until it was too late. Most Americans in any event believed that the U.S. military could force a satisfactory conclusion to the war in a politically acceptable amount of time. The limits of public patience with the war's prolonged indecisiveness and rising costs as well as the limits of U.S. military conventionality in Indochina's operational setting were insufficiently appreciated.

Finally, America's Vietnamese client failed to satisfy the minimal political and military requirements necessary to assume the primary responsibility for its own survival. This failure might not have mattered had the Vietnam War's Americanization in 1965 dealt a decisive and permanent blow to Hanoi's determination and ability to reunify Vietnam under communist auspices. But Americanization simply provoked Hanoi's counterescalation and a resulting military stalemate, which in turn prompted eventual U.S. unilateral withdrawal from the fight, leaving the helpless Republic of Vietnam exposed to certain extinction at the hands of communist revolutionaries for whom protracted war was a way of life and strategic stalemate also a strategic advantage.

All of this now appears obvious. Today, few Americans would claim that events in Indochina in the 1960s engaged objectively vital U.S. interests, or that American policymakers had a clear appreciation of communist and U.S. strengths and weaknesses, or that the Republic of Vietnam was worthy of significant American sacrifice.

For many Americans then and now, however, there is, and can be, no satisfactory explanation of the Vietnam War's outcome that does not encompass an inquiry into the depth and consequences of civil-military antagonisms over the war's conduct. This chapter addresses those antagonisms, especially as they shed light on apportioning responsibility within the U.S. decision-making establishment for the war's loss.

The civil-military struggle within the American government over the war's prosecution was in some respects as intense and bitter as the actual fighting in Vietnam itself. To be sure, legally mandated and politically customary civilian control over the conduct of the war was never directly challenged; there were no McClellans or MacArthurs openly disputing the president's authority as commander in chief. But from the Vietnam War's inception, profound differences separated civilian and military opinion within the Executive Branch over how the war should be fought. Washington's war policy did indeed suffer from manifest official indecision and internal division, though whether the absence of both would in and of itself have been sufficient to overcome the other obstacles to a decisive American military victory in Vietnam remains an open question. Some believe that such a victory was in the cards but that it was self-denied by civilian authority. Others believe that, with or without civilian trespass on the military, victory would still have eluded the United States because of other factors present in the war. All agree that civil-military tensions were high during the war, especially in the years preceding the Tet Offensive.

Those tensions derived primarily from two sources: civilian-imposed restrictions on the mobilization of U.S. military power and its application in Indochina, and civilian disdain—even contempt—for professional military opinion. It is also important to recognize that civil-military relations were by 1965 already embittered for reasons having nothing to do with the worsening war in Vietnam.

The principal restrictions that rankled the military—and understandably so—were: (1) Lyndon Johnson's unprecedented refusal to mobilize Guard and Reserve forces and (2) the Johnson administration's prohibition of U.S. ground force operations in Laos and Cambodia; (3) limitation of bombing targets and rules of engagement in North Vietnam; and (4) pursuit of an incremental escalation strategy. Professional military antagonism toward these restrictions was inflamed by what was often an ill-concealed contempt for military opinion on the part of Johnson himself as well as McNamara and the young "whiz kid" economists and systems analysts he brought with him to the OSD.

This contempt, however, had been a feature of civil-military relations during the Kennedy administration. Kennedy felt betrayed by the Joint Chiefs of Staff in the wake of the Bay of Pigs fiasco, and rejected much of the military advice he subsequently received during the Cuban Missile crisis; he regarded most of the Chiefs as insensitive to the delicate political-military demands of Cold War crisis management; and in appointing McNamara as secretary of defense, he imposed upon the Pentagon, among other things, a centralization of decision-making authority within OSD that outraged many senior military leaders. Johnson exhibited a southern populist's innate distrust of military men, and as a young senatorial ringside observer of the Truman administration and the Korean War, he believed that Gen. Douglas MacArthur—vain, insubordinate, and disastrously wrong on the matter of Chinese intervention and military effectiveness—had poorly served his president.

The restrictions the Johnson administration imposed on the application of U.S. military power in Indochina were driven by four main considerations. The first was a fear of provoking direct Russian, and especially Chinese, intervention in the war. Johnson was determined to avoid a Korean surprise in Vietnam, and he regarded North Vietnam as little more than an extension of Chinese imperial ambitions in Southeast Asia. Second was a conviction, or at least hope, that Hanoi would be cowed by a limited display of U.S. military power designed not so much to hurt as to threaten to inflict real pain. Third was a desire not to arouse public opinion in a manner that could torpedo Johnson's ambitious domestic social agenda; whipping up war passions would play into the hands of both conservative opponents at home as well as those who wanted to pull out all the stops in Vietnam. Fourth was a determination to retain control of the war's conduct. Johnson bullied his generals and micromanaged military operations in part because he was—in today's parlance—a control freak, and in part because he wished to deter any attempt, à la MacArthur, to usurp his presidential authority as commander in chief. White House intrusion upon the military's operational prerogatives was the best insurance against the threat of military intrusion upon the White House's grand strategic and strategic prerogatives.

Senior military opinion tended to dismiss prospects for direct Chinese intervention, and to hold that even if the Chinese did come in, they could be effectively stalemated by U.S. air power employed against both Chinese forces in Indochina and their staging bases along the Sino-Vietnamese border. The Johnson White House's "China syndrome" clearly served to inhibit the more vigorous and extensive use of force favored by the JCS, CINCPAC, and MACV.

But what rankled the military even more was civilian authority's embrace of a gradualist limited war theory. The civilians, it seemed, could never quite bring themselves to recognize that what was going on in Indochina was a real war, and not just a crisis management problem of unusual proportions; what mattered was real, not suggestive, uses of force. Johnson's view of the purposes served by bombing North Vietnam underscores the chasm that separated White House and military convictions on how force should be used in Indochina. "I saw our bombs as my *political resources for negotiating a peace*," he told Doris Kearns. "On the one hand, our planes and our bombs could be used as carrots for the South, strengthening the morale of the South Vietnamese and pushing them to clean up their corrupt house, by demonstrating the depth of our commitment to the war. On the other hand, our bombs could be used as sticks against the North, pressuring North Vietnam to stop its aggression. By keeping a lid on all the designated targets," Johnson continued, "I knew I could keep control of the war in my hands. If China reacted to our slow escalation by threatening to retaliate, we'd have plenty of time to ease off the bombing. But this control—so essential for preventing World War III—would be lost the moment we unleashed a total assault on the North—for that would be rape rather than seduction—and then there would be no turning back."[1] The military, whose senior leaders had fought to a decisive victory in World War II, was understandably perplexed: How was one expected to gain a conclusive military victory over North Vietnam if denied the latitude of undertaking an early and sharp use of air power against the DRV, of entering and cleaning out communist sanctuaries in Laos and Cambodia, and of at least threatening to invade North Vietnam itself? Indeed, what, in the way of specific military objectives, did civilian authority expect the armed services to fulfill in Indochina? The White House and OSD were always very specific and assertive when it came to telling the military what not to do in Indochina, but were vague on what they wanted the military to do—other than not to lose.

The consequences of this disparity between specific "don'ts" and ambiguous "do's" were manifestly pernicious. The disparity alerted Hanoi to an extraordinary measure of U.S. self-restraint that could be interpreted as half-heartedness. It eliminated for North Vietnamese military planners the necessity of having to grapple with the worst-case scenario of a U.S. invasion of the DRV itself, which would place Hanoi on the strategic and operational defensive and compel the withdrawal of PAVN forces from the rest of Indochina. (Until May 1972 the United States refrained from bombing the critical North Vietnamese port of Haiphong, through which transited, especially after the Tet Offensive, mountains of Soviet war materiel, including the sophisticated surface-to-air missile launchers that claimed so many U.S. aircraft.) It forced the United States to embrace a negative strategy of defeat avoidance, a strategy ultimately doomed against a totalitarian enemy that displayed astonishing patience and capacity for sacrifice. Finally, it played into the hands of Johnson's domestic war critics, most of whom favored a less restrained use of military power in Indochina.

But it was the Johnson White House's refusal to mobilize the reserves that more than anything else offended military opinion and hobbled the Pentagon's war effort. Johnson's refusal was not just unprecedented. It was also an act of strategic recklessness: in depriving the United States of the services of over one million men trained precisely for the purpose of bridging the wartime mobilization gap separating active-duty forces and the newly-trained draftees, it accelerated the Pentagon's depletion of the U.S. strategic reserve (uncommitted active-duty forces withheld in the United States) as well as its desperate cannibalization of NATO and other U.S. force deployments overseas, producing the great U.S. military manpower crisis of early 1968. (It is not unreasonable to assume that America's manifest strategic over-commitment to the Vietnam War by 1968 entered the calculations that prompted North Korea's seizure of the USS *Pueblo* in January and the Soviet Union's invasion of Czechoslovakia in August.) And because the absence of reserve mobilization necessitated early and heavy reliance on a highly inequitable conscription regime, it also transformed the reserve components into havens for draft dodgers, and the Selective Service System itself into a lightning rod for domestic war critics, in the process inflaming ugly class divisions. "For the first time in the history of the United States," observed Don Oberdorfer, "it was considered normal and even fashionable for leading families of government and business not to send their sons abroad to war under the nation's flag. . . . The American elite tended increasingly to think it was a bad war which did not merit their participation or support. Even the hawks were frustrated—win or get out."[2]

Indeed, class division was no stranger to the White House. Lyndon Johnson and Richard Nixon, both impoverished sons of "outlanders," detested the liberal Eastern Establishment and its draft-dodging, war-protesting children. In his last years, Nixon railed to Monica Crowley against intellectually smug antiwar protesters who believed that "our enemies should win because their cause was more just." Nixon condemned even Bill Clinton, hardly a child of privilege though a beneficiary of student deferments from the draft: "When he evaded the draft, he cheated the country and the people. . . . As I was out there trying to end the goddamned war, he was running around, claiming privilege, avoiding service, and demonstrating against it. He was no conscientious objector; he was a selfish, spoiled brat. He made my job so much harder, and he sent God knows how many men to their death in his place."[3]

As the United States prepared to intervene directly and in force in the Vietnam War in the spring of 1965, the Joint Chiefs had every reason to expect that the reserves would be called up, as they had been in every other major foreign war. They—and initially Secretary of Defense McNamara—were dismayed by Johnson's refusal to do so, and the JCS continued to press strongly for mobilization right on up through the Tet Offensive. Johnson's decision denied the Pentagon access to a great reservoir of trained men, and perhaps worse still, excused the president from reserve mobilization's imperative of taking the case for war before the public and Congress in a vigorous and convincing manner. A reserve call-up mandated a more intense political engagement of the electorate than did the alternative of relying on young draftees, most of whom, like those young men who sought collegiate refuge from the clutches of the Selective Service System, were not even eligible to vote.[4] The Joint Chiefs of Staff "felt that it would be desirable to have a reserve call-up in order to make sure that the people of the United States knew that we were in a war and not engaged in some two-penny military adventure," observed JCS Chairman Earl Wheeler in retrospect.[5] But in 1965 Lyndon Johnson was averse to recognizing the struggle into which he was about to plunge the United States as a real war. He certainly did not want a free-for-all debate over U.S. policy in Southeast Asia. "You know," he told McNamara in 1967, "when I go up [to Congress] and ask for authority to call up the reserves, the debate will not be about that issue. The debate will be whether or not we ought to be in Vietnam. And we'll lose that vote. And therefore there is no point in trying to get it."[6] Johnson wanted two things, and he wanted them simultaneously: to keep the South Vietnamese domino from toppling with the least possible and manifest investment, and to enact his ambitious and controversial Great Society legislative agenda. But he could mobilize neither the country nor the Congress for a war on poverty, ignorance, and social injustice at home and a real shooting war overseas. Johnson had to choose, and the choice for the Texas populist who was committed to eliminating want and racial segregation was never in doubt. He refused not just to call up the reserves; he refused to seek a declaration of war or national emergency, to take the case for war to the country, or even to disclose the full extent of his planned military buildup in Vietnam. By not doing all of these things, he managed to buy some time for the Great Society, but he also bought into an open-ended land war on the Asian mainland and laid the foundation for the ultimate destruction of his presidency. Johnson ended up paying the price for trying to do something that American democracy will not tolerate: fight a large and long hot war in cold blood.

The depth of the military's anguish over the reserve mobilization issue was manifest in an ambitious albeit failed attempt by the JCS to compel Johnson to order a call-up in the wake of the Tet Offensive (discussed below), and in the army's post-Vietnam War adoption of a Total Force Policy, which sought to integrate that service's active-duty and reserve components so intimately as to preclude any future president from committing the army in force overseas without a reserve mobilization. "The political argument for greater integration of the Reserves had its roots in Vietnam," declares the official Army history of the Gulf

War, which begins with a review of organizational and other reforms prompted by the Vietnam War and subsequently displayed in the Gulf.

President Johnson chose to rely on the draft alone to prosecute the war in order to cause as little disruption on the home front as possible and thereby dampen popular opposition. While successful during the early years, Johnson's policy created an army in the field made up largely of the very young, the poor, and the disaffected. As the war dragged on and the casualties mounted, a rift was inevitable between the people and this unfamiliar, unrepresentative body of men fighting an unpopular war. For that reason, [Creighton] Abrams, during his short tenure as Chief of Staff [1972–74], had insisted that the Army could not go to war again without the involvement and tacit approval of the American people. A call-up of Reserves would bring home to Americans from the beginning that they had a personal stake in the conflict. Therefore, Abrams had sought to weave Reserve forces so inextricably into established deployment schemes that no force would be able to fight a major war in the future without them.[7]

Johnson's unwillingness to mobilize the reserves or public opinion testifies to what was civilian authority's greatest single deficiency during the Vietnam War: lack of moral courage. This lack was manifest in numerous actions and inactions, but most importantly in an unwillingness to cut U.S. losses in Vietnam or, failing that, to confront head-on the gut issues posed by intervention. Both Kennedy and Johnson were extremely skeptical over the wisdom and feasibility of direct U.S. intervention, but both also placed domestic political considerations—including their own reelection prospects—ahead of strategic considerations. Even though the commitment to South Vietnam's defense inherited by Kennedy from Eisenhower and by Johnson from Kennedy was conditional upon South Vietnamese political reform and capacity to carry the main burden of the ground war, neither man was prepared to cut U.S. losses in Vietnam even when it became apparent that Saigon's political and military behavior had become irretrievably self-defeating. In May 1964, for example, just a year before he authorized the commitment of U.S. ground combat forces to the war, Johnson told his mentor and friend, Sen. Richard Russell of Georgia, that Vietnam was "the biggest damn mess I ever saw." He further—and quixotically—lamented that, "I don't think it's worth fighting for, and I don't think we can get out."[8] To be sure, Johnson could have cut U.S. losses, but the contrary advice he was receiving seemed to be what he wanted to hear. "If Johnson had wanted different advice, or a wider range of opinion at the top, he could have changed his group of advisers," concludes Doris Kearns. "He could have dismissed Dean Rusk and elevated George Ball to Secretary of State. He could have replaced McGeorge Bundy with Bill Moyers. He could have promoted Westmoreland out of Vietnam and appointed a new commander more congenial to withdrawal. Moreover, many of those advocating escalation had taken that position as it became clearer that escalation would be the President's own decision. If he had shifted, most of them would have shifted. None of this would have been easy. Leading the country out of war in 1965 would have required delicate planning on the order, in reverse, of FDR's masterful job of leading the country into war in 1939–1941. The point is Lyndon Johnson never tried."[9]

Neither Kennedy nor Johnson were well served by their secretaries of state and defense, which they shared. Rusk argued for staying the course in Vietnam come hell or high water on the basis of blind adherence to a 1954 SEATO Treaty that at the time of its signing he himself regarded as a dangerous mistake because it invited the very kind of open-ended land war on the Asian mainland whose avoidance had long been a strategic principle of American statecraft.[10] Of all of the Kennedy-Johnson senior lieutenants, Rusk, who served as an influential field grade officer in the China-Burma-India theater during the Second World War and subsequently as assistant secretary of state for Far Eastern Affairs, should have had reason to grasp the grave risks of intervention, but he was so mesmerized by the Munich analogy, and so deferential to McNamara and the military, that he became the epitome of American officialdom's group-think syndrome that propelled the United States into such a strategically foolhardy war. As for McNamara, he managed, within the space of no more than about nine months, to move from the chief and most influential cabinet advocate of a prompt military solution to the struggle in Vietnam to the chief cabinet doubter that a military solution existed. (In 1984, he admitted, under examination at the Westmoreland-CBS libel trial, that he had concluded "as early as the latter part of 1965" that the Vietnam War could not be won militarily,[11] although even in his 1995 book on Vietnam, *In Retrospect: The Tragedy and Lessons of Vietnam*, he still could not bring himself to explain how he could go on, for over two more years, running a war—and serving as its principal public cheerleader before an increasingly skeptical Congress—that he no longer believed could be won.)

Only one senior official in the Johnson administration, Under Secretary of State George Ball, had the courage to confront his peers with the tough questions posed by intervention. McNamara in retrospect mourns that "We failed to ask the most basic questions: Was it true that the fall of South Vietnam would trigger the fall of Southeast Asia? Would that constitute a grave threat to the West's security? What kind of war—conventional or guerrilla—might develop? Could we win it with U.S. troops fighting alongside the South Vietnamese? Should we not know the answers to all these questions before deciding whether to commit troops? It seems beyond all understanding, incredible, that we did not force ourselves to confront such issues head-on."[12] This particular McNamara lament is extraordinary for two reasons: first, George Ball, encouraged by President Johnson, did ask these very questions—and more—at numerous cabinet meetings at which McNamara was present. But Ball received from McNamara and his lieutenants nothing but emphatic counterarguments, followed by astonishing private visits by McNamara to Ball in which (according to Ball) McNamara declared his "full agreement with Ball's reservations about the war."[13] Second, McNamara went out of his way to squelch dissent on the war within the administration; such doubting or dissenting genuine Asian experts in the State Department, Central Intelligence Agency, and elsewhere in the government as Paul Kattenberg, Roger Hilsman, Desmond Fitzgerald, Allen Whiting, and Jim Thompson were effectively eased out of the decision-making process, "or, in the case of Kattenberg [who served as State's Vietnam desk officer in 1952–56 and as director of Vietnam Affairs in 1963–64], perhaps the most fearless of them, hammered by either McNamara, [Maxwell] Taylor or John McNaughton."[14] A willingness to listen to opinions contrary to his own, especially if those opinions were unattended by quantitative analytical "proof," was not a trademark of McNamara, who once took pride in the Vietnam War's being called "McNamara's War."[15] Indeed, McNamara appears to have understood as little about the domestic political considerations underlying U.S. intervention as he did about the Vietnam War itself. "Every president quite properly considers domestic politics," wrote McNamara thirty years after the United States took the plunge into Vietnam, "but I do not believe that the Kennedy and Johnson administrations' errors in Vietnam can be explained on that basis."[16]

If McNamara brooked no dissent from Asia hands who actually knew something about Vietnam, he was no more tolerant of professional military opinion. Indeed, McNamara was the focal point of a period of acute civil-military tensions that began with the arrival of the Kennedy administration in Washington in January 1961. Senior U.S. military leaders had come to detest McNamara long before the August 1964 Gulf of Tonkin incident. Not only did McNamara and his OSD assert an unprecedented (and long overdue) measure of direct civilian control over the management and funding of the armed services as well as over the formulation of nuclear and conventional military strategy; he also served two presidents who deeply distrusted military advice. Unlike his predecessors, McNamara was not content simply to referee rival service requests. With the strong backing of President Kennedy, McNamara centralized defense decision making in the OSD, and chose to rely primarily on the advice not of the Joint Chiefs of Staff, but rather his young civilian aides, most of them economists or management experts by training, and many of them enamored of the limited war theory fashionable in the late 1950s and early 1960s. Air Force Chief of Staff Gen. Curtis LeMay despised the whiz kids as "the most egotistical people that I ever saw in my life. They had no faith in the military; they had no respect for the military at all. They felt that the Harvard Business School method of solving problems would solve any problem in the world. . . . They were better than all the rest of us; otherwise they wouldn't have gotten their superior education, as they saw it."[17]

McNamara shared Kennedy's suspicion of military judgment.[18] In mid-1961, in an undisguised affront to the Chiefs, Kennedy had appointed retired general Maxwell Taylor as his personal military representative and advisor, in part because he felt the JCS had failed to apprise him fully of the potential for folly inherent in the CIA's crackbrained scheme to overthrow Castro by depositing a small invasion force of Cuban exiles at the remote Bay of Pigs. Kennedy and McNamara were also dismayed by the Chiefs' performance during the subsequent Cuban Missile Crisis. The Chiefs favored direct U.S. military action against Soviet forces in Cuba rather than what they regarded as the tepid naval quarantine Kennedy finally settled upon, and they angrily resisted McNamara's attempt to micromanage U.S. naval commanders on the spot.[19] After the Russians had backed down, Air Force Chief of Staff Curtis LeMay told Kennedy to his face, "We have been had. It's the greatest defeat in our history. We should invade today." McNamara, who was present, recalled that Kennedy was shocked and stuttered in reply.[20] "Walking out on generals was a Kennedy specialty," and Kennedy displayed his contempt for the quality of the Chiefs' professional advice, which he regarded as "narrow and stupid,"[21] not only by bringing Taylor to the White House (and later appointing him chairman of the JCS), but also by breaking precedent in not reappointing Adm. George Anderson to a customary second term as chief of naval operations and in extending LeMay's term as air force chief of staff by only one rather than the customary two years. Kennedy is reported once to have remarked that "the first advice I'm going to give my successor is to watch the generals and to avoid the feeling that just because they are military men their opinion on military matters is worth a damn."[22]

Kennedy need not have worried. Lyndon Johnson distrusted generals as much if not more than Kennedy; he regarded them as narrow-minded, even as warmongers. "It's hard to be a hero without a war," he once said. "That's why I'm so suspicious of the military." He also once cautioned Westmoreland, "General, I have got a lot riding on you. . . . I hope you don't pull a MacArthur on me."[23] Johnson severely restricted the military's direct access to him, compelling the JCS to present all their recommendations to the president through the OSD. Astoundingly, even Earl Wheeler, the chairman of the Joint Chiefs of Staff during the Vietnam War, was barred, until 1967, from regularly attending the Johnson-established Tuesday Lunch meetings in which Vietnam War policy was discussed and decisions made.[24] It was as if

Franklin Roosevelt had not come to consult George Marshall regularly on war matters until over two years after Pearl Harbor.

The point here is not whether the Johnson White House and McNamara OSD or the Joint Chiefs of Staff were right or wrong in their differing views on the way the war should be fought; rather, it is that the profound suspicion each harbored of the other severely impeded the formulation of a coherent military policy. To be sure, military opinion is as fallible as any other, and generals have on occasion given their civilian superiors very bad advice. However, as Stephen Peter Rosen has argued, "The military was fighting the war and had the data and personal experience that were crucial to the formulation of good strategy. Bad relations meant that the civilians and the soldiers were less likely to work together to develop good strategy. Instead, the civilians were inclined to turn to limited war theory. It enabled them to make strategy of a sort without help from the generals. It gave them power over the generals, which is what they wanted."[25]

Civil-military tensions have been present in all of America's wars, but they were exceptionally bitter during the Vietnam War. Lincoln had legitimate reasons to distrust the insubordinate, professionally timid, and politically ambitious McClellan, but in Grant he subsequently found a repository of sound strategic and operational judgment upon which he could rely and to which he deferred. Woodrow Wilson relied heavily on John J. Pershing, as did Franklin D. Roosevelt on George Marshall; in both world wars, civil-military tensions were modest, paling (especially in World War II) in comparison to tensions between U.S. and Allied military leaderships over strategy. Truman disliked and distrusted MacArthur, but then so too did most of the Joint Chiefs of Staff, whose counsel Truman respected and whose strong support politically enabled him to fire the imperious general. George Bush and Secretary of Defense Dick Cheney delegated to Colin Powell and Norman Schwarzkopf great latitude in planning and conducting Operation Desert Storm, although the White House established clear limits on the political and territorial scope of military operations, and—in the opinion of some—prematurely halted those operations. But Lyndon Johnson could never bring himself either to respect the military as a profession or to view his professional military advisors as anything other than adversaries out to wrest control of the war from him, and with it his Great Society hopes.

It is to be noted that the Vietnam War was neither the first nor the last instance in which civilian authority imposed significant limitations on the military's operational latitude. For the United States, the Vietnam War was, like the Korean and Gulf wars, limited in terms of both objectives sought and means employed. In the Korean War, the Truman administration, though at one point encouraged by spectacular military success (Inchon and the rout of the North Korean army) to seek reunification of the entire peninsula under Western auspices, ended up settling for its initial war aim—i.e., restoration of South Korea's territorial integrity. The source of MacArthur's insubordination was his increasingly public opposition during the winter of 1950–51 and following spring to operational restrictions placed on his command by Truman and the JCS. Following China's intervention in the conflict, a humiliated MacArthur pressed for authority to conduct air operations across the Yalu River against both Chinese forces and Manchurian industrial targets. (Throughout the Korean War, the White House placed virtually no restrictions on U.S. military operations inside the Korean peninsula.) MacArthur also argued for a naval blockade of China's ports and the "unleashing," via the withdrawal of elements of the U.S. Seventh Fleet from the Formosa Strait, of Formosa-based Kuomintang forces for possible operations against the Chinese mainland. Neither Truman nor the JCS, who until China's intervention had granted MacArthur's every wish (including approval of what the Chiefs regarded as a very risky proposed amphibious landing at Inchon), wanted an expansion of the Korean War at a time when Western Europe remained open to Soviet invasion and when U.S. conventional military power was just beginning to recover from a half-decade of almost criminal neglect. MacArthur's relief from command and dramatic appearance before a joint session of Congress created a domestic political firestorm replete with charges that Truman, the civilian amateur, had snatched defeat from the jaws of certain victory—a charge echoed over the past quarter century by those who believe such a victory was no less self-denied in Vietnam. In the case of Korea, however, critics were quickly and effectively disarmed by the fact that

MacArthur's views were not shared by any of the Chiefs, including the popular and professionally prestigious Chairman, Omar Bradley, who forcefully made their own views known in highly publicized congressional hearings just weeks after MacArthur's relief.[26]

With respect to the Gulf War, it remains commonplace to regard that conflict as almost everything the Vietnam War was not, including, in the arena of civil-military relations, a more or less tension-free conflict. To be sure, the Bush White House did wage a war for limited objectives; it aimed to liberate Kuwait and cripple Iraq's offensive military power. But it did not seek to destroy central political authority in Iraq (though it hoped for Saddam Hussein's removal); it rejected any idea of invading and occupying the country for the purposes of destroying dictatorial rule in Iraq—even if such restraint meant, as it did in the end, living with Saddam still in power and standing by while he crushed the Shia and Kurdish rebellions that erupted at the conclusion of Operation Desert Storm. The Bush administration was just as prepared to accept the survival of a hostile and territorially intact Iraq as was the Johnson administration prepared to accept a hostile and territorially intact North Vietnam. Yet, in contrast to the LBJ White House, the Bush White House laid down clear and attainable military objectives—though not grand strategic ones in terms of what kind of postwar Iraq would be acceptable. It then proceeded to give the military what the professionals in uniform thought they needed to fulfill those objectives, and stayed out of the way while the military went about winning the war. The result was the kind of clear-cut military victory that many Johnson White House critics believe could have been obtained in Vietnam if only Johnson and McNamara's OSD had butted out of the military's professional business.

Comparisons of the Vietnam and Gulf wars are as seductive as they are plentiful, but they are also inherently tenuous because of the vast differences separating virtually every aspect of the two conflicts. In the first place, there was a considerable amount of civil-military tension during the Gulf crisis of 1990–91, though it was modest by Vietnam standards. For example, in late July 1990 the White House and State Department overruled the reluctant Joint Chiefs of Staff to place a U.S. aircraft carrier (USS *Independence*) in the Arabian Sea as a caution to Saddam against taking the very action he launched against Kuwait in early August. In September, Secretary of Defense Dick Cheney relieved Air Force Chief of Staff Michael J. Dugan for publicly affronting the other services as well as General Powell by presciently suggesting that air power alone could win a war against Iraq. In February 1991, following the air force's destruction of a public bomb shelter thought to be a military command post, Cheney and Powell revoked Schwarzkopf's authority to select strategic targets without clearance from Washington. Cheney and Powell previously had deleted other air war targets from the U.S. Central Command's list, including a giant statue of Saddam and a huge arch celebrating Iraq's victory over Iran in 1988. Indeed, the desire to avoid collateral damage produced the establishment, in the judgment of one thorough analysis, of the "tightest rules of [air attack] engagement in military history."[27] The strategic bombing campaign against Iraq "operated without effective guidance in terms of political direction and grand strategy" in part because the choice between satisfying the demand to restrict collateral damage and that of maximizing the political impact of high levels of damage to Iraq "was not made clearly and consistently during the Gulf War."[28]

There was also, of course, the White House's declaration of a U.S. cease-fire absent any request for terms by Iraq, a declaration several U.S. commanders on the ground correctly regarded as premature. Rarely in history has a victorious army unilaterally stopped fighting in the absence of any request for terms by the vanquished, and Saddam Hussein almost certainly interpreted Bush's haste in unilaterally calling off the war as a sign of weakness. "It was George Bush with his own will who decided to stop the fighting," declared Saddam in a speech "celebrating" the first anniversary of Desert Storm's beginning. "Nobody asked him to do so."[29] Additionally and perhaps most unsettling of all was President Bush's casual public expansion, just three days after Iraq's invasion of Kuwait, of the central U.S. objective in the Gulf crisis from that of preserving Saudi Arabia's territorial integrity to that of liberating Kuwait, by force if necessary. Bush made the announcement without bothering to consult JCS Chairman Powell on its military implications, even though Powell was known to have serious professional reservations about employing U.S. military power in the Gulf for purposes other than deterring an attack on Saudi Arabia.[30]

In the second place, though Desert Storm succeeded in ejecting Iraqi forces from Kuwait—in stark contrast to the failure of the U.S. military to compel the PAVN's withdrawal from South Vietnam—Desert Storm failed to drive Saddam Hussein from power or to cripple the Iraqi military beyond the point of recovery. The Bush administration clearly—and mistakenly—believed that the magnitude of the Coalition's victory would prompt Saddam's overthrow and eliminate any future Iraqi threats to its southern neighbors. Ironically, it was Bush who was turned out of office. Saddam made remarkable progress in rebuilding Iraqi military power—to the point of again seriously threatening Kuwait in 1994. The Bush administration overestimated Iraq's fighting power before the war as well as the damage the Coalition inflicted on Iraq and Iraqi military forces during the war. The Gulf War, in short, may have been a stunning operational success, but it was hardly an enduring strategic triumph.

Third, though the Bush administration's avoidance of operationally crippling political intrusion upon the Gulf War's conduct undoubtedly contributed to Desert Storm's successful outcome, it is nonetheless hard to avoid the conclusion that the diplomatic, strategic, and operational environments in which U.S. military power was employed in the Gulf in 1990–91 were so radically more favorable to the success of American arms than those confronting the United States in Indochina in the 1960s that the Vietnam War's outcome probably would have been no different had U.S. military leaders of the 1960s been granted the professional latitude their successors enjoyed in the Gulf. Simply to list the differences is to begin to grasp the chasm separating the challenge of Vietnamese revolutionary war in Indochina and that posed by Iraq's half-baked attempt to challenge Western power on its own terms in the Persian Gulf a quarter of a century later. Unlike North Vietnam, Iraq was diplomatically and militarily isolated; virtually the entire world community was arrayed against Baghdad, whereas North Vietnam enjoyed powerful political and material support from the Soviet Union and China. Unlike the Vietnamese communists, Saddam elected to wage a straight conventional fight against the Coalition, thereby pitting Iraqi weakness against irresistible U.S. strength—exactly the reverse of the course pursued against the Americans by the Vietnamese communist leadership, whose grasp of grand strategic and strategic imperatives dwarfed that of the strategically incompetent Iraqi leader. Unlike North Vietnam, Iraq presented a robust array of economic and military infrastructure targets whose destruction could—and did—strategically paralyze the Iraqi war effort; Iraq's thoroughly conventional forces in the field, in contrast to the elusive PAVN and Viet Cong, also provided rich grist for U.S. firepower. Unlike Indochina's topography and weather, that of the Kuwaiti theater of operations seemed tailor-made for a decisive application of U.S. air power. And unlike the superbly motivated and disciplined PAVN—and the professional All-Volunteer U.S. armed forces in the Gulf—the Iraqi army in the Kuwaiti theater of operations was a poorly led force composed largely of demoralized conscripts and sullen reservists.

No discussion of civilian authority's role in Vietnam War decision making would be complete without at least a passing reference to Congress, which is, after all, a major component of civilian authority and which has the power to deny funding for any presidential military enterprise overseas. In the critical years separating the Gulf of Tonkin incident and the Tet Offensive, Congress could have acted to block, or—as it later did—limit America's strategic liability in Vietnam. That it did not do so is testimony to an abdication of its Constitutional responsibilities. The combination of Cold War anticommunist conformity and abject deference to the executive branch on matters of national security had, long before the Gulf of Tonkin incident of 1964, effectively removed Congress as a check on presidential strategic recklessness overseas. Between the end of the Korean War and the beginning of the Vietnam War, Congress got into the habit of routinely granting presidential requests for broad authority to use force in advance of any actual decision to use force. During the Formosa Strait crisis of 1955, for example, Congress overwhelmingly passed a resolution by which President Eisenhower was "authorized to employ the Armed Forces of the United States as he deems necessary" in defense of Formosa and the Pescadores. So it was with the Gulf of Tonkin Resolution ("To Promote the Maintenance of International Peace and Security in Southeast Asia"), which on 7 August 1964 passed the House of Representatives unanimously and the Senate with two dissenting votes. The resolution, which was floor-managed by none other than Sen. J. William Fulbright, chairman of the Senate Foreign Relations Committee and later the Senate's most outspoken critic of the Vietnam War, authorized the president, "*as the President determines,* to take all necessary steps, *including the use of armed force,* to assist any member or protocol state of the Southeast Asia Collective Defense Treaty requesting assistance in defense of its freedom."[31] The depth of congressional docility—and gullibility—in 1964 was manifest in Fulbright's reply on the Senate floor to Sen. John Sherman Cooper's question, "If the President decided to use such force as could lead into war, we will give that authority by this resolution?" Fulbright: "That is the way I would interpret it. . . . I have no doubt that the President will consult with Congress in case a major change in present policy becomes necessary."[32]

To be sure, Fulbright later chaired impressive and highly publicized hearings that examined the questionable premises and potential consequences of U.S. intervention in Vietnam. Fulbright's Foreign Relations Committee could take credit for confronting, if somewhat belatedly, the very same fundamental questions posed by intervention that the Johnson administration's group-think White House and cabinet only skirted. But it was not until the spring of 1970, two years after the Tet Offensive, that Congress began to muster the courage to restrict presidential authority in Indochina. Outraged by Nixon's invasion of Cambodia, and emboldened by rising disgust with the war even among conservatives, Congress voted to repeal the Tonkin Gulf Resolution and to ban any further U.S. ground force operations in Cambodia and Laos. But it was not until 1973, after the Paris Peace Accords had been signed, mandating the withdrawal of remaining U.S. forces in South Vietnam, that Congress banned any further U.S. military operations in Indochina. (Congress also passed the War Powers Act.)

Clearly, neither the White House nor Capitol Hill provided profiles of political courage during the Vietnam War. But it is no less disappointing to observe that the U.S. professional military leadership also displayed little moral fortitude. Napoleon once said, with respect to a military commander's disagreement with "his sovereign," that "every general is culpable who undertakes the execution of a plan which he considers faulty. It is his duty to represent his reasons, to insist upon a change of plan; in short, to give his resignation rather than allow himself to become the instrument of his army's ruin."[33] Given the magnitude of the civil-military disagreement over how the Vietnam War should be waged, the military as a corporate body had only two legitimate choices before it: (1) accept White House-imposed restrictions on the use of force in Indochina and attempt to devise a viable strategy within those restrictions; or should it conclude that such a strategy was unavailable, (2) confront the president directly and demand change on pain of resignation. Unfortunately for their own personal and professional reputations, U.S. military leaders chose neither to accept the restrictions nor to resign, preferring instead to pursue a protracted and ultimately futile quest to compel the White House to abandon its constraints on military operations.

The issue here is not the validity—or invalidity—of those constraints; rather, it is the willingness of senior U.S. military leaders, especially the Joint Chiefs of Staff, to swallow their professional judgment and continue to serve as instruments of a war policy they regarded as self-defeating (and therefore entailing, among other things, the vain loss of American lives).

Critics of the LBJ White House and McNamara OSD contend that the absence of a reserve call-up, the constraints imposed upon the air war against North Vietnam, and the prohibition against U.S. ground force operations in Laos and Cambodia all left the MACV no real strategy choices other than those of attrition and population protection/nation building inside South Vietnam, and that neither option was attractive. The critics are right: Westmoreland's options were severely limited. Moreover, I have argued that the attrition strategy the MACV did elect to pursue was doomed by the combination of North Vietnam's birth rate and of communist forces' fighting power and ability to control their own losses. I have also argued that the population protection alternative, though a better fit to the war's character in 1965, was politically unsustainable by a hopelessly corrupt GVN, and in any event offered South Vietnam, absent the presence of massive U.S. military power, no effective solution to the challenge posed by the DRV's shift to massive conventional military operations in the early 1970s.

The conclusion that the Vietnam War was probably unwinnable as it was fought does not, ipso facto, mean that it would have been winnable had the military been given a freer hand—a subject the next chapter addresses. Nor does it absolve the MACV of responsibility for actions that exacerbated the consequences of the very political constraints the military opposed. I have noted, for example, Westmoreland's personnel rotation policies, which further diluted the quality of a U.S. military performance already plagued by White House-denied access to hundreds of thousands of trained reservists. I also have noted the profligate waste of U.S. manpower inside South Vietnam stemming from the MACV's reliance on lavish base camps. Did beating the PAVN really require the construction of swimming pools, movie theaters, and ice cream factories? Could not U.S. forces have lived in the field, as they did in World War II and Korea? Had Westmoreland squeezed more combat power out of the troops he was granted, he could have applied greater pressure against PAVN and VC units in the field while at the same time stopping his constant demands to Washington for still more troops—demands that helped pave the way for the war effort's ultimate loss of public support.

Nor can the military be excused responsibility for the profound disunity of command with which it prosecuted military operations. The refusal of the JCS and PACOM to permit the creation, at least for the war's duration, of a separate and authoritative "U.S. Southeast Asian Command"—equivalent to the U.S. Central Command with which Gen. H. Norman Schwarzkopf later and so effectively waged the Gulf War—testified to the military establishment's inability to subordinate peacetime bureaucratic considerations even to the imperative of wartime maximization of operational effectiveness. The latter was certainly not permitted to interfere with the interservice rivalry–driven disorganization of the air war against North Vietnam. Indeed, it was the military's unwillingness to place its own bureaucratic house in order that probably drove the most important nail into the coffin of the idea of a combined U.S.-GVN military command. Such a command would have required a truly unified U.S. command as a prerequisite, but "the JCS apparently believed that the gain to be had by unifying the command was not worth the inevitable interservice hassle and upheaval it would bring about."[34] H. R. McMaster, in his revealing *Dereliction of Duty:*

Lyndon Johnson, Robert McNamara, the Joint Chiefs of Staff, and the Lies That Led to Vietnam, argues convincingly that the quality and timeliness of the military advice the JCS provided during the war was crippled by the "Chiefs' chronic inability to transcend interservice rivalry" and the organizational debilities of the JCS itself—especially its weak chairmanship, which reduced advice to that of the lowest common denominator acceptable to the powerful individual service chiefs.[35]

In sum, to the extent that a U.S. victory in the Vietnam War was self-denied—if indeed it was—it was denied not only by civilian-imposed political restrictions on the use of force in Indochina, but also by the U.S. military establishment's own self-inflicted wounds. Edward N. Luttwak's judgment is harsh, but on the mark:

> It was not the civilians who insisted that the war be shared among all the bureaucratic segments of the armed forces. . . . It was not the civilians who willed the hundreds of daily sorties of the fighter-bombers and the almost *4 million* helicopter-gunship sorties of 1966–1971, whose bombs, rockets, and cannon shells would have destroyed all the armies in history had even a small fraction been aimed at worthy targets. . . . It was not the civilians whose poverty of operational thinking and atrophied tactics were revealed by such futile use of so much firepower. It was not the civilians who condemned the enlisted men to fight and die among strangers by making every unit a mere transit pool for individual soldiers, each on his own twelve-month Vietnam tour. It was not the civilians who laid down six-month duty tours for unit commanders, thus ensuring . . . the constant renewal of inexperience. . . . It was not the civilians who impeded the improvement of Vietnamese forces by denying promotion to officers who chose to serve as advisers instead of "punching their tickets" in the customary command slots needed for career advancement. Finally, it was not the civilians who decided that every service unit and base, every headquarters and depot, be built on a lavish scale and administered by crowds of desk-bound officers. . . .[36]

The question remains why the Chiefs, above all, stayed on the job, serving a war policy they clearly regarded as ruinous to prospects for victory, and serving a president and secretary of defense who had ill-concealed contempt for their professional judgment. One answer is that principled resignation is foreign to the American military tradition of military subservience to civil authority, a tradition that promotes the very idea of resignation as an act of unconscionable disloyalty if not outright insubordination. Neither McClellan nor even MacArthur, both of whom had profound war policy disagreements with the presidents they served, were prepared to resign; on the contrary, both hung on to their commands until they were fired. No senior military officer who served during the Vietnam War, including ones who, like Adm. U.S. Grant Sharp, commander of the U.S. Pacific Command, spent much of their retirement fulminating in print against civilian interference in what would have otherwise been victorious military operations in Vietnam, saw fit to place their careers on the line. In this respect, these officers behaved very much like the secretary of defense whom they so despised; by late 1965, McNamara had also come to believe—for reasons different than the JCS and CINCPAC—that Johnson's war policy was fatally flawed, but he could think of nothing better to do than continue to serve that policy, at least until Johnson finally eased him out of office. (To this day, McNamara claims that he doesn't know whether he resigned or was fired. He also makes the astonishing claim that to have resigned in protest "would have been a violation of my responsibility to the president and my oath to uphold the Constitution.")[37]

Another answer may be embedded in the strident "can do," "zero-defects" psychology that pervaded U.S. military culture from the last year of World War II until it began to run aground on Vietnamese shoals twenty years later. The U.S. military came off of V-E Day and V-J Day believing that there was nothing it could not accomplish on the battlefield. Senior military commanders undoubtedly believed, at least in the early days of the war, that American military power would prevail, notwithstanding the political controls placed upon it; Westmoreland seemed to believe (if some of his professional colleagues did not) that attrition would work to the point of forcing the North Vietnamese "to desist" in the South simply by "demonstrat[ing] that they could not win in the South," and by having the South Vietnamese make "real progress in pacification."[38] In any event, "can do" did not encompass resignation, which was, among other things, a confession of failure to make one's view prevail. Better to stay in uniform and continue fighting the two-front war in Indochina and Washington. "Not once during the war did the JCS advise the commander-in-chief or secretary of defense that the strategy being pursued most probably would fail and that the United States would be unable to achieve its objectives," observed Gen. Bruce Palmer Jr. in retirement. "The only explanation of this failure is that the chiefs were imbued with the 'can do' spirit and could not bring themselves to make such a negative statement or appear to be disloyal."[39]

That at least the Joint Chiefs of Staff should have resigned is the post-Vietnam War judgment of many influential officers. "Somewhere in 1967 or early 1968," argues Phillip B. Davidson, Westmoreland's chief intelligence officer, "one or more of the Chiefs should have stood up and told the president publicly that what he was doing in Vietnam would not work, and then resigned."[40] Harry Summers believes it "was the duty and responsibility of his military advisors to warn [the president] of the likely consequences of his actions, to recommend alternatives, and, as Napoleon put it, to tender their resignations rather than be an instrument of their army's downfall."[41] Army Chief of Staff Harold K. Johnson himself later regretted his failure to resign: "I should have gone to see the president. I should have taken off my stars. I should have resigned. It was the worst, the most immoral decision I've ever made."[42] Chief of Naval Operations Adm. David McDonald also lamented (in retirement), "Maybe we military men were all weak. Maybe we should have stood up and pounded the table. . . . I was part of it and I'm sort of ashamed of myself too. At times I wonder, 'why did I go along with this kind of stuff?'"[43]

Indeed, some accounts claim that the Chiefs, at JCS Chairman Wheeler's suggestion, came very close to resigning en masse (and then holding a press conference) in August 1967, but quickly had second thoughts when Wheeler himself changed his mind, arguing: "We can't do it. It's mutiny. . . . If we resign they'll just get someone else. And we'll be forgotten. Twenty-four hours from now there will be new guys sitting in our places and they'll do what they're told."[44] The military in effect chose to keep quiet in the face of what it regarded as disastrous civilian ineptitude that had saddled the country—and their own profession—with what increasingly appeared to be a lost war. It is hard to resist

McMaster's conclusion that "The 'five silent men' on the Joint Chiefs of Staff made possible the way the United States went to war in Vietnam."[45] Surely, a collective threat to resign, to say nothing of actual resignation, would have been political dynamite to a president whose worst nightmare was an open alliance between right-wing enemies of his Great Society and a disaffected military leadership. Lyndon Johnson was many things, including a bully, and bullies are known for their aversion to showdowns with genuinely courageous adversaries.

Probably the main reason the Chiefs stayed on was a conviction that the war's steady escalation would at some point compel Johnson both to mobilize the reserves and to lift at least some of the bombing and other operational restrictions in Indochina. Vietnam War historian George C. Herring has concluded that the JCS "seem to have assumed that once the United States was committed in Vietnam they could maneuver the president into giving them what they wanted."[46] The evidence is now clear, for example, that JCS Chairman Wheeler attempted to exploit the shock of the Tet Offensive to bring Johnson around. From the very inception of U.S. intervention in Vietnam, "Wheeler continued to work tirelessly for full mobilization, crafting a policy that made troop increases look incremental but brought the administration inevitably closer to full mobilization," concludes Mark Perry. "In retrospect, this unstated strategy was one of the most elegant and astute maneuvers in JCS history: by agreeing to an ever larger commitment of U.S. forces, Wheeler realized he was moving closer to the upper limit of U.S. troop availability; when he reached the upper level, he believed, Johnson would have little choice but to mobilize the nation."[47]

Wheeler and his fellow Chiefs perceived a golden opportunity in the Tet Offensive's exposure of the dangerous degree to which the Vietnam War had strategically overstretched U.S. military resources. Wheeler in effect conned a gullible Westmoreland into submitting a request that another 206,000 troops be made available for combat in Vietnam (108,000 to deploy to South Vietnam by 1 September 1968; the remaining 98,000 to be withheld in the United States for possible later deployment) to respond effectively to the consequences of the Tet Offensive. In fact, Westmoreland did not believe that such additional manpower was necessary because he correctly regarded Tet as a military disaster for the communists. Wheeler may have shared the MACV's assessment, but his agenda was much broader: to force Johnson's hand on the reserve mobilization issue, which would permit the Chiefs not only to meet escalation demands in Southeast Asia but also to reconstitute the dangerously depleted U.S. strategic reserve. Wheeler visited Vietnam while the Tet Offensive was still playing out and returned to Washington, where he set about creating the "perception that General Westmoreland needed reinforcements as a result of the Tet Offensive and the threat at Khe Sanh. From the beginning, the 'troop request issue' (as it came to be called) would grow into one of the most devious and damaging episodes in American military history."[48] The Defense Department's own history of U.S. Vietnam War decision making supports the conclusion that the JCS were after far bigger game than simply the dispatch of yet another increment of U.S. troops to Vietnam: "The tactic the Chiefs were using was clear: by refusing to scrape the bottom of the [manpower] barrel any further for Vietnam they hoped to force the President to 'bite the bullet' on the call-up of reserves—a step they had long thought essential, and that they were determined would not now be avoided."[49]

Unfortunately for Wheeler, the troop request issue, like a crude pipe bomb in the hands of an amateur terrorist, exploded in his face. Word of the 206,000-man request promptly leaked to the *New York Times,* and a political firestorm ensued that ultimately provoked Johnson, not to mobilize the reserves, but rather to abandon the search for a military victory in Vietnam in favor of a negotiated settlement. Johnson chose in effect to abdicate (i.e., not seek reelection) rather than to capitulate to the Chiefs' agenda. Wheeler misjudged both Johnson and the Tet Offensive's corrosive impact on presidential, congressional, and public support for the war's continuation.

Yet Johnson's refusal to be ensnared by the trap Wheeler laid for him offered the military absolution for the ultimate defeat in Vietnam. By rejecting the JCS troop request for an additional 206,000 men, Johnson provided potent ammunition to those who continue to claim that the military was denied sufficient resources to win the war. Robert Buzzanco contends that the JCS had no real hope that Johnson would grant the troop request, but instead sought "to immunize themselves from greater culpability for the U.S. failure in Indochina" and to provide the military "an alibi for future failures" in Vietnam.[50] Moreover, Johnson's decision not to stand for reelection in 1968 opened the possibility that the next president might be prepared to lift or at least ease the Johnson White House–imposed restrictions on military operations in Vietnam. And so it was that the Nixon administration did indeed permit U.S. ground forces to enter Cambodia, and U.S. air forces eventually to close Haiphong harbor and attack long-proscribed targets in the Hanoi area. But the intent of granting such wider latitude was not to gain a military victory—Nixon was no more prepared to mobilize the reserves than his predecessor—but to orchestrate a U.S. military withdrawal in circumstances that maximized U.S. bargaining leverage while protecting U.S. and South Vietnamese forces from significant battlefield defeat. Both the JCS and MACV recognized "Vietnamization" for what it was: a political smoke screen to obscure U.S. failure to compel Hanoi to cease its attempt to reunify Vietnam under communist auspices.

The civil-military struggle waged along the Potomac from the Gulf of Tonkin incident of August 1964 through Johnson's "abdication" speech of 31 March 1968 compromised not only the moral integrity of both sides but also chances for establishing a coherent and whole-hearted war effort. Civilian authority, on whose shoulders most historians rightly place the primary burden of responsibility for the disaster that befell the United States in Vietnam, could never quite bring itself to recognize that the United States confronted in Vietnam a real war being waged by a foe for whom the stakes involved were not to be denied by a limited application of U.S. military power. To Hanoi, U.S. strategy appeared to consist of hesitant and half-hearted military responses driven by alien concepts of nuclear- war- fear-driven demonstrative uses of military force and crisis management techniques. The Kennedy administration–assembled leadership that witlessly propelled the United States into the Vietnam War may have been "the best and the brightest" by the fashionable standards of "Camelot," but it also displayed a fatal combination of hubris and ignorance. Sheer brain power—epitomized by Robert S. McNamara, who bears personal responsibility second only to Lyndon Johnson's for what happened to the United States in Vietnam—proved no substitute for informed judgment, common sense, and moral fortitude. Nor was it a substitute for professional military training and experience, for which McNamara and his "whiz kids" as well as the Johnson White House displayed nothing but contempt.

The military, by virtue of its Constitutional role as an instrument of civilian authority, was relegated to the role of accomplice in what amounted to the most strategically reckless American enterprise of the twentieth century. The JCS, PACOM, and MACV did not make the decisions to put U.S. military power in Indochina and to keep it there for eight years; nor did they make the decisions—on the contrary, they opposed them—that constrained the application of that power. Yet the record reveals no instance of the Joint Chiefs of Staff counseling the president to cut U.S. losses in Vietnam rather than embrace the substantial risks of full-blown intervention. In 1964–65, there was present nowhere in the senior U.S. military leadership a Matthew Ridgway, who in 1954 orchestrated within the JCS compelling arguments against intervention in French Indochina, a course of action favored by Vice President Nixon, Secretary of State John Foster Dulles, and JCS Chairman Arthur Radford. (Ridgway also opposed subsequent U.S. intervention in Vietnam.) At every juncture on the road to disaster in Vietnam, the Chiefs pushed for earlier use of more force. Nor does the record reveal an instance of the Chiefs, once the intervention decision had been made, confronting Lyndon Johnson with the military consequences of his political decisions affecting the war's conduct. They lacked the courage of their convictions when it came to the point of having to decide whether to continue to serve a war policy that their own professional judgment told them was a recipe for military failure. If the country was poorly served in Southeast Asia in the 1960s by its civilian leaders, those leaders in turn were poorly served by the professional military.

7. Lost Victory?

IN APRIL 1961, the Kennedy administration sponsored an attempted invasion of Cuba by fourteen hundred anti-Castro Cuban exiles. Planned and conducted by the Central Intelligence Agency, Operation Zapata, as it was known, was quickly crushed on its beachhead at the Bay of Pigs by Castro's military forces. It became clear within hours after going ashore that the beleaguered invaders, only 10 percent of whom were professional soldiers, could not even hope to survive without immediate U.S. air support, which was available from the carrier USS *Essex* just a few miles offshore. President Kennedy refused to authorize direct U.S. intervention, and the invaders subsequently surrendered or died fighting.

Kennedy's decision to withhold air support was opposed at the time by Chief of Naval Operations Arleigh Burke, and later condemned by Gen. Lyman Lemnitzer, chairman of the Joint Chiefs of Staff, and even by retired president Dwight Eisenhower. The issue continued to plague Kennedy for the remainder of his presidency; both American political conservatives and the Cuban exile community in the United States accused Kennedy of betraying the invasion. The implication was clear: the invasion would have succeeded had U.S. air support been provided.

It was clear at the time that the invasion could not possibly have succeeded without American air support. But it was no less clear to many at the time, as has been the judgment of almost every retrospective analysis, that the invasion would have failed even with that support. The argument over Kennedy's decision is irrelevant because the premises and planning of the Bay of Pigs invasion were so faulty that no amount of air support would have made a decisive difference. Aside from the invasion's fatal lack of secrecy and violation of every principle of amphibious assault, it was ludicrous to expect a force of fourteen hundred to hold its own against the twenty thousand Cuban army regulars and local militia that Castro could—and did—assemble to lock the invaders down on their beachhead. But an invasion of ten times as many exiles also would have been doomed from the start because of the CIA's disastrous assumption that Operation Zapata would spark a mass popular uprising against the Castro government; the CIA apparently assumed that Castro was as unpopular at home as he was in the Cuban exile community in the United States. In fact, in 1961 the Cuban Revolution and Castro were still immensely popular on the island. Cuban communism's appeal, like that of its Vietnamese counterpart, rested first and foremost on its nationalist credentials, and Castro was swift to exploit the Bay of Pigs as yet another Yankee bid to reenslave Cuba to American capitalism. In the final analysis, it made no difference in April 1961 what the USS *Essex* did not do off Cuba's shores.[1]

But can the same be said of U.S. military power in Southeast Asia just a few years later? Could the United States have won the Vietnam War had the military been granted early on the operational latitude it vainly sought from the White House?

There can be no definitive answer to this question because no one—including the North Vietnamese—can say for sure how the Vietnamese communist leadership would have reacted in 1965 to a no-holds-barred air war against the DRV coupled with a U.S. invasion and occupation of southern Laos—the military's two prime and most persistent desiderata in Indochina. But an affirmative answer to the question of whether a U.S. victory in Vietnam was self-denied rests on three assumptions. The first is that the relative influence of the Vietnam War's military dimension vis-à-vis that of its political aspects was such as to permit preservation of a noncommunist South Vietnam by military means. The second assumption is that an operational definition of military victory was available. Closely related is the third assumption: that the operational latitude the military believed to be imperative would have in fact provided an enduring military solution to the Vietnam War. Specifically, could victory have been achieved had the military in 1965 been granted the authority to mine North Vietnam's deep-water ports and inland waterways; bomb all militarily significant targets and lines of communication inside the DRV (including Hanoi and its environs) to within five miles of the Chinese border; and inject U.S. ground combat forces into Laos and Cambodia as necessary to disrupt communist base areas there and interdict the Ho Chi Minh Trail?[2] This last question poses yet another: if the military had in fact gotten what it wanted from the White House but still failed to produce a victory, were there other operational choices available that were not pushed by the military but that nonetheless might have produced a decisive victory?

With respect to the first assumption, the fact that the Vietnam conflict began as a revolutionary war in which the struggle for the peasantry's political allegiance was paramount does not mean that the conflict ended as such or that even a revolutionary war was immune to defeat via a combination of military pressure and political reform. Certainly by the time of the Tet Offensive, the military dimension of the Vietnam War had come to dominate the political. Indeed, the war's Americanization during the preceding three years had established U.S. military power—not the South Vietnamese government and its supporters—as the main obstacle to a communist victory, and that power could be forced out of Vietnam, if at all, only through very costly and protracted military operations aimed at sapping U.S. will. Peasant political loyalties remained important, but they were no longer decisive. On the contrary, in the years after Tet, communist political support in the countryside sharply receded, and communist forces, now dominated by the PAVN, turned increasingly to conventional military solutions, whose attractiveness rose as the United States began unilaterally withdrawing its military forces from the conflict.

U.S. military power successfully denied South Vietnam to Hanoi for eight years, and proved lethal to communist forces when they sought to take and hold territory in a manner that exposed them en masse to American firepower. Moreover, there is every reason to believe that the communists' successful offensive of 1975 could have been thwarted, as was their so-called "Easter Offensive" of 1972, had U.S. air power been available in 1975 in the quantities employed three years earlier. It was not U.S. military power but rather the political will to use it in Indochina that collapsed between 1972 and 1975, though the quality of American military forces worldwide suffered greatly in the decade following the Tet Offensive in no small part because of the Vietnam War itself. Had that will remained intact, Hanoi probably would have reconsidered the wisdom of the 1975 offensive, perhaps opting for an even greater protraction of hostilities at a lower level of violence.

Thus, if the problem of the Vietnam War was how to prevent a forcible communist takeover of South Vietnam, the substitution of massive U.S. for puny South Vietnamese power beginning in 1965 provided a military solution. The PAVN and VC could whip the RVNAF, but they could not directly defeat the MACV and PACOM. Yet such a solution could never endure against a determined Hanoi and capable PAVN absent a permanent and significant U.S. force presence in South Vietnam and a constant U.S. willingness to reenter the war whenever it was necessary to forestall a decisive South Vietnamese defeat. The United States could not have picked a more intractable enemy and a feebler ally than it did in Indochina, and while the United States was never prepared to accept the Vietnam War's permanent Americanization, neither was it able to build a South Vietnamese nation capable of surviving without a massive U.S. military presence. In Vietnam by 1965, permanent defeat avoidance meant permanent Americanization of the war. Unfortunately, this unpleasant reality was not grasped by U.S. decision makers who propelled the United States into the war. "American forces initially were deployed to Vietnam in order to prevent the South Vietnamese from losing the war, to ensure that aggression from the north would not succeed," observes *The Pentagon Papers* narrative. "Having deployed enough troops to insure that [North Vietnamese] aggression would not succeed, it had been almost a reflex action to start planning on how much it would take to 'win' the war. Lip service was given to the need for developing South Vietnamese political institutions, but no one at high levels seemed to question the assumption that U.S. political objectives in South Vietnam could be attained through military victory."[3] Stanley Hoffman believes that a U.S. military victory in Vietnam could have been gained only "by destroying the North, or alternatively being perpetually willing to reintervene," choices the United States was simply unwilling to make.[4]

What, in any event, constituted a military victory? Clearly it did not encompass North Vietnam's destruction or the overthrow of its communist regime. Nor did it include the establishment of GVN political authority in every square meter of communist-controlled territory in South Vietnam. It did include, for the Democratic Kennedy and Johnson administrations, the negative domestic political imperative of avoiding outright defeat, which was sustainable as long as U.S. forces remained in South Vietnam. The imperative of defeat avoidance, however, offered no military guidance other than simply keeping sufficient U.S. military power in and around Indochina to prevent a decisive communist victory in the South; between 1965 and 1968, this meant escalating the ground war to offset greatly increased North Vietnamese infiltration down the Ho Chi Minh Trail.

The declared object of U.S. military intervention was to preserve a noncommunist South Vietnam from the threat posed by North Vietnam to South Vietnam's political and territorial integrity, and the nub of that threat after 1965 was the growing presence in South Vietnam of regular North Vietnamese military forces. The operating assumption of U.S. intervention was that Hanoi was the backbone of the communist military challenge in the South, and that absent a PAVN presence in the South, that challenge would be manageable by a properly trained and equipped RVNAF. Thus the operational aim of the U.S. military was to destroy—or compel the permanent retirement of—the PAVN presence in the South. In July 1965, McNamara sent President Johnson a memorandum in which he defined a "favorable outcome" of the war as including PAVN's withdrawal from the South, a reduction of VC attacks and terrorism, an independent South Vietnam, and withdrawal of U.S. combat forces from the South (though not U.S. military advisors).[5]

Westmoreland believed that the United States could compel a unilateral or negotiated PAVN withdrawal by demonstrating to Hanoi's leaders, via an attrition strategy that would threaten to grind the PAVN down at a pace faster than it could reconstitute itself, that North Vietnam could not hope to win a decisive military victory. Westmoreland also believed that granting authority to the MACV to conduct ground operations in southern Laos would increase the PAVN's difficulties in South Vietnam by disrupting the flow of men and materiel from North Vietnam. He and the Joint Chiefs of Staff persistently—albeit vainly— pressed the Johnson White House for such authority. The Chiefs and the PACOM also pressed, without success until 1972 (after the United States had not only abandoned the search for a military victory but also was in the process of withdrawing the last of its ground combat forces from South Vietnam), for authority to mine the DRV's ports and inland waterways as well as to conduct a more or less unrestricted air campaign against military and transportation targets inside the DRV.

The White House's denial of such operational latitude continues to elicit condemnation from military and civilian critics alike. Westmoreland believes that "Washington policy decisions forced us to fight with but one hand."[6] U.S. Grant Sharp, who commanded the U.S. Pacific Command from 1964 to 1968, subsequently charged that "we were not permitted to fight this war to win" because of the restrictions imposed upon the bombing of the DRV; "with the proper use of air power we could bring the North Vietnamese to heel."[7] Ronald Reagan made civilian betrayal of the military an issue in the 1980 presidential election campaign; the Vietnam War was a war from which American soldiers "came home without a victory, not because they'd been defeated but because they'd been denied permission to win."[8]

It is far from clear, however, that White House accession to the military's requests for greater operational latitude in the air over, and the ground in, Indochina alone would have either strangled PAVN forces in the South or otherwise compelled Hanoi to abandon its bid to reunify all of Vietnam under communist auspices. To be sure, an early mining of the DRV's ports and inland waterways coupled with more or less unrestricted U.S. air attacks on the DRV military targets and internal lines of communications (roads, rail lines, canals) could have severely impeded the flow of Chinese and Soviet war materiel into North Vietnam and its movement through that country into Laos. With such operational authority the military almost certainly could have stymied any attempt by Hanoi to move from guerrilla to large-scale conventional military operations; it could have denied to Hanoi the option of both the 1972 and 1975 conventional offensives. And to be sure, a U.S. invasion of southern Laos would have imposed significant additional logistical burdens on Hanoi's support of the war in the South, and together with an earlier and much sharper air war against the DRV uninterrupted by politically motivated bombing pauses, probably have conveyed to Hanoi a measure of American resolve substantially greater than that transmitted by the gradualist strategy Washington actually pursued.

But the strategic effectiveness in 1965 of a more robust air and ground war must be weighed in the political and military context of the pre-Tet years of the Vietnam War. First, with respect to signaling to Hanoi a convincing measure of resolve to win the war, nothing could have been as powerful as a U.S. mobilization of its reserve forces, an invasion of North Vietnam, or both (the latter would have dictated the former). It is most unlikely that an earlier and more brutal bombing campaign would have erased Hanoi's determination to reunify the country by force or threatened the communist regime's grip on its population, a judgment supported by the U.S. strategic bombing experience against such other police states as different in time and place as Nazi Germany, Imperial Japan, and Baathist Iraq. Moreover, shutting down Haiphong and other North Vietnamese deep-water ports might have done little more than channel delivery of the bulk of Soviet and Chinese war materiel into overland lines of communication along the Sino-Vietnamese border. The U.S. air interdiction experience against German ground forces in Europe in World War II, and especially against the transit of supplies across the relatively open Yalu River valley to Chinese forces in Korea during the Korean War, strongly suggest that air power could impair but not decisively break those lines of communication.

Second, an attempted interdiction of the Ho Chi Minh Trail in southern Laos via ground combat operations would have also probably reduced, but almost certainly not eliminated, the flow of communist troops and supplies from the North into the South. Given the terrain and topography of the Annamite cordilerra that dominates southern Laos and northern former South Vietnam, there was no prospect of constructing a leak-proof barrier, notwithstanding McNamara's predictable infatuation with stringing across the Ho Chi Minh Trail what amounted to an electronic Maginot Line of sensors and mines designed to detect and disrupt movement down the trail.[9] The MACV could never halt the flow of communist supplies inside South Vietnam, where it enjoyed unfettered operational latitude. Ground force operations in Laos, moreover, would have been irrelevant to curbing infiltration by sea, upon which North Vietnam increasingly relied during the war, using either small coastal craft to move materiel directly to secret reception points along the South Vietnamese coast, or ocean-going vessels to deliver much larger quantities of supplies to the Cambodian port of Sihanoukville.

A third and much more important obstacle to the strategic effectiveness in 1965 of a more robust U.S. air and ground war was the very nature of the Vietnam War before the Tet Offensive. During the years of the U.S. military buildup in Vietnam, and certainly in 1965, the war was still a predominantly southern-based and manned insurgency that was not critically dependent on manpower and supplies from the North. In 1965, there was simply not much to interdict along the Ho Chi Minh Trail in Laos or anywhere else, certainly when compared to the logistical avalanche that poured down the trail in 1972 and 1975. U.S. conventional military operations, however more they might have been expanded in the mid-1960s than they were, were still unsuited to the character of the war at hand. The irony, of course, is that although such operations became increasingly effective in the years following the Tet Offensive against an increasingly conventional communist military threat, their potential strategic decisiveness was voided by the Tet-induced U.S. abandonment of its search for a military solution in Vietnam and the unilateral withdrawal of American forces from that country.

Fourth, not even an early grant of the broadest operational latitude to the military could have compensated for what in the long run Vietnam War historian George C. Herring has correctly identified as the single greatest obstacle to the preservation of a noncommunist South Vietnam: the "fundamental and apparently unsolvable problem" of "the weakness of the South Vietnamese government."[10] Unless communist military forces, especially the PAVN, could have been permanently crushed, or unless the United States was prepared to stay in the war indefinitely, the GVN was ultimately in a an irremediable situation. John Prados has rightly recognized that "any victory had to utilize what was there, what was available in South Vietnam, and since the national identity and the aspirations of the Vietnamese favored the other side, any potential strategy had an extra obstacle to overcome."[11] As noted, if the United States could not have picked a tougher and more obstinate adversary anywhere in the world than it did in the communist Democratic Republic of Vietnam, it also could not have chosen a more feckless ally than it did in the noncommunist Republic of Vietnam. "The war not only had to be won in South Vietnam, but it had to be won by the South Vietnamese. Unfortunately, to the end the South Vietnamese performance remained the Achilles' heel of the allied effort," concludes Guenter Lewy.[12] Even the Chinese in the Korean War proved more politically tractable than did their counterparts in North Vietnam in the 1960s, and the South Korean government and military forces had considerably more vitality and staying power than did their counterparts in South Vietnam. Clark Clifford, who in 1965 counseled President Johnson against intervention in Vietnam and later replaced McNamara as secretary of defense, observed after the war that, "From its beginning, . . . we were constrained by the fact that our South Vietnamese allies were corrupt, inefficient, and poorly motivated. This was critical: in the final analysis, American objectives in Vietnam depended more on the capabilities of our allies in Saigon than on our own efforts. And the more we did for them, the more dependent and ineffectual they became. It was on this very point that our policy would ultimately fail."[13]

There was always a political limit to the duration of direct military intervention in the Vietnam War, even though few senior U.S. military leaders in the mid-1960s seem to have recognized this critical fact. John Prados notes that from the beginning of direct intervention, the "clock was running, not only as North Vietnam and the Viet Cong improved their infrastructure and fighting power, but also domestically. American politics permitted only a certain amount of time for the perfect solution to be found, after which reversal of political support would occur."[14] Richard Nixon made the same point: "When a president sends American troops to war, a hidden timer starts to run. He has a finite period of time to win the war before the people grow weary of it."[15] Hanoi certainly recognized America's political clock: the strategy of protracted war was based on it. Former National Security Council staff member James C. Thompson, testifying before Senator Fulbright's Foreign Relations Committee in 1972, observed that the North Vietnamese "have always known from the beginning of time that they live there and we don't, and that eventually we will go home; and even back in early 1965 when people were discussing the possibility of a bombing track, it was suggested by wiser men who knew Vietnam that even if we bombed them back to the stone age, the North Vietnamese would with reluctance permit the destruction of what they had built over the last 10 years, retreat back into the bush, and reappear once we had gone home."[16]

Finally, it should be observed that the military's desire to increase U.S. forces' operational effectiveness via greater operational authority was not accompanied by a willingness to tackle its self-imposed obstacles to operational effectiveness. It was—and remains—disingenuous of the military and their conservative political supporters to whine about civilian intrusion upon potential U.S. military effectiveness in Vietnam when the U.S. military itself was hobbling that effectiveness through disunity of command, a faulty attrition strategy, rear-area bloat, and idiotic personnel rotation policies. The military's appeal to civilian authority for more operational latitude in Indochina clearly would have carried with it greater moral force had the military first put its own house in order.

Were there nonetheless other operational options available that might have altered the Vietnam War's outcome, but which for one reason or another were never seriously considered by either civilian or military decision makers? With respect to destroying the PAVN's military effectiveness or at least compelling the withdrawal of PAVN forces from South Vietnam, there were at least two. The first would have been an invasion of North Vietnam. Nothing concentrates the mind—and resources—of an enemy more intensely than an invasion of his homeland. An invasion of North Vietnam almost certainly would have produced the PAVN's swift departure from the South in order to defend the motherland. It would have placed North Vietnam on the strategic defensive by threatening the one piece of territory it valued above all others. Moreover, shifting the ground war from South Vietnam to North Vietnam would have afforded the former early on the opportunity to build durable political institutions and implement the kind of agrarian reforms that Saigon finally implemented after it was too late for them to have a decisive bearing on the war's outcome. (Whether the GVN could and would have effectively acted on that opportunity is an unanswerable question, although there is nothing in its actual performance during the war that encourages an affirmative answer.)

The strategic logic of invasion is unassailable: it is always better to make the enemy fight on his territory than to permit him to fight on one's own. Moreover, an invasion would force the North Vietnamese to stand and defend territory, thereby forcing them to wage at least some set-piece battles of the kind for which American commanders long prayed. In 1954, U.S. Army Chief of Staff Matthew Ridgway, who commanded U.S. forces in Korea after MacArthur's departure, opposed U.S. intervention to save the French in Indochina precisely because he foresaw that any chance of reversing the communist tide there would require what in effect amounted to a massive U.S. invasion (seven to twelve divisions) of northern Vietnam, then as in 1965 the great communist stronghold of Indochina.[17] Because Ridgway regarded such a huge commitment to a place of marginal strategic importance to the United States as a mindless enterprise, he opposed U.S. intervention in Vietnam throughout the 1950s and 1960s.

Yet the risks of an invasion of North Vietnam almost certainly would have outweighed its operational dividends, which undoubtedly explains why it was never seriously considered by U.S. decision makers. Invasion would have constituted a major escalation of the war, necessitating a U.S. reserve call-up; the commitment to military operations in Southeast Asia of perhaps as many as 1 million U.S. military personnel (or almost twice actual U.S. peak military strength in the region in 1969); and the political preparation of the American public for a large war of indefinite duration. Much would depend on the invasion's declared purpose; an invasion to overthrow the communist regime in Hanoi and reunify all of Vietnam under noncommunist auspices obviously would require considerably more effort than one aimed at simply forcing the PAVN out of South Vietnam pursuant to a negotiated settlement in which Hanoi recognized South Vietnamese independence. In either case, the North Vietnamese could be expected to fight even longer and harder to defend their homeland than they did to conquer South Vietnam. Of course, all bets would be off if invasion, whatever its purpose, provoked Chinese intervention, as it probably would have. A much wider and infinitely more costly war would have ensued (as it did in Korea) in which South Vietnam's ultimate fate would take a distant back seat to far more important strategic considerations.

The absence within the White House and the Pentagon of any enthusiasm for an invasion is understandable. "The best thing that can be said about the option of invading North Vietnam," concludes one assessment, "is that it is a good thing that no one tried it."[18] Unlike the air war and Laotian options vainly sought by the JCS, PACOM, and MACV, however, the invasion option did strike directly—and tellingly—at the primary source of the threat to South Vietnam's preservation as a noncommunist state. The air war and Laotian options favored by U.S. military leaders were useful. But they were also peripheral. U.S. military leaders moreover either failed to recognize them as peripheral, which speaks poorly of their strategic insight, or worse, understood the options to be peripheral but were either afraid to confront their civilian superiors with the harsh facts or saw in their denial by the White House a persuasive alibi for a lost war. The United States paid an enormous price for not having a Matthew Ridgway at the national military helm in the 1960s. Approaching the Vietnam War required the combination of a sound sense of strategic priorities, the ability to recognize a bad fight when one appeared, and the moral courage to speak the truth to those in power.

Another unsought operational option that probably would have rid South Vietnam of the PAVN—albeit more slowly than the invasion option—was that of a massive bombing campaign conducted directly against North Vietnam's population. Sustained bombing of population centers and the Red River dike system not only would have killed or injured hundreds of thousands of North Vietnamese and placed additional millions at risk. It also would have compelled the diversion of enormous human and other resources into homeland air defense— far more than were diverted by the bombing campaign the United States actually pursued. Such an air campaign sooner or later probably would have crippled the PAVN's recruiting base inside North Vietnam, offering a far more effective means of decimating PAVN forces in South Vietnam than Westmoreland's vain pursuit of attrition through search and destroy on the ground. (Because the Americans always enjoyed the initiative in the air, North Vietnam would not have been able to control its population losses to homeland air attack, in contrast to its ability to control its military manpower losses in the ground war in South Vietnam.) A "countervalue" bombing campaign had precedent in the brutal U.S. firebombing—and ultimately atomic bombing—of Japanese cities in 1945. The North Vietnamese population, like Japan's, was highly concentrated and vulnerable to air attack, and North Vietnam's capacity to feed itself rested on the highly regulated flow of water in the Red River delta. U.S. antiwar protesters who claimed that the United States was pursuing a policy of deliberate saturation bombing on North Vietnamese population centers were ignorant not only of actual policy but also of the real capacity of U.S. air power, if unchecked, to inflict an aerial holocaust on the country.

Saturation bombing was never considered because most civilian and military leaders considered it both immoral and unnecessary, as well as incompatible with both declared U.S. Air Force doctrine and the limited nature (for the United States) of the Vietnam War itself. A civilian authority that refused to permit U.S. pilots to attack enemy surface-to-air missile sites until they were operational and firing on U.S. aircraft was not about to authorize the carpet-bombing of residential areas. Saturation bombing, which is not easily distinguishable from genocide, also would have outraged much of American and most of international opinion.

It is difficult to avoid the conclusion that the United States lacked any strategically decisive and morally acceptable war-winning military options in the Vietnam War. Options considered—and not considered— were either peripheral or, if potent and at least theoretically decisive, unacceptable. The military's vain push for ground war options in Laos and Cambodia and expanded air war options against North Vietnam was a push, in effect, for an extension of the military stalemate in Indochina at a higher and more costly level of violence, though these rebuffed options continue to serve the cause of those who believe that the Vietnam War was a case of American self-defeat.

The history of U.S. escalatory military moves from the Gulf of Tonkin incident to the Tet Offensive shows that Hanoi and its Soviet and Chinese patrons were able and willing to respond effectively to each step the United States took up the escalation ladder. There is simply no convincing evidence that an earlier and less restrained American use of force in Indochina, absent the subsequent emergence of a politically and militarily viable South Vietnam, could or would have dissuaded or blocked Hanoi from successfully pursuing its goal of reunifying Vietnam under communist auspices. To accept the judgment that a U.S. victory in Vietnam was self-denied "requires a great leap of faith," concludes Herring. "To justify American intervention on the simple grounds of anti-Communism or on the basis of Hanoi's postwar actions ignores a great deal of history and evades some hard questions. That the war was winnable in any meaningful sense is at best an unprovable proposition, and the notion that America's defeat was largely self-inflicted, the result of a faulty strategy or lack of will, reduces a complex historical issue to the most simplistic terms."[19] I share Norman Podhoretz's view that winning the Vietnam War was "beyond the reasonable capabilities of the United States," but "that it *was* within the reasonable capabilities of the United States to deny victory to the Communists,"[20] though I believe that Podhoretz surely must know that an enduring denial of communist victory would have required the war's more or less permanent—and ipso facto politically intolerable—Americanization.

Whether the Vietnam War was winnable or not, there seems to be a near consensus today that U.S. intervention in the war was strategically stupid. The sage, Asia-wise Mike Mansfield, who succeeded Lyndon Johnson as Senate Majority Leader and who opposed U.S. intervention from its inception, later reflected that the war "was unnecessary, uncalled for, it wasn't tied to our security or vital interest. It was just a misadventure in a part of the world we should have kept our nose out of."[21] But perhaps there is no characterization of the war more apt than that made by Omar Bradley of MacArthur's proposed expansion of the Korean War into a general war with China: "The wrong war, at the wrong place, at the wrong time, and with the wrong enemy."[22]

Notes

INTRODUCTION

1. Quoted in Fisher, "Reopening the Wounds of Vietnam," 10.
2. During the Vietnam War a total of 2,850,000 U.S. military personnel served in Southeast Asia, 2,150,000 of them in Vietnam. See Baksir and Strauss, *Chance and Circumstance*, 53.
3. Quoted in Steel, "Blind Contrition," 35.
4. Dole, acceptance speech, sec. A, 13.
5. Podhoretz, *Why We Were in Vietnam*, 62.
6. Ibid., 210.
7. Kearns, *Lyndon Johnson*, 252.
8. Quoted in testimony of Arthur M. Schlesinger Jr., in *Causes, Origins, and Lessons of the Vietnam War*, 63.
9. McNamara with VanDeMark, *In Retrospect*, xvi, xviii.
10. Hanson Baldwin, "Forward," in U. S. G. Sharp, *Strategy for Defeat*.
11. Westmoreland, *A Soldier Reports*, 145.
12. Nixon, *No More Vietnams*, 97, 165.
13. "When South Vietnam was taken over by the North Vietnamese army, American combat troops had departed some two years earlier. This is very important, and everybody should know it, but there are many people in this country who do not." William C. Westmoreland, "Vietnam in Perspective," in *Vietnam: Four American Perspectives*, ed. Patrick J. Hearnden, 44.
14. Le Gro, *Vietnam from Cease-Fire to Capitulation*, 2.
15. Tang with Chanoff and Tai, *A Vietnam Cong Memoir*, 214–15.
16. Vien, *The Final Collapse*, 6.
17. Kissinger, *Diplomacy*, 632.
18. Nixon, *The Real War*, 119.
19. Isaacson, *Kissinger: A Biography*, 485.
20. Westmoreland, "Vietnam in Perspective," 48.

21. Dean Rusk with Richard Rusk and Papp, *As I Saw It,* 491.
22. Mandlebaum, "Vietnam: The Television War," 165.
23. Powell with Persico, *My American Journey,* 149.

1. THE REASONS WHY

1. von Clausewitz, *On War,* 88.
2. *The Pentagon Papers* (Senator Gravel ed.), vol. 2, 90–92.
3. Quoted in Foot, *The Wrong War,* 23.
4. Dean Rusk with Richard Rusk and Papp, *As I Saw It,* 427.
5. Quoted in Herring, ed., *The Pentagon Papers* (abridged ed.), 115.
6. Ibid., 138.
7. Statement and testimony of George F. Kennan before the Senate Foreign Relations Committee, 10 February 1966, reprinted in *The Vietnam Hearings,* 108.
8. JCS memorandum to the secretary of defense, reprinted in Herring, *The Pentagon Papers* (abridged ed.), 16.
9. Kissinger, *Diplomacy,* 621.
10. Quoted in Reeves, *President Kennedy,* 444.
11. Quoted in Buzzanco, *Masters of War,* 143.
12. Kearns, *Lyndon Johnson,* 252.
13. Quoted in VanDeMark, *Into the Quagmire,* 204.
14. Robert Thompson, "Squaring the Error," 442.
15. Quoted in Herring, *The Pentagon Papers* (abridged ed.), 112.
16. Quoted in Gardner, *Pay Any Price,* 185.
17. Neil Sheehan and David Halberstam, quoted in *Where the Domino Fell,* Olson and Roberts, eds., 110.
18. Statement by Secretary of State Dean Rusk before the House Foreign Affairs Committee, 3 August 1965, reprinted in *Why Vietnam,* 9.
19. Quoted in Kattenburg, *The Vietnam Trauma,* 113.
20. Powell with Persico, *My American Journey,* 149.
21. Statement of Secretary of State Dean Rusk before the Senate Foreign Relations Committee, 18 February 1966, reprinted in *The Heart of the Problem,* 6.
22. Ball, "The Issue in Vietnam," 9–10.
23. See Jian, "China's Involvement in the Vietnam War," 356–87; and John Garver, "The Tet Offensive and Sino-Soviet Relations," in *The Tet Offensive,* Gilbert and Head, eds., 45–61.
24. President Kennedy's NBC interview, 9 September 1963, reprinted in *Department of State Bulletin,* 30 September 1963, 499. See *The Pentagon Papers* (Senator Gravel ed.), vol. 2, 829.
25. Secretary of Defense Robert S. McNamara, "U.S. Policy in Vietnam," 26 March 1964, reprinted in *Department of State Bulletin,* 13 April 1964, 562. See *The Pentagon Papers* (Senator Gravel ed.), vol. 3, 713.

26. Address by President Johnson at Johns Hopkins University, Baltimore, Maryland, 7 April 1965, reprinted in *Department of State Bulletin*, 26 April 1965, 607. See *The Pentagon Papers* (Senator Gravel ed.), vol. 3, 730.

27. Quoted in Gelb and Betts, *The Irony of Vietnam*, 42.

28. Galbraith, *How to Get Out of Vietnam*, 19.

29. Quoted in Kahn, *The China Hands*, 23.

30. Quoted in Herring, *The Pentagon Papers* (abridged ed.), 18.

31. Asprey, *War in the Shadows*, 595.

32. See *The Pentagon Papers* (Senator Gravel ed.), vol. 1, 132–39, 148–49, 169–72.

33. See Duiker, *Sacred War*, 179–81; and Kahin, *Intervention*, 228–341.

34. *The Vietnam Hearings*, 136.

35. President's radio report to the American people on Korea and U.S. policy in the Far East, 11 April 1951, Public Papers of the Presidents, 233, in *The Pentagon Papers* (Senator Gravel ed.), vol. 1, 588–89.

36. President Eisenhower's remarks at Governors' Conference, 4 August 1953, Public Papers of the Presidents, 1953, 540, in *The Pentagon Papers* (Senator Gravel ed.), vol. 1, 592.

37. Eisenhower, letter to Churchill, 1954, excerpted in *Major Problems*, McMahon, ed., 121 ff.

38. Quoted in Kearns, *Lyndon Johnson*, 252.

39. Dean Rusk with Richard Rusk and Papp, *As I Saw It*, 404.

40. Speech of Senator John F. Kennedy, June 1956, excerpted in Lewy, *America in Vietnam*, 12.

41. Interview with Secretary Rusk and Secretary McNamara on CBS Television News program, 9 August 1965, published as "Political and Military Aspects of U.S. Policy in Vietnam" in *Department of State Bulletin*, 30 August 1965, 342. See *The Pentagon Papers* (Senator Gravel ed.), vol. 4, 636.

42. "SEATO's principal purpose was to provide our President legal authority to intervene in Indochina." John Foster Dulles, quoted in Bator, *Vietnam, a Diplomatic Tragedy*, 200.

43. Quoted in Young, *The Vietnam Wars*, 47.

44. Clifford with Holbrooke, *Counsel to the President*, 451.

45. Gardner, *Approaching Vietnam*, 331.

46. See Schulzinger, *A Time for War*, 76.

47. Quoted in McMahon, *Major Problems*, 169.

48. Quoted in Gettlemen, et al., eds., *Vietnam and America*, 241.

49. Morgenthau, "We Are Deluding Ourselves in Vietnam," excerpted in *The Vietnam Reader*, Raskin and Fall, eds., 44.

50. Summers, *On Strategy*, 113.

51. Westmoreland, "Vietnam in Perspective," 42.

52. Nixon, *No More Vietnams*, 47.

53. Ellsberg, *Papers on the War*, 172.

54. Gelb and Betts, *The Irony of Vietnam,* 343.
55. Robert Thompson, *No Exit from Vietnam,* 116.
56. Draper, "The Revised Version," 31.
57. *Aggression from the North,* 3.
58. Total based on figures appearing in ibid., 38–42.
59. Robert Thompson, *No Exit from Vietnam,* 45.
60. Cited in Clodfelter, *The Limits of Air Power,* 134.
61. Quoted in Hilsman, *To Move a Nation,* 426.

2. STAKES, STAMINA, AND FIGHTING POWER

1. Fall, *Viet-Nam Witness,* 244–45.
2. Quoted in Kahin, *Intervention,* 249.
3. Quoted in Wells, *The War Within,* 99.
4. Dean Rusk with Richard Rusk and Papp, *As I Saw It,* 472.
5. Interview with Tom Wells, in Wells, *The War Within,* 99.
6. Westmoreland, *A Soldier Reports,* 306.
7. Quoted in Blair, *The Forgotten War,* 348.
8. Kissinger, *Diplomacy,* 632.
9. Mueller, "'Breaking Point' in Vietnam," 514.
10. Quoted in Isaacson, *Kissinger: A Biography,* 246.
11. Mueller, "'Breaking Point' in Vietnam," 507.
12. Cited in Lewy, *America in Vietnam,* 450–51.
13. Fallaci, *Interview with History,* 82.
14. Ibid., 59.
15. See Webb, "Robert McNamara," 48.
16. Lawrence E. Grinter, "Vietnam: The Cost of Ignoring the Political Requirements," in *The American War in Vietnam,* Grinter and Dunn, eds., 38–39.
17. Mueller, "'Breaking Point' in Vietnam," 507–9.
18. The figure of 13 million dead equals 5 percent times 260 million; the figure 3.9 million missing equals 1.5 percent (300,000 communist missing divided by 20 million total population base) 260 million.
19. Quoted in Asprey, *War in the Shadows,* 476.
20. Salisbury, *Behind the Lines—Hanoi,* 196.
21. Duiker, *Sacred War,* 3.
22. Quoted in Summers, *Historical Atlas of the Vietnam War,* 96.
23. McNamara, *In Retrospect,* 109.
24. See Duiker, *Sacred War,* 179–80; Lomperis, *The War Everyone Lost—and Won,* 138–40; and Papp, *Vietnam,* 77–78.
25. Dean Rusk with Richard Rusk and Papp, *As I Saw It,* 456.
26. Quoted in Podhoretz, *Why We Were in Vietnam,* 80.
27. See, for example, Osgood, *Limited War,* and Schelling, *The Strategy of Conflict.*

28. Schelling, *Arms and Influence*, 2–3.
29. In his famous Johns Hopkins University address of April 1965, President Johnson dangled before Hanoi the prospect of a U.S-sponsored Tennessee Valley Authority–style hydroelectric program for the entire Mekong River region if only North Vietnam would cease its sponsorship of the war in South Vietnam. Seven years later, the Nixon administration secretly pledged the United States to pay reparations to Hanoi as an inducement to accept the Paris peace agreement that was finally signed in January 1973. Hanoi's acceptance of that agreement, however, was stimulated less by the promise of money than by the U.S. commitment to depart South Vietnam and abandonment of its insistence that the North Vietnamese Army do likewise.
30. Bill Moyers's interview with Michael Janeway, late 1967, reprinted in "Bill Moyers Talks About the War and LBJ," in *Who We Are*, Manning and Janeway, eds., 262.
31. *The Pentagon Papers* (Senator Gravel ed.), vol. 3, 64–65.
32. Quoted in Gardner, *Pay Any Price*, 154.
33. Quoted in VanDeMark, *Into the Quagmire*, 115.
34. Quoted in Gelb with Betts, *The Irony of Vietnam*, 256.
35. Gardner, *Pay Any Price*, 162.
36. Cooper, "The Day It Became the Longest War," 80.
37. Westmoreland, *A Soldier Reports*, 154.
38. McNamara, with VanDeMark, *In Retrospect*, 322.
39. Hoffmann, et al., "Vietnam Reappraised," 13.
40. Hackworth and Sherman, *About Face*, 598.
41. Cooper, *The Lost Crusade*, 224.
42. Krepinevich, *The Army and Vietnam*, 4.
43. Quoted in McNamara, with VanDeMark, *In Retrospect*, 212.
44. Quoted in Lanning and Cragg, *Inside the VC and NVA*, 233.
45. Schulzinger, *A Time for War*, 181.
46. Cooper, *The Lost Crusade*, 422.
47. Halberstam, *The Best and the Brightest*, 250.
48. McNamara, with VanDeMark, *In Retrospect*, 322.
49. Ibid., 153.
50. van Creveld, *Fighting Power*, 3.
51. Ball, *The Past Has Another Pattern*, 370.
52. Interview with Oriana Fallaci, in Fallaci, *Interview with History*, 83–84.
53. Karnow, "Giap Remembers," 36.
54. Dean Rusk with Richard Rusk and Papp, *As I Saw It*, 497.
55. See Lorell and Kelley, *Casualties, Public Opinion, and Presidential Policy*.
56. JCS memorandum to the secretary of defense, reprinted in *The Pentagon Papers* (abridged ed.), George C. Herring, ed., 16.
57. Podhoretz, *Why We Were In Vietnam*, 127.

58. Kissinger, *The White House Years*, 298.
59. Davidson, *Vietnam at War*, 477.
60. Nixon, *No More Vietnams*, 202.
61. Nunn, *Vietnam Aid: The Painful Options*, 5.
62. Thieu, interview by Oriana Fallaci, in Fallaci, *Interview with History*, 60–61.
63. Heinl, "The Collapse of the Armed Forces," 30.
64. Davidson, *Vietnam at War*, 542.

3. THE WAR IN THE SOUTH

1. Quoted in Olson and Roberts, *Where the Domino Fell*, 25.
2. Quoted in Berman, *Planning a Tragedy*, 137.
3. Quoted in Podhoretz, *Why We Were in Vietnam*, 113–14.
4. Nixon, *No More Vietnams*, 56.
5. See Warner, *Shooting at the Moon*, 88–89; and McMaster, *Dereliction of Duty*, 90–91, 155–58.
6. Pike, *Viet Cong*, 38.
7. Giap, *Big Victory, Great Task*, 74.
8. See John M. Gates, "If at First You Don't Succeed, Try to Rewrite History: Revisionism and the Vietnam War," in *Looking Back on the Vietnam War*, Head and Grinter, eds., 179.
9. Salisbury, *Behind the Lines—Hanoi*, 144.
10. Robert Thompson, "Squaring the Error," 447.
11. Quoted in Oberdorfer, *Tet!*, 93.
12. Millett and Maslowski, *For the Common Defense*, 70.
13. Nixon, *No More Vietnams*, 31.
14. Nixon, *The Real War*, 105–6.
15. Testimony excerpted in *The Pentagon Papers* (Senator Gravel ed.), vol. 3, 35, 36.
16. Taylor, cable to State Department, excerpted in *The Pentagon Papers* (Senator Gravel ed.), vol. 3, 446.
17. Sheehan, *A Bright Shining Lie*, 90–91.
18. *The Pentagon Papers* (Senator Gravel ed.), vol. 2, 413; and Hunt, *Pacification*, 59.
19. *The Pentagon Papers* (Senator Gravel ed.), vol. 2, 433.
20. Quoted in Krepinevich, *The Army and Vietnam*, 37.
21. Gen. William Dupuy, quoted in *America's Longest War*, Herring, ed., 168.
22. Quoted in Lewy, *America in Vietnam*, 73.
23. Westmoreland, *A Soldier Reports*, 185.
24. Palmer, *Summons of the Trumpet*, 147.
25. Westmoreland, *A Soldier Reports*, 185.
26. Earl H. Tilford Jr., "Bombing Our Way Back Home: The Commando Hunt and Menu Campaigns of 1969–1973," in *Looking Back on the Vietnam War*, Head and Grinter, eds., 123.

27. Tang with Chanoff and Tai, *A Viet Cong Memoir,* 167, 168.
28. Palmer, *Summons of the Trumpet,* 148.
29. Kinnard, *The War Managers,* 45.
30. Buzzanco, *Masters of War,* 230–31; and Sorley, *Thunderbolt,* 201, 224–25.
31. Westmoreland, *A Soldier Reports,* 156
32. Ibid., 180.
33. *The Pentagon Papers* (Senator Gravel ed.), vol. 3, 396.
34. Buzzanco, *Masters of War,* 8.
35. For an account and discussion of PROVN, see *The Pentagon Papers* (Senator Gravel ed.), vol. 2, 501–2, 576–80; Buzzanco, *Masters of War,* 261–63, 272; and Bergerud, *The Dynamics of Defeat,* 110–14.
36. Excerpted in *The Pentagon Papers* (Senator Gravel ed.), vol. 2, 578.
37. Ibid., 548.
38. Quoted in Krepinevich, *The Army and Vietnam,* 174.
39. See Lewy, *America in Vietnam,* 84; and Robert Thompson, "Squaring the Error," 445.
40. Robert Thompson, *No Exit from Vietnam,* 60.
41. Excerpted in *The Pentagon Papers* (Senator Gravel ed.), vol. 4, 457.
42. Ibid., 458; and Stanton, *Rise and Fall,* 86.
43. Wirtz, *The Tet Offensive,* 117.
44. See ibid., 158–79; Berman, *Lyndon Johnson's War,* 27–31; and Adams, *War of Numbers.*
45. Adams, *War of Numbers,* 105; and Young, *The Vietnam Wars,* 73.
46. Ebert, *A Life in a Year,* 189.
47. David Hackworth, introduction to Adams, *War of Numbers,* xvi.
48. Buzzanco, *Masters of War,* 283.
49. Quoted in Berman, *Lyndon Johnson's War,* 81.
50. McNamara, *In Retrospect,* 48.
51. Stanton, *Rise and Fall,* 272–73.
52. This is the judgment, for example, of Prados and Stubbe, *Valley of Decision;* Pisor, *The End of the Line;* and Duiker, *Sacred War.* "The absurdity of Khe Sanh," wrote Sir Robert Thompson, "will rate a book by itself. Holding it, relieving it, and evacuating it were all regarded as victories." Quoted in Pisor, *The End of the Line,* 267.
53. Oberdorfer, *Tet!,* 34.
54. Kolko, *Anatomy of a War,* 200–205.
55. Young, *The Vietnam Wars,* 177.
56. Huntington, "The Bases of Accommodation," 649, 650.
57. Larry E. Cable, "Everything Is Perfect and Getting Better: The Myths and Measures of the American Ground War in Indochina, 1965–1968," in *Looking Back,* Head and Grinter, eds., 201–2.
58. Kolko, *Anatomy of a War,* 250.

59. Quoted in Krepinevich, *The Army and Vietnam*, 84.
60. Robert Thompson, "Squaring the Error," 453.
61. Bernard B. Fall, *Street without Joy*, 267.
62. The incident is recounted in Record, "Maximizing COBRA Utilization."
63. *The Pentagon Papers* (Senator Gravel ed.), vol. 3, 419.
64. Colby, *Lost Victory*, 179.
65. Summers, *The New World Strategy*, 161; see also *The Pentagon Papers*(Senator Gravel ed.), vol. 2, 533–36.
66. Bergerud, *The Dynamics of Defeat*, 3.
67. Lomperis, *The War Everyone Lost—and Won*,158.
68. Stuckey and Pistorius, "Mobilization for the Vietnam War," 26.
69. Quoted in "Discussion Issues," in *Second Indochina War Symposium: Papers and Commentary*, Schlight, ed., 266.
70. Stanton, *Rise and Fall*, 366–68.
71. Appy, *Working-Class War*, 6–7.
72. Krepinevich, *The Army and Vietnam*, 205.
73. Hackworth and Sherman, *About Face*, 524.
74. Westmoreland, *A Soldier Reports*, 358.
75. Cincinnatus, *Self-Destruction*, 155.
76. Moore and Galloway, *We Were Soldiers Once—and Young*, 405.
77. Thayer, *War without Fronts*, 94.
78. Ebert, *A Life in a Year*, 1.
79. Spector, *After Tet*, 43.
80. Stanton, *Rise and Fall*, 23.
81. Ebert, *A Life in a Year*, 89.
82. Palmer, *The Twenty-five-Year War*, 69.

4. THE WAR AGAINST THE NORTH

1. Quoted in Asprey, *War in the Shadows*, 938.
2. Kissinger, *The White House Years*, 232.
3. See Momyer, *Air Power in Three Wars*, 13.
4. Quoted in Coffey, *Iron Eagle*, 435.
5. Quoted in Clodfelter, *The Limits of Air Power*, 145.
6. Sharp, *Strategy for Defeat*, xvii.
7. Robert Thompson, *No Exit from Vietnam*, 139.
8. Quoted in Berman, *Planning a Tragedy*, 45.
9. See, for example, Record, *Hollow Victory*, 103–5.
10. Interview with Mary-Ann Bendel, *USA Today*, 23 July 1986, sec. A, 9.
11. Frisbee, "The Practice of Professionalism," 113.
12. Mitchell, *Winged Defense*, xvi.
13. De Seversky, *Victory through Air Power*, 5.

14. *United States Strategic Bombing Survey,* 30 September 1945, 72.

15. Ibid., 108.

16. Clodfelter, *The Limits of Air Power,* 9.

17. MacDonald, *Korea: The War Before Vietnam,* 238.

18. *Air Force Manual 1-1. Basic Aerospace Doctrine,* 3-2.

19. Momyer, *Air Power in Three Wars,* 249.

20. Werrell, "Air War Victorious," 43–44.

21. Mrozek, *Air Power and the Ground War in Vietnam,* 64.

22. Nichols and Tillmann, *On Yankee Station,* 16.

23. Coffey, *Iron Eagle,* 428.

24. Quoted in ibid., 428.

25. Momyer, *Air Power in Three Wars,* 15–16.

26. Broughton, *Going Downtown,* 174.

27. Nichols and Tillmann, *On Yankee Station,* 26–28.

28. Broughton, *Going Downtown,* xvi.

29. Ibid., 84.

30. Westmoreland, *A Soldier Reports,* 418.

31. For an extensive discussion of the issue of centralized air power in Vietnam see Schlight, *The War in South Vietnam,* 139–65.

32. Momyer, *Air Power in Three Wars,* 95.

33. Kissinger, *The White House Years,* 1112.

34. *The Pentagon Papers* (Senator Gravel ed.), vol. 3, 269.

35. Ibid., 311.

36. Ibid., vol. 4, 116.

37. Ibid., 223 (emphasis original).

38. Ibid., 224.

39. Ibid., 225–28.

40. Ibid., 201.

41. Clodfelter, *The Limits of Air Power,* 318.

42. Tilford, *Setup,* 154–55.

43. Quoted in *The Lessons of Vietnam,* W. Scott Thompson and Frizzell, eds., 127.

44. *The Pentagon Papers* (Senator Gravel ed.), vol. 4, 118.

45. Salisbury, *Behind the Lines—Hanoi,* 222.

46. Kahn, "If Negotiations Fail," 629.

47. Spector, *After Tet,* 188.

48. Enthoven and Smith, *How Much Is Enough,* 304.

49. Tilford, *Setup,* xvii.

50. Franklin, *MIA, or Mythmaking in America,* 99.

51. Tilford, *Setup,* 291–92.

52. See Papp, *Vietnam,* 141–44.

53. Ambrose, "The Christmas Bombing," 557.

54. Ibid., 555.

55. Herring, *America's Longest War,* 280.
56. Tilford, *Setup,* 264.
57. Ibid., 280, 281.
58. *The Pentagon Papers* (Senator Gravel ed.), vol. 4, 57.
59. For other judgments, see Stephen Peter Rosen, "Vietnam and the American Theory of Limited War," in Foerster and Wright, *American Defense Policy,* 92; and Lewy, *America in Vietnam,* 416.

5. HOLLOW CLIENT

1. Vien, *The Final Collapse,* 155.
2. Hammer, *A Death in November,* 203.
3. Kattenburg, *The Vietnam Trauma in American Foreign Policy,* 52.
4. *The Pentagon Papers* (Senator Gravel ed.), vol. 1, 253.
5. Quoted in Newman, *JFK and Vietnam,* 355.
6. *The Pentagon Papers* (Senator Gravel ed.), vol. 1, 252.
7. Bergerud, *The Dynamics of Defeat,* 55.
8. Tang with Chanoff and Tai, *A Viet Cong Memoir,* 64. Also see Bergerud, *The Dynamics of Defeat,* 14–17, and Kolko, *Anatomy of a War,* 93.
9. Bergerud, *The Dynamics of Defeat,* 3.
10. Quoted in *Vietnam and America: A Documented History,* Gettleman, et al., eds., 142.
11. Quoted in Gardner, *Pay Any Price,* 54–55.
12. *The Pentagon Papers* (Senator Gravel ed.), vol. 2, 456.
13. Quoted in Prochau, *Once upon a Distant War,* 49.
14. See Hilsman, *To Move a Nation,* 494–96.
15. Draper, *Abuse of Power,* 50.
16. *The Pentagon Papers* (Senator Gravel ed.), vol. 4, 398–99.
17. Quoted in Olson and Roberts, *Where the Domino Fell,* 220.
18. Kinnard, *The War Managers,* 97.
19. Hosmer, Kellen, and Jenkins, *The Fall of South Vietnam,* 31.
20. Herrington, *Peace with Honor?,* 40.
21. Bergerud, *The Dynamics of Defeat,* 81.
22. Lewy, *America in Vietnam,* 218.
23. Isaacs, *Without Honor,* 502.
24. Spector, *The U.S. Army in Vietnam,* 126.
25. *The Pentagon Papers* (Senator Gravel ed.), vol. 2, 359–60, 413, 478–79.
26. Thomas, *The Very Best Men,* 328.
27. Bergerud, *The Dynamics of Defeat,* 95.
28. Kissinger, "The Vietnam Negotiations," 230.
29. Herring, *America's Longest War,* 298.
30. Kolko, *Anatomy of a War,* 107.

6. THE WAR ALONG THE POTOMAC

1. Kearns, *Lyndon Johnson,* 254–65 (emphasis added).
2. Oberdorfer, *Tet!,* 82.
3. Crowley, *Nixon off the Record,* 69, 114.
4. The minimum voting age in federal elections during the Vietnam War was 21; it was reduced to 18 only with the ratification of the Twenty-sixth Amendment to the Constitution in 1971.
5. Quoted in Berman, *Planning a Tragedy,* 126.
6. Quoted in Wells, *The War Within,* 153.
7. *Certain Victory: The U.S. Army in the Gulf War* (Washington, D.C.: Office of the Chief of Staff, United States Army, 1993), 18.
8. Michael Holmes, "Johnson in '64: Vietnam 'Biggest Mess I Ever Saw,'" *Atlanta Journal Constitution,* 15 February 1997.
9. Kearns, *Lyndon Johnson,* 263.
10. Dean Rusk with Richard Rusk and Papp, *As I Saw It,* 42.
11. Hendrickson, *The Living and the Dead,* 196.
12. McNamara with VanDeMark, *In Retrospect,* 39.
13. Hendrickson, *The Living and the Dead,* 153.
14. Halberstam, "Vietnam: Why We Missed the Story," 9.
15. McNamara with VanDeMark, *In Retrospect,* 118.
16. Ibid., 135.
17. Quoted in McMaster, *Dereliction of Duty,* 20.
18. See Sorensen, *Kennedy,* 602–8.
19. Reeves, *President Kennedy,* 401–2.
20. Beschloss, *The Crisis Years,* 543–44.
21. Reeves, *President Kennedy,* 182, 306.
22. Quoted in Keegan, "The Human Face of Deterrence," 147.
23. Quoted in Rosen, "Vietnam and the American Theory of Limited War," in Foerster and Wright, *American Defense Policy,* 314.
24. Herring, *LBJ and Vietnam,* 40.
25. Rosen, "Vietnam and the American Theory of Limited War," in Foerster and Wright, *American Defense Policy,* 314.
26. See Rovere and Schlesinger, *The MacArthur Controversy;* Spanier, *The Truman-MacArthur Controversy;* and *Testimony of General Douglas MacArthur.*
27. Cordesman and Wagner, *The Lessons of Modern War,* vol. 4, *The Gulf War,* 496.
28. Ibid., 541.
29. Quoted in Bernd Debusman, "Saddam Jeers at Bush, Claims Iraq Won War," *Washington Times,* 17 January 1992.
30. See Record, *Hollow Victory,* 119–25; and Gordon and Trainor, *The Generals' War,* 31–38.
31. Emphasis added.
32. Quoted in Schlesinger, *The Imperial Presidency,* 180.

33. Chandler, *The Military Maxims of Napoleon*, 79.
34. Davidson, *Vietnam at War*, 357.
35. McMaster, *Dereliction of Duty*, 114.
36. Luttwak, *The Pentagon and the Art of War*, 41–42.
37. McNamara, with VanDeMark, *In Retrospect*, 311.
38. Westmoreland, *A Soldier Reports*, 135.
39. Bruce Palmer Jr., *The Twenty-five-Year War*, 46.
40. Davidson, *Vietnam at War*, 462–63.
41. Summers, *On Strategy*, 121.
42. Quoted in Perry, *Four Stars*, 152.
43. Quoted in McMaster, *Dereliction of Duty*, 262.
44. Ibid., 163–65. See also Buzzanco, *Masters of War*, 300–301.
45. Ibid., 330.
46. George C. Herring, "The Johnson Administration's Conduct of Limited War in Vietnam," in *Looking Back on the Vietnam War*, Head and Grinter, eds., 82.
47. Perry, *Four Stars*, 158–59.
48. Davidson, *Vietnam at War*, 442.
49. *The Pentagon Papers* (Senator Gravel ed.), vol. 4, 238. For further discussion of the issue, see Davidson, *Vietnam at War*, 442–56; Buzzanco, *Masters of War*, 313–14; Perry, *Four Stars*, 158–59; Herring, *LBJ and Vietnam*, 155–58; and Berman, *Lyndon Johnson's War*, 164–66.
50. Buzzanco, *Masters of War*, 339.

7. LOST VICTORY?

1. See Hilsman, *To Move a Nation*, 30–34; Reeves, *President Kennedy*, 70–102; Patterson, *Grand Expectations*, 492–500; and Thomas, *The Very Best Men*, 169–241.
2. For a detailed list of expanded military options favored by the Joint Chiefs of Staff by late 1967, see *The Pentagon Papers* (Senator Gravel ed.), vol. 4, 533–36.
3. Ibid., vol. 4, 604.
4. Hoffman, et al., "Vietnam Reappraised," 18.
5. Gettleman, et al., *Vietnam and America*, 286–87.
6. Westmoreland, *A Soldier Reports*, 102.
7. Sharp, *Strategy for Defeat*, 4, 67.
8. Quoted in Kimball, "The Stab-in-the-Back Legend," 439.
9. Gibson, *The Perfect War*, 396.
10. Herring, "Vietnam Remembered," 163.
11. Prados, *Hidden History*, 296.
12. Lewy, *America in Vietnam*, 438.
13. Clifford with Holbrooke, *Counsel to the President*, 404.
14. Prados, *Hidden History*, 296.

15. Nixon, *No More Vietnams,* 88.
16. Testimony of James C. Thompson in *Causes, Origins, and Lessons of the Vietnam War,* 45.
17. See Davidson, *Vietnam at War,* 237–40; Buzzanco, *Masters of War,* 25–53; and Krepinevich, *The Army and Vietnam,* 17–19.
18. Prados and Stubbe, *Valley of Decision,* 197.
19. Herring, "Vietnam Remembered," 162–63.
20. Podhoretz, *Why We Were in Vietnam,* 115.
21. Quoted in Fromkin and Chase, "What *Are* the Lessons of Vietnam?," 729.
22. Quoted in Foot, *The Wrong War,* 23.

Works Cited

BOOKS AND REPORTS

Adams, Sam. *War of Numbers: An Intelligence Memoir.* South Royalton, Vt.: Steerforth Press, 1994.

Appy, Christian G. *Working-Class War: American Combat Soldiers and Vietnam.* Chapel Hill: University of North Carolina Press, 1993.

Asprey, Robert B. *War in the Shadows: The Guerrilla in History.* New York. William Morrow, 1994.

Baksir, Lawrence M., and William A. Strauss. *Chance and Circumstance: The Draft, the War, and the Vietnam Generation.* New York: Random House, 1978.

Ball, George W. *The Past Has Another Pattern: Memoirs.* New York: W. W. Norton, 1982.

Bator, Victor. *Vietnam, a Diplomatic Tragedy: Origins of U.S. Involvement.* London: Faber and Faber, 1965.

Bergerud, Eric M. *The Dynamics of Defeat: The War in Hau Nghia Province.* Boulder, Colo.: Westview Press, 1991.

Berman, Larry. *Lyndon Johnson's War.* New York: W. W. Norton, 1989.

———. *Planning a Tragedy: The Americanization of the War in Vietnam.* New York: W. W. Norton, 1982.

Beschloss, Michael. *The Crisis Years: Kennedy and Khrushchev, 1960–1963.* New York: Simon and Schuster, 1991.

Blair, Clay. *The Forgotten War.* New York: Times Books, 1987.

Broughton, Jack. *Going Downtown: The Air War against Hanoi and Washington.* New York: Orion Books, 1988.

Buzzanco, Robert. *Masters of War: Military Dissent and Politics in the Vietnam Era.* New York: Cambridge University Press, 1996.

Chandler, David G. *The Military Maxims of Napoleon.* New York: Macmillan, 1988.

Cincinnatus [Cecil B. Curry]. *Self-Destruction: The Disintegration and Decay of the U.S. Army during the Vietnam War.* New York: W. W. Norton, 1981.

Clifford, Clark, with Richard Holbrooke. *Counsel to the President: A Memoir.* New York: Random House, 1991.

Clodfelter, Mark. *The Limits of Air Power: The American Bombing of North Vietnam.* New York: Free Press, 1989.

Coffey, Thomas M. *Iron Eagle: The Turbulent Life of General Curtis LeMay.* New York: Avon Books, 1986.

Colby, William. *Lost Victory: A Firsthand Account of America's Sixteen-Year Involvement in Vietnam.* New York: Contemporary Books, 1989.

Cooper, Chester L. *The Lost Crusade: America in Vietnam.* New York: Dodd, Mead, 1970.

Cordesman, Anthony H., and Abraham R. Wagner. *The Lessons of Modern War.* Vol. 4, *The Gulf War.* Boulder, Colo.: Westview Press, 1996.

Crowley, Monica. *Nixon off the Record: His Candid Commentary on People and Politics.* New York: Random House, 1996.

Davidson, Philip B. *Vietnam at War: The History, 1946–1975.* Novato, Calif.: Presidio Press, 1988.

Draper, Theodore. *Abuse of Power.* New York: Viking Press, 1966.

Duiker, William J. *Sacred War: Nationalism and Revolution in a Divided Vietnam.* New York: McGraw-Hill, 1995.

Ebert, James R. *A Life in a Year: The American Infantryman in Vietnam, 1965–1972.* Novato, Calif.: Presidio Press, 1993.

Ellsberg, Daniel. *Papers on the War.* New York: Simon and Schuster, 1972.

Enthoven, Alain C., and K. Wayne Smith. *How Much Is Enough: Shaping the Defense Program, 1961–1969.* New York: Harper and Row, 1971.

Fall, Bernard B. *Street without Joy.* Harrisburg, Pa.: Stackpole Books, 1961.

———. *Viet-Nam Witness.* New York: Praeger, 1966.

Fallaci, Oriana. *Interview with History.* Translated by John Shepley. Boston: Houghton Mifflin, 1976.

Foerster, Schuyler, and Edward N. Wright. *American Defense Policy.* 6th ed. Baltimore: Johns Hopkins University Press, 1990.

Foot, Rosemary. *The Wrong War: American Policy and the Dimensions of the Korean Conflict, 1950–1953.* Ithaca: Cornell University Press, 1985.

Franklin, H. Bruce. *MIA, or Mythmaking in America.* New Brunswick, N.J.: Rutgers University Press, 1992.

Galbraith, John Kenneth. *How to Get Out of Vietnam.* New York: Signet Books, 1967.

Gardner, Lloyd C. *Approaching Vietnam: From World War II through Dienbienphu.* New York: W. W. Norton, 1988.

———. *Pay Any Price: Lyndon Johnson and the Wars for Vietnam.* Chicago: Ivan R. Dee, 1995.

Gelb, Leslie H., and Richard K. Betts. *The Irony of Vietnam: The System Worked.* Washington, D.C.: Brookings Institution, 1979.

Gettleman, Marvin E., et al., eds. *Vietnam and America: A Documented History.* New York: Grove Press, 1995.

Giap, Vo Nguyen. *Big Victory, Great Task.* New York: Praeger, 1968.

Gibson, James William. *The Perfect War: Technowar in Vietnam.* Boston: Atlantic Monthly Press, 1986.

Gilbert, Marc Jason, and William Head, eds. *The Tet Offensive.* Westport, Conn.: Praeger, 1996.

Gordon, Michael R., and Bernard E. Trainor. *The Generals' War: The Inside Story of the Conflict in the Gulf.* Boston: Little, Brown, 1995.

Grinter, Lawrence E., and Peter M. Dunn, eds. *The American War in Vietnam: Lessons, Legacies, and Implications for Future Conflicts.* New York: Greenwood Press, 1987.

Hackworth, David, and Julie Sherman. *About Face: The Odyssey of an American Warrior.* New York: Simon and Schuster, 1989.

Halberstam, David. *The Best and the Brightest.* New York: Ballantine Books, 1969.

Hammer, Ellen J. *A Death in November: America in Vietnam, 1963.* New York: Oxford University Press, 1987.

Head, William, and Lawrence E. Grinter, eds. *Looking Back on the Vietnam War: A 1990s Perspective on the Decisions, Combat, and Legacies.* Westport, Conn.: Praeger, 1993.

Hearnden, Patrick J., ed. *Vietnam: Four American Perspectives.* West Lafayette, Ind.: Purdue University Press, 1990.

Hendrickson, Paul. *The Living and the Dead: Robert McNamara and Five Lives of a Lost War.* New York: Knopf, 1996.

Herring, George C. *America's Longest War: The United States and Vietnam, 1950–1975.* 3d ed. New York: McGraw-Hill, 1996.

———. *LBJ and Vietnam: A Different Kind of War.* Austin: University of Texas Press, 1994.

———, ed. *The Pentagon Papers.* Abridged ed. New York: McGraw-Hill, 1993.

Herrington, Stuart A. *Peace with Honor? An American Reports on Vietnam, 1973–1975.* Novato, Calif.: Presidio Press, 1983.

Hilsman, Roger. *To Move a Nation: The Politics of Foreign Policy in the Administration of John F. Kennedy.* Garden City, N.Y.: Doubleday, 1967.

Hosmer, Stephen T., Konrad Kellen, and Brian M. Jenkins. *The Fall of South Vietnam: Statements by Vietnamese Military and Civilian Leaders.* Santa Monica, Calif.: Rand Corporation, 1978.

Hunt, Richard A. *Pacification: The American Struggle for Vietnam's Hearts and Minds.* Boulder, Colo.: Westview Press, 1995.

Isaacs, Arnold R. *Without Honor: Defeat in Vietnam and Cambodia.* New York: Vintage Books, 1984.

Isaacson, Walter. *Kissinger: A Biography.* New York: Simon and Schuster, 1992.

Kahin, George McT. *Intervention: How America Became Involved in Vietnam.* New York: Knopf, 1986.

Kahn, E. J. *The China Hands: America's Foreign Service Officers and What Befell Them.* New York: Viking Press, 1972.

Kattenburg, Paul M. *The Vietnam Trauma in American Foreign Policy, 1945–1975.* New Brunswick, N.J.: Transaction Books, 1980.

Kearns, Doris. *Lyndon Johnson and the American Dream.* New York: Harper and Row, 1976.

Kinnard, Douglas. *The War Managers: American Generals Reflect on Vietnam.* New York: Da Capo Press, 1977.

Kissinger, Henry. *Diplomacy.* New York: Simon and Schuster, 1994.

———. *The White House Years.* Boston: Little, Brown, 1979.

Kolko, Gabriel. *Anatomy of a War: Vietnam, the United States, and the Modern Historical Experience.* New York: New Press, 1985.

Krepinevich, Andrew F. *The Army and Vietnam.* Baltimore: Johns Hopkins University Press, 1986.

Lanning, Michael Lee, and Dan Cragg. *Inside the VC and NVA: The Real Story of North Vietnam's Armed Forces.* New York: Ivy Books, 1992.

Le Gro, William E. *Vietnam from Cease-Fire to Capitulation.* Washington, D.C.: U.S. Army Center of Military History, 1985.

Lewy, Guenter. *America in Vietnam.* New York: Oxford University Press, 1978.

Lomperis, Timothy J. *The War Everyone Lost—and Won: America's Intervention in Vietnam's Twin Struggles.* Rev. ed. Washington, D.C.: Congressional Quarterly Press, 1993.

Lorell, Mark, and Charles Kelley Jr. *Casualties, Public Opinion, and Presidential Policy during the Vietnam War.* Santa Monica, Calif.: Rand Corporation, 1985.

Luttwak, Edward N. *The Pentagon and the Art of War.* New York: Simon and Schuster, 1984.

MacDonald, Callum A. *Korea: The War before Vietnam.* New York: Free Press, 1987.

Manning, Robert, and Michael Janeway, eds. *Who We Are: An* Atlantic *Chronicle of the United States and Vietnam.* Boston: Little, Brown, 1969.

McMahon, Robert J., ed. *Major Problems in the History of the Vietnam War.* 2d ed. Lexington, Mass.: D. C. Heath, 1995.

McMaster, H. R. *Dereliction of Duty: Lyndon Johnson, Robert McNamara, the Joint Chiefs of Staff, and the Lies That Led to Vietnam.* New York: Harper Collins, 1997.

McNamara, Robert S., with Brian VanDeMark. *In Retrospect: The Tragedy and Lessons of Vietnam.* New York: Random House, 1995.

Millett, Allan R., and Peter Maslowski. *For the Common Defense: A Military History of the United States of America.* Rev. ed. New York: Free Press, 1994.

Mitchell, William. *Winged Defense: The Development and Possibilities of Modern Air Power—Economic and Military.* New York: G. P. Putnam's Sons, 1925.

Momyer, William W. *Air Power in Three Wars.* Washington, D.C.: Office of History, U.S. Air Force, 1978.

Moore, Harold G., and Joseph L. Galloway. *We Were Soldiers Once—and Young: Ia Drang, the Battle That Changed the War in Vietnam.* New York: Random House, 1992.

Mrozek, Donald M. *Air Power and the Ground War in Vietnam.* Washington, D.C.: Pergamon-Brassey's, 1989.

Newman, John M. *JFK and Vietnam: Deception, Intrigue, and the Struggle for Power.* New York: Warner Books, 1992.

Nichols, John B., and Barrett Tillmann. *On Yankee Station: The Naval Air War over Vietnam.* Annapolis, Md.: Naval Institute Press, 1987.

Nixon, Richard. *No More Vietnams.* New York: Avon Books, 1985.

———. *The Real War.* New York: Warner Books, 1980.

Nunn, Sam. *Vietnam Aid: The Painful Options.* Report to the U.S. Senate Committee on Armed Services. Washington, D.C.: U.S. Government Printing Office, 1975.

Oberdorfer, Don. *Tet!* Garden City, N.Y.: Doubleday, 1971.

Olson, James S., and Randy Roberts. *Where the Domino Fell: America and Vietnam, 1945–1990.* New York: St. Martin's Press, 1991.

Osgood, Robert. *Limited War.* Chicago: University of Chicago Press, 1957.

Palmer, Bruce, Jr. *The Twenty-five-Year War: America's Military Role in Vietnam.* Lexington: University of Kentucky Press, 1984.

Palmer, Dave Richard. *Summons of the Trumpet: A History of the Vietnam War from a Military Man's Viewpoint.* New York: Ballantine Books, 1978.

Papp, Daniel S. *Vietnam. The View from Moscow, Peking, Washington.* Jefferson, N.C.: McFarland and Co., 1981.

Patterson, James T. *Grand Expectations: The United States, 1945–1974.* New York: Oxford University Press, 1996.

The Pentagon Papers: The Defense Department History of United States Decisionmaking on Vietnam. Senator Gravel ed. Boston: Beacon Press, 1971.

Perry, Mark. *Four Stars: The Inside Story of the Forty-Year Battle between the Joint Chiefs of Staff and America's Civilian Leaders.* Boston: Houghton Mifflin, 1989.

Pike, Douglas. *Viet Cong: The Organization and Techniques of the National Liberation Front of South Vietnam.* Cambridge: MIT Press, 1966.

Pisor, Robert. *The End of the Line: The Siege of Khe Sanh.* New York: W. W. Norton, 1982.

Podhoretz, Norman. *Why We Were in Vietnam.* New York: Simon and Schuster, 1982.

Powell, Colin, with Joseph E. Persico. *My American Journey.* New York: Random House, 1995.

Prados, John. *The Hidden History of the Vietnam War.* Chicago: Ivan R. Dee, 1995.

Prados, John, and Ray W. Stubbe. *Valley of Decision: The Siege of Khe Sanh.* Boston: Houghton Mifflin, 1991.

Prochau, William. *Once upon a Distant War: Young War Correspondents and the Early Vietnam Battles.* New York: Times Books, 1995.

Raskin, Marcus G., and Bernard B. Fall, eds. *The Vietnam Reader: Articles and Documents on American Foreign Policy and the Vietnam Crisis.* New York: Vintage Books, 1965.

Record, Jeffrey. *Hollow Victory: A Contrary View of the Gulf War.* Washington, D.C.: Brassey's, 1993.

Reeves, Richard. *President Kennedy: Profile of Power.* New York: Simon and Schuster, 1993.

Rovere, Richard, and Arthur M. Schlesinger Jr. *The MacArthur Controversy and American Foreign Policy.* New York: Farrar, Straus and Giroux, 1951.

Rusk, Dean, with Richard Rusk and Daniel S. Papp. *As I Saw It.* New York: W. W. Norton, 1990.

Salisbury, Harrison E. *Behind the Lines—Hanoi.* New York: Harper and Row, 1967.

Scales, Robert H., Jr. *Certain Victory: The U.S. Army in the Gulf War.* Washington, D.C.: Office of the Chief of Staff, U.S. Army, 1993.

Schelling, Thomas C. *Arms and Influence.* New Haven: Yale University Press, 1966.

———. *The Strategy of Conflict.* Cambridge, Mass.: Harvard University Press, 1963.

Schlesinger, Arthur M., Jr. *The Imperial Presidency.* Boston: Houghton Mifflin, 1973.

Schlight, John, ed. *Second Indochina War Symposium: Papers and Commentary.* Washington, D.C.: U.S. Army Center of Military History, 1986.

———. *The War in South Vietnam: The Years of the Offensive.* Washington, D.C.: Office of History, U.S. Air Force, 1988.

Schulzinger, Robert D. *A Time for War: The United States and Vietnam, 1941–1975.* New York: Oxford University Press, 1997.

Seversky, Alexander P. De. *Victory through Air Power.* Garden City, N.Y.: Garden City Publishing, 1943.

Sharp, U. S. G. *Strategy for Defeat: Vietnam in Retrospect.* San Rafael, Calif.: Presidio Press, 1978.

Sheehan, Neil. *A Bright Shining Lie: John Paul Vann and America in Vietnam.* New York: Random House, 1988.

Sorensen, Theodore C. *Kennedy.* New York: Harper and Row, 1965.

Sorley, Lewis. *Thunderbolt: From the Battle of the Bulge to Vietnam and Beyond: General Creighton Abrams and the Army of His Times.* New York: Simon and Schuster, 1992.

Spanier, John W. *The Truman-MacArthur Controversy and the Korean War.* Cambridge, Mass.: Belknap Press, 1959.

Spector, Ronald H. *After Tet: The Bloodiest Year of the War.* New York: Free Press, 1993.

———. *The U.S. Army in Vietnam: Advice and Support—the Early Years, 1941–1960.* Washington, D.C.: U.S. Army Center for Military History, 1983.

Stanton, Shelby. *The Rise and Fall of an American Army: U.S. Ground Forces in Vietnam, 1965–1973.* Novato, Calif.: Presidio Press, 1985.

Summers, Harry G., Jr. *Historical Atlas of the Vietnam War.* Boston: Houghton Mifflin, 1995.

———. *The New World Strategy: A Military Policy for America's Future.* New York: Touchstone Books, 1995.

————. *On Strategy: A Critical Analysis of the Vietnam War*. Novato, Calif.: Presidio Press, 1982.

Tang, Truong Nhu, with David Chanoff and Doan Van Tai. *A Viet Cong Memoir: An Inside Account of the Vietnam War and Its Aftermath*. New York: Vintage Books, 1985.

Testimony of General Douglas MacArthur before the Armed Services and Foreign Relations Committees of the U.S. Senate. 82d Congress, 1st sess., 3–5 May 1951. Reprint, Paterson, N.J.: Hour-Glass Publishers, 1966.

Thayer, Thomas C. *War without Fronts: The American Experience in Vietnam*. Boulder, Colo.: Westview Press, 1985.

Thomas, Evan. *The Very Best Men—Four Who Dared: The Early Years of the CIA*. New York: Simon and Schuster, 1995.

Thompson, Robert. *No Exit from Vietnam*. New York: David McKay, 1969.

Thompson, W. Scott, and Donaldson D. Frizell, eds. *The Lessons of Vietnam*. New York: Crane Russak and Co., 1977.

Tilford, Earl H., Jr. *Setup: What the Air Force Did in Vietnam and Why*. Maxwell Air Force Base, Ala.: Air University Press, 1991.

U.S. Department of State. *Aggression From the North: The Record of North Viet-Nam's Campaign to Conquer South Vietnam*. Washington, D.C.: U.S. Government Printing Office, 1965.

————. *The Heart of the Problem*. Washington, D.C.: U.S. Government Printing Office, 1966.

U.S. Department of the Air Force. *Air Force Manual 1-1: Basic Aerospace Doctrine*. Washington, D.C.: U.S. Government Printing Office, 1984 (16 March).

U.S Senate Committee on Foreign Relations. *Causes, Origins, and Lessons of the Vietnam War*. 92d Congress, 2d sess., 9–11 May 1972.

The United States Strategic Bombing Survey—Over-all Report (European War). Washington, D.C.: U.S. Government Printing Office, 1945 (30 September).

van Creveld, Martin. *Fighting Power: German and American Military Performance, 1939–1945*. Westport, Conn.: Greenwood Press, 1982.

VanDeMark, Brian. *Into the Quagmire: Lyndon Johnson and the Escalation of the Vietnam War*. New York: Oxford University Press, 1995.

Vien, Cao Van. *The Final Collapse*. Washington, D.C.: U.S. Army Center of Military History, 1983.

The Vietnam Hearings. New York: Vintage Books, 1966.

von Clausewitz, Carl. *On War*. Ed. and trans. Michael Howard and Peter Paret. Princeton: Princeton University Press, 1976.

Warner, Roger. *Shooting at the Moon: The Story of America's Clandestine War in Laos*. South Royalton, Vt.: Steerforth Press, 1996.

Wells, Tom. *The War Within: America's Battle over Vietnam*. New York: Henry Holt, 1994.

Westmoreland, William C. *A Soldier Reports*. Garden City, N.Y.: Doubleday, 1976.

Why Vietnam. Washington, D.C.: U.S. Government Printing Office, 1965.

Wirtz, James J. *The Tet Offensive: Intelligence Failure in War.* Ithaca: Cornell University Press, 1991.

Young, Marilyn B. *The Vietnam Wars, 1945–1990.* New York: HarperPerennial, 1991.

ARTICLES AND SPEECHES

Ambrose, Stephen E. "The Christmas Bombing." In *America at War: An Anthology of Articles from MHQ, the Quarterly Journal of Military History,* ed. Calvin L. Christman. Annapolis, Md.: Naval Institute Press, 1995.

Ball, George W. "The Issue in Vietnam." Washington, D.C.: U.S. Department of State, 1966.

Cooper, Charles G. "The Day It Became the Longest War." *U.S. Naval Institute Proceedings* 122 (May 1996): 77–80.

Dole, Robert J. Acceptance speech at the 1996 Republican National Convention. Reprinted in the *New York Times,* 16 August 1996.

Draper, Theodore. "The Revised Version." *New Republic,* 10 March 1982.

Fisher, Marc. "Reopening the Wounds of Vietnam." *Washington Post National Weekly Edition,* 1–7 May 1995.

Frisbee, John L. "The Practice of Professionalism." *Air Force Magazine* 69 (August 1986): 113.

Fromkin, David, and James Chase. "What *Are* the Lessons of Vietnam?" *Foreign Affairs* 63 (1985): 722–46.

Halberstam, David. "Vietnam: Why We Missed the Story." *Washington Post National Weekly Edition,* 22–28 May 1995.

Heinl, Robert D., Jr. "The Collapse of the Armed Forces." *Armed Forces Journal,* 7 June 1971.

Herring, George C. "Vietnam Remembered." *Journal of American History* 73 (1986): 152–64.

Hoffman, Stanley, et al. "Vietnam Reappraised." *International Security* 6 (summer 1981): 3–26.

Huntington, Samuel P. "The Bases of Accommodation." *Foreign Affairs* 46 (1968): 642–56.

Jian, Chen. "China's Involvement in the Vietnam War, 1964–1969." *China Quarterly,* no. 142 (1995): 356–87.

Kahn, Herman. "If Negotiations Fail." *Foreign Affairs* 46 (1968): 627–41.

Karnow, Stanley. "Giap Remembers." *New York Times Magazine,* 23 June 1990.

Keegan, John. "The Human Face of Deterrence." *International Security* 6 (summer 1981): 136–51.

Kimball, Jeffrey P. "The Stab-in-the-Back Legend and the Vietnam War." *Armed Forces and Society* 14 (1988): 433–58.

Kissinger, Henry A. "The Vietnam Negotiations." *Foreign Affairs* 47 (1969): 211–34.

Mandlebaum, Michael. "Vietnam: The Television War." *Daedalus* 111 (fall 1982): 157–69.

Morgenthau, Hans J. "We Are Deluding Ourselves in Vietnam." *New York Times Magazine,* 18 April 1965.

Mueller, John E. "The Search for the 'Breaking Point' in Vietnam: The Statistics of a Deadly Quarrel." *International Studies Quarterly* 24 (1980): 497–519.

Record, Jeffrey. "Maximizing COBRA Utilization." *Washington Monthly,* April 1971.

Steel, Ronald. "Blind Contrition." *New Republic,* 5 June 1995.

Stuckey, John D., and Joseph H. Pistorius. "Mobilization for the Vietnam War: A Political and Military Catastrophe." *Parameters* 15 (spring 1985): 26–38.

Thompson, Sir Robert. "Squaring the Error." *Foreign Affairs* 46 (1968): 442–53.

Webb, James. "Robert McNamara, the Anti-War Left, and the Triumph of Intellectual Dishonesty." *Strategic Review* 23 (fall 1995): 47–50.

Werrell, Kenneth P. "Air War Victorious: The Gulf War vs. Vietnam." *Parameters* 22 (summer 1992): 41–54.

Index

About the Author

Jeffrey Record is an internationally respected defense analyst. He has served as a legislative assistant to both Sen. Sam Nunn and Sen. Lloyd Bentsen, as a professional staff member of the Senate Armed Services Committee, as a Rockefeller Younger Scholar at the Brookings Institution, as a senior research fellow at the BDM International Corporation, and as a senior fellow with the Institute of Foreign Policy and Analysis and the Hudson Institute. Record has written numerous books, including *Hollow Victory: A Contrary View of the Gulf War, Revising U.S. Military Strategy: Tailoring Means to Ends,* and *The Perils of Reasoning by Historical Analogy: Munich, Vietnam, and American Use of Force since 1945.* He lives in Atlanta with his wife, Leigh.

The Naval Institute Press is the book-publishing arm of the U.S. Naval Institute, a private, nonprofit, membership society for sea service professionals and others who share an interest in naval and maritime affairs. Established in 1873 at the U.S. Naval Academy in Annapolis, Maryland, where its offices remain today, the Naval Institute has members worldwide.

Members of the Naval Institute support the education programs of the society and receive the influential monthly magazine *Proceedings* and discounts on fine nautical prints and on ship and aircraft photos. They also have access to the transcripts of the Institute's Oral History Program and get discounted admission to any of the Institute-sponsored seminars offered around the country.

The Naval Institute also publishes *Naval History* magazine. This colorful bimonthly is filled with entertaining and thought-provoking articles, first-person reminiscences, and dramatic art and photography. Members receive a discount on *Naval History* subscriptions.

The Naval Institute's book-publishing program, begun in 1898 with basic guides to naval practices, has broadened its scope in recent years to include books of more general interest. Now the Naval Institute Press publishes about 100 titles each year, ranging from how-to books on boating and navigation to battle histories, biographies, ship and aircraft guides, and novels. Institute members receive discounts of 20 to 50 percent on the Press's nearly 600 books in print.

Full-time students are eligible for special half-price membership rates. Life memberships are also available.

For a free catalog describing Naval Institute Press books currently available, and for further information about subscribing to *Naval History* magazine or about joining the U.S. Naval Institute, please write to:

Membership Department
U.S. Naval Institute
118 Maryland Avenue
Annapolis, MD 21402-5035
Telephone: (800) 233-8764
Fax: (410) 269-7940
Web address: www.usni.org